I Know Your Dog
Is a Good Dog

## "Dogs in Our World" Series

*Police Dogs of Trinidad and Tobago:
A 70-Year History* (Debbie Jacob, 2024)

*We Saved Each Other: How Rescue Dogs Help Us
Through Hardship* (Christopher Dale, 2024)

*Dogs of the Railways: Canine Guardians, Companions
and Mascots Since the 19th Century* (Jill Lenk Schilp, 2023)

*The Force Free Dilemma: Truth and Myths in Modern
Dog Training* (Fallon Wilson, 2023)

*Horror Dogs: Man's Best Friend as Movie Monster*
(Brian Patrick Duggan, 2023)

*I Know Your Dog Is a Good Dog: A Trainer's Insights on Reactive,
Aggressive or Anxious Behavior* (Linda Scroggins, 2023)

*The Most Painful Choice: A Dog Owner's Story
of Behavioral Euthanasia* (Beth Miller, 2023)

*Your Service Dog and You: A Practical Guide* (Nicola Ferguson, 2023)

*Dog of the Decade: Breed Trends and What They Mean
in America* (Deborah Thompson, 2022)

*Laboratory Dogs Rescued: From Test Subjects
to Beloved Companions* (Ellie Hansen, 2022)

*Beware of Dog: How Media Portrays
the Aggressive Canine* (Melissa Crawley, 2021)

*I'm Not Single, I Have a Dog: Dating Tales
from the Bark Side* (Susan Hartzler, 2021)

*Dogs in Health Care: Pioneering Animal-Human
Partnerships* (Jill Lenk Schilp, 2019)

*General Custer, Libbie Custer and Their Dogs:
A Passion for Hounds, from the Civil War to Little Bighorn*
(Brian Patrick Duggan, 2019)

*Dog's Best Friend: Will Judy, Founder of National Dog Week
and Dog World Publisher* (Lisa Begin-Kruysman, 2014)

*Man Writes Dog: Canine Themes in Literature,
Law and Folklore* (William Farina, 2014)

*Saluki: The Desert Hound and the English Travelers
Who Brought It to the West* (Brian Patrick Duggan, 2009)

# I Know Your Dog Is a Good Dog

## A Trainer's Insights on Reactive, Aggressive or Anxious Behavior

LINDA SCROGGINS

**DOGS IN OUR WORLD**
*Series Editor* Brian Patrick Duggan

McFarland & Company, Inc., Publishers
*Jefferson, North Carolina*

ISBN (print) 978-1-4766-9366-8
ISBN (ebook) 978-1-4766-5145-3

Library of Congress and British Library
cataloguing data are available

Library of Congress Control Number 2023050220

© 2024 Linda Scroggins. All rights reserved

*No part of this book may be reproduced or transmitted in any form or by any means, electronic or mechanical, including photocopying or recording, or by any information storage and retrieval system, without permission in writing from the publisher.*

Front cover image: © Joop Snijder Photography/Shutterstock

Printed in the United States of America

*McFarland & Company, Inc., Publishers
Box 611, Jefferson, North Carolina 28640
www.mcfarlandpub.com*

For all of the dog guardians who opened their hearts
and their homes to contribute to this book.
The tears and laughter will stay with me forever.
And most of all, for all of the good dogs.

# Table of Contents

*Prologue: Pink* — 1
*Introduction: This Is Not a Book About Training* — 9

1. Jack — 15
2. What Is Happening to the Dogs? — 18
3. Finding Help — 23
4. Maya — 33
5. The Behavior Modification Plan—Part 1 — 38
6. Maizy — 47
7. The Behavior Modification Plan—Part 2 — 53
8. Freckles — 79
9. The Behavior Modification Plan—Part 3 — 86
10. Even More Help — 102
11. Arlo — 115
12. Becoming an Advocate — 123
13. Walt — 136
14. Help for the Human — 142
15. When You Can No Longer Live with Your Dog — 144
16. Grady — 151
17. Behavioral Euthanasia — 156
18. Tex — 158
19. Quality of Life — 164
20. Champ — 168
21. Saying Goodbye — 176

## Table of Contents

| | |
|---|---|
| 22. Should I Get Another Dog? | 180 |
| 23. Celebrate Your Dog | 188 |
| *Recommended Reading* | 193 |
| *Chapter Notes* | 195 |
| *Bibliography* | 200 |
| *Index* | 203 |

# Prologue
## *Pink*

"She is a challenge," that's what they told Lori, about this dog named Pink. This "difficult-to-handle" dog had been in the shelter for eight months. Her wild behavior had been a deterrent to adoption. Her unruliness was even too much for most of the volunteers at the shelter. In fact, only two of the most experienced volunteers were comfortable taking Pink out of her kennel for walks. Because of her behavior and the length of time she had been at the shelter, the volunteer staff worried that Pink was going to end up on the euthanasia list. They wanted her to find a home, but Pink could be a "difficult-to-like" type of dog.

But for Lori, it was love at first sight. Lori was at the shelter on that fated day, to return two small puppies she had been fostering. The puppies had grown old enough to be placed for adoption and Lori was there to set them on their journey to find their new homes. An experienced volunteer and foster parent, Lori was leaving through the lobby of the shelter, when she saw one of the volunteer dog walkers standing near the door, holding the leash of a beautiful tan, pit bull type dog.

"Who is this?" Lori asked as she bent down to look into the dog's deep brown eyes. "This is Pink," the volunteer offered. As Lori knelt to say hello, Pink buried her block-like head into Lori's chest for snuggles. She is not sure why, but Lori had a sudden feeling that she and Pink were meant to be together.

Lori eagerly inquired about Pink on the volunteer message boards. "Well," some said, "she can be a little, challenging? And hard to walk." "You may want to think about it," others said. "She has a lot of, um, energy." But Lori could not stop thinking about Pink, she went back to the shelter to see her again.

"I will give it to you straight," one of the shelter trainers told Lori.

# Prologue

"She is a handful. When the volunteers are in her kennel trying to put on her leash, she grabs their arms and hands in her mouth. And if they can get her out of the kennel for a walk, she doesn't just pull on the leash, she jumps on the person holding the leash and anyone else she can reach. She bolts off like a car at the beginning of a drag race. When the volunteers try to cross the street in front of the shelter to enter the park, she likes to stop in the middle of the road, it is her favorite trick. And while traffic is at a standstill, with awe-struck drivers watching you, she will bite your feet or try to knock you down. More than one person has been injured trying to handle her."

The trainer took a deep breath and continued, "Volunteers have been bruised and battered and some frightened. Most of them do not want to walk with her. They are afraid she will either get away from them or hurt them." "But," the trainer said, "if you are truly interested, the shelter may consider adopting her to you since we know you, but the adoption would have to be approved by a manager." That was all Lori needed to hear. She began the process to adopt Pink.

Pink would be Lori's first pit bull. She had lived with other power breeds. Her past dogs included a mastiff and more than one Chow Chow. She was sure she could handle Pink and make it work. It was obvious to everyone involved that Lori was Pink's last chance, so home with Lori she went.

When Pink first joined Lori's family, she was an angel. She got along with Lori's other dogs and loved people. Until.... Until she got comfortable. Then Pink began to show her true colors. And that is where I came in. Lori had heard about me through the shelter chain of communication. I was new to the training world. My certification as a Certified Professional Dog Trainer was freshly minted. My dream was to train dogs to be great family pets. I was confident by teaching owners and their dogs basic skills I could help to improve the relationship between human and dog. If dogs could learn manners, how to sit and lie down on cue and how to wait before rushing out of a door, then life would be smooth. I was ready to get started, and here was a customer.

I knew Lori casually as we both volunteered at the same shelter. Though our paths did not cross often, we had been on some committees together and had worked on several fundraising events. So, when Lori called asking for help with her new dog, I thought it would be a favor for a fellow volunteer and good experience for me. I drove to Lori's house to meet Pink.

## *Prologue*

I was introduced to a 45-pound tan should-be pittie with a white muzzle and the sweetest face. You could practically see the halo hovering above her head. Pink greeted me at the door with wiggles and kisses. "So," I asked Lori, "what concerns are you having?" "Well," Lori said, "she is kind of wild. If I try to walk her, she pulls in all directions, then she will lie down on the ground and do alligator rolls, wrapping herself in the leash. Then, she jumps up and grabs my arms and legs with her mouth."

"In the backyard, she will run and slam into me. She has almost knocked me down." Lori continued, "In the house, if I walk from room to room, she bites my ankles, and it is impossible to move around." "Really?" I asked, looking at the calm dog offering a perfect sit for the treats I had with me. "Yes," Lori said. "I need help."

I walked across the room and called Pink to me. She bunny-hopped to my side. "Does she know anything yet?" I asked Lori. "She knows how to sit," Lori said with a bit of a sigh. "Then let's start with some basics," I instructed. On that first visit, and on our second visit, we worked on common skills, such as sit, stay, and leave it. Pink was doing so well that I knew we would soon start working on her much-needed leash-walking skills.

As I drove to my third visit with Pink and Lori, I thought about what a nice dog Pink was and how much fun she was to work with. I thought about how happy I was to get to know Lori better and that we had become friends. I wondered how soon we would be able to have Pink take the Canine Good Citizen test. Sponsored by the American Kennel Club, it's a test that shows a dog can maneuver through the community with good manners. That will show all those people who thought Pink was a "challenge," I smugly thought.

When I arrived at the house, I was met at the door by Lori looking a little haggard. Her eyes were tired and peculiarly, her hair was a little disheveled. "Today is not a good training day," she said. "She will not do anything for me." "Okay, let's see what the trainer can do," I said with confidence. I sat on the couch and Pink appeared with a twinkle in her eye. The minute I said, "Hi Pink!" she started grabbing my ankles in her large vice-like jaws. It hurt. She grabbed at my shoes, and when I reached down to save my shoelaces, she grabbed my wrists in what I could only think of as a T-Rex-type grip. When I stood up to move away, she grabbed the tail of my shirt and held on, a tug of war I was not going to win. "Huh, let's try outside," I said, "and let's bring her mat."

Over the last few weeks, we had been working on an exercise called "relax on mat." This exercise is meant to help dogs learn how to be calm.

## Prologue

It involves slowly dropping treats on a rug (the mat), and if Pink showed any relaxed body language, such as sitting or lying on the rug we would rain treats down upon her, to hopefully reinforce that relaxed behavior. The idea was that the "mat" would be a place the dog would recognize as a station they would lie on and just chill out.

I carried the mat as I moved towards the back door, all the while dodging teeth. Once outside, Pink grabbed the rug from me, she held it in her teeth and shook it, hard. Then with what I can only describe as glee, she ran across the yard with her rug in her mouth. So much for relaxing on that mat.

Once Pink was on the other side of the yard, she dropped the rug and looked at Lori and me with a gleam in her eye. "Watch out," Lori warned. Pink began running toward us at full speed. We held on to the handrail of the deck like Dorothy during a tornado and dodged out of the way as Pink flew past us. I had no doubt she had the ability to break bones if her potato-shaped, torpedo body made full contact. "Okay," I said, "I see what you mean, not a good day for training." We spent the rest of that morning eating bagels and drinking mimosas. I did not charge for that visit!

Now, many years later, with barely suppressed laughter, Lori recalls that as one of the best days of her life because I got to see the real Pink! Lori was relieved I didn't run out of the door there and then. I knew at that time, that I was in over my head. After that first of many bagel and mimosa days, I talked to one of my mentors about Pink. "What is she trying to tell you?" this very experienced trainer asked me, "What is her body language saying?"

I began to watch Pink closely on my visits. Pink seemed happy most of the time; she was a cheerful dog. But one day we were working on short sit-stays, asking Pink to sit, then not move until we gave her a release word. Pink did great, for about 3 repetitions. On the fourth try, Lori gave the cue to sit, and once Pink sat, Lori gave the cue to stay. Immediately Pink stood up, she moved to a small table that was a few feet away and began sniffing the legs of the table. We reset and tried again. Again, at the cue to stay, Pink got up and sniffed the table, and then looked around the room. The table was not new and there was nothing on the table that should be particularly interesting to a dog. I was puzzled at why this table would be suddenly attracting her attention.

With a sigh and a mental slap to my forehead, I realized that Pink was showing a displacement behavior. Our training was stressing her

## Prologue

out. Displacement behaviors can be thought of as normal behaviors that happen out of context. Sniffing is a normal thing for dogs to do, but why was Pink doing it now, at this moment? Displacement behaviors typically happen when a dog is feeling conflicted or stressed.

I did not think we were asking that much of Pink; the sit-stay was a simple exercise. "What is she trying to tell you?" my mentor had said. With that little sniff of a table, Pink's life, Lori's life, and my life changed forever. We finally heard what Pink was trying to tell us. Pink was a people pleaser. She was a good dog and wanted to do the right thing, but she had no idea how.

I had attempted to apply a general training plan for Lori and Pink. I pushed for the behaviors I thought Pink should know. We knew very little about Pink's background before she came to the shelter. I realized Pink was not a blank slate. I was not considering the needs the dog in front of me may have. From that moment, instead of asking Pink to do things for us, we began to listen to what she needed from us.

We learned a lot about Pink over the months we worked with her, we learned she could only tolerate very short training sessions. Sometimes these sessions were four minutes followed by a 15-minute break. We learned that Pink was an expert at reading human body language and tone of voice. Now that we were looking, we could see that at the first sign of disappointment from her human that Pink would start to worry. I am sure this was a survival tactic that had served her well in her previous life. We learned that Pink loved to have fun and we learned that she loved her people.

Lori was a natural at dog training and learned much about Pink's communication style. She began to recognize what triggered Pink's unwanted behavior. She learned that if they were out for a walk and Pink dropped to the ground, the alligator roll would come next. She learned that when Pink dropped, she was telling us she had had too much, too much stimulation, too much sensory input. Lori learned to stop where she was, as long as it was not the middle of the street, and speak calmly to Pink and give her gentle pets until Pink was through this moment of panic. Soon Pink was able to continue her walk instead of rolling like a canine reptile.

We studied Pink. We would spend whole training sessions discussing canine body language; sometimes we would spend 15–20 minutes on just watching her nose or tail. Pink was quiet in her communication, but she had important things to say.

# Prologue

And Pink learned how to have fun. She loved platform work. Platform work for dogs is a technique using an elevated surface and teaching a dog to put parts of her body on the platform. This may be front paws or back paws or all four paws. Platform work can be used to teach dogs tricks, to have them station their body in a specific position for husbandry care, or to condition canine athletes.

I had found an empty, wooden, electrical cord spool and covered it with duct tape. When we weighted the bottom, the spool became our platform. Pink learned to put her front paws on the platform, and it wasn't long before she learned to walk in a circle around the platform while keeping her front feet on the top. I really believe that Pink loved platform work because it was free of pressure. These silly tricks were a way for Pink to learn about the process of learning without the fear of making a mistake. After all, not many people feel pressure to teach their dog to walk around a platform while wearing a pink tutu.

In the process of platform training, Lori learned about shaping a behavior and marking and reinforcing a behavior. She became a great dog trainer. And I learned to listen, listen to the dog in front of me, what are they telling me, what am I asking of them? What is their emotional state? How do they learn and what is important for them to learn? Training is a process of two-way communication. It takes time. Lori and I went through a lot of bagels and mimosas in the early days, and I lost a lot of shoelaces and several t-shirts to Pink's teeth. But it was worth it for the lessons we learned.

Pink was always a good dog, and she grew into a great dog. She made wonderful progress. She remained enthusiastic but learned to calmly greet visitors. No more jumping. As she grew comfortable in her world, her anxiousness dissipated, and she stopped using her jaws to

**Pink sporting her fancy clothes**

*Prologue*

**The author with Pink, who started it all.**

express herself. Lori would always remain tuned in to Pink's emotional state and was mindful of Pink's need to decompress now and then. But as time went on the outbursts grew less and Pink became a solid, dependable dog.

As for me, I never did have those classes with lines of owners and dogs in fancy heel positions. But I did go on to work with many dogs who had behavior concerns. My practice developed into working with dogs who had been diagnosed with anxiety, reactivity, or aggression. I have worked with veterinarians and mentored new trainers. It all started with a dog named Pink.

## Prologue

Pink lived a good life and now that she is gone, we talk about her often. We talk about how funny she was. We remember the time she was so excited about a new donut-shaped toy, that she ran in circles with the toy in her mouth and looped over her muzzle across her eyes. In her excitement, she ran right into the television because she could not see. We talk about how sweet she was and how hard she worked to be a better dog. I know that every behavior-challenged dog I have been able to help started with Pink. It is her legacy.

# Introduction

*This Is Not a Book About Training*

This is not a book on how to train your dog. There are many good books that help owners learn how to train their dogs, and I will be sharing a few of my favorites.[1*] This is not that book. But I am a dog trainer, so why did I write this book? Because of the grumpy dogs, the scared dogs, the wild dogs. The dogs who just don't quite have their act together, the dog who cannot make sense of the world. I wrote this book because those dogs and their people need help. I wrote this book so you, the human living with that dog, would know you are not alone. Most of all, I wrote this book because I know your dog is a good dog.

In this book, you will see me refer to dogs that have behavior problems, or behavior issues, or even behavior concerns. All these terms mean the same thing. Dogs whose behavior may not be a problem for them but is a problem for their families or the community at large. Dogs whose behavior is going to get them into big trouble. Dogs that cannot seem to fit in. Dogs who may be dangerous. Dogs who may not have the best quality of life. I like to think of them as special dogs. The dogs who have shaped my career as a trainer and behavior consultant.

I have loved dogs all my life. My path to becoming a dog trainer started early. The first dog I attempted to train was my Dalmatian, Snoopy. I was about ten years old and knew nothing about teaching a dog anything, except that repetition and Velveeta® cheese should be part of the plan. Armed with those two tools, I went about training Snoopy. With my juvenile enthusiasm, or more likely despite it, Snoopy learned several tricks. He was a smart dog, and I was hooked on training.

There were other dogs after Snoopy and much of my joy in living

---

\* A list of recommended reading is at the back of this book. Numbered notes hereafter are together at the back of the book.

## Introduction

with dogs grew from what I could teach them and what they taught me. But, alas, as I grew into an adult, my life took many paths. I became a mother. I became a registered nurse. There was not a lot of time in my day for working with dogs, but my love for dogs and my interest in training never waned. Once my children had grown and I had more time of my own I was able to pursue more "doggy" things. I began volunteering at my local animal shelter.

At the shelter, I was able to see firsthand the importance of training, especially for these homeless dogs. Many of the dogs at the shelter had been dropped off or returned after adoption due to unwanted behavior. We volunteers found that often a little training set the dogs up for success. Dogs that could learn to sit at the kennel door instead of jumping, or those who could do a trick, such as shaking hands, attracted more interest and were often adopted faster. My interest in training was renewed.

I began to seek out resources that would help me learn how to be a real trainer and move past the Velveeta cheese stage. Through my contacts at the shelter, I was introduced to a local training club that offered a program for beginning trainers. I jumped in with both feet. I completed the program and became an assistant trainer and then a lead trainer for the club's family dog classes. I loved helping other people train their dogs and seeing dogs become good pets was thoroughly rewarding.

Eventually, I pursued a more formal path in training and decided to "go pro." I began working on certification with the Certification Council for Professional Dog Trainers®. I was proud when I completed the long process and was able to add the letters, CPDT-KA®, standing for Certified Professional Dog Trainer-Knowledge Assessed, behind my name.

Once I had completed my certification, I decided to hang out my shingle and started my own small business. I partnered up with a colleague and through our local parks department, began holding weekend classes to teach basic obedience skills to family dogs. The classes were a success. We had fun and earned a little pocket money.

## *My Dog Needs Your Help*

Then the calls started coming in. Calls from people who had been turned down by other trainers, people who had been told their dog couldn't be trained, that their dog was dangerous. I received calls

*Introduction*

from people who were worried their dog was going to bite or who had already bitten. These dog owners were not calling me because of my reputation or advertising. They were calling me because they were calling everyone. They were working their way through lists of trainers, looking for help.

For every call I received from someone wanting to join a class to teach their dog how to walk nicely on a leash, I received a dozen calls from desperate owners begging for my help with dogs that were experiencing behavior issues.

I had lived with dogs that had similar issues and had great empathy for these pet guardians. I wanted to help and found myself entering the world of behavior consulting and working with reactive and anxious dogs. In the process of helping these special dogs, I pursued further education and a new certification. In addition to my CPDT-KA credential, I eventually added CBCC-KA (Certified Behavior Consultant, Canine-Knowledge Assessed).

You will hear the word reactive or reactivity a lot if you have, well, a reactive dog. The word reactive is used because it is a better descriptor than aggressive. In the behavior world, the term aggression is meant to describe an action, and carries with it the intent to do harm. Reactive dogs may be aggressive, and they can intend to do harm, they may even be dangerous. But the word reactive is better at describing the motivation for the behavior. When we think of problem behaviors we are thinking of a dog "reacting" to a trigger. A trigger is something that creates or increases stress, anxiety, or fear in the dog. The dog wants the trigger to go away and "reacts" based on their emotional state and by using tools that have worked for them in the past, such as pulling, lunging, barking, growling, and even biting.

Not all behavior problems in dogs create reactivity. There is a multitude of issues that the "behavior problem" label can describe. There are dogs whose lives are ruled by anxiety. Separation anxiety is one of the most common anxiety disorders in dogs. These dogs suffer from an honest-to-goodness panic disorder.[2] Being left alone is intolerable for these dogs. It would be a hard-hearted person that would not be touched by the pain these dogs experience.

There are dogs whose life experience has taught them that the best way to handle a dangerous world is to shut down, pretend you are not there and do not let anyone notice you. Their depression overwhelms them.

These are the dogs that need help, and if you live with one of these dogs, I want to help you too. By understanding why dogs act this way

# Introduction

and how we set about helping these dogs, I hope to give you a better relationship with your dog. I want to provide a guide to finding the people that can help you help your dog. And in the end, if you have to say goodbye to your dog, I want you to know you are not alone.

## *You Are Not Alone*

Since I began focusing my training business on dogs with behavior issues I have worked with hundreds of families. Almost every one of the families I work with is surprised to hear that there are other dogs like theirs and other families dealing with the same issues. Owners are startled when I tell them, "Yes, I've seen this behavior before."

There is an interesting dichotomy created. From my viewpoint as a trainer, there is an ever-growing number of dogs with behavior problems, because that is what I see in my world. For the owner, their dog is an unusual and singular problem. I'm betting neither of us is completely right.

I think these different viewpoints grow in part due to owners not talking about their dog's difficulties to anyone other than their veterinarian. They may be embarrassed or ashamed to talk about their dog to friends and neighbors. When my brother-in-law goes on and on about how his Bernese Mountain Dog was the star of the July 4 BBQ, it can be hard for me to add, "Well, we had to stay home with the curtains closed and give our dog drugs to get through the day." The result is that no one is talking about their problem dogs. Consequently, families living with these dogs can feel very isolated.

But I guarantee you, you are not alone. My behavior colleagues and I have so many calls for help that our waiting lists are months long. Would you be surprised to know that inside the behavior world the topic of dogs with problem behavior supports a whole industry? Books are being written and workshops given. There are international experts who travel around the world teaching trainers like me to work with reactive dogs. But outside of the dog training and behavior world, a dog with behavior problems can become a hidden secret.

## *I Know Your Dog Is a Good Dog*

"They're good dogs, Brent." This quip became popular when used by the X account @dog_rates to shut down a commenter complaining

## *Introduction*

that the account consistently rated dogs at 12/10 or 13/10. The account, now known on social media as We Rate Dogs, is used to share pictures of funny, amazing, adorable dogs. All in fun. When the commenter complained that it didn't make sense to give ratings over 10 in a 10/10 system the page owner's response was, "They're good dogs, Brent."[3]

They are good dogs. The influence of social media has given us many colloquialisms to describe dogs and all things dog; doggo, smol, treatos. A good dog is no longer so much a judgment of behavior as it is of value. They're good dogs because they are appreciated and loved, and they make someone happy. They are funny and brighten someone's day.

But when a dog has a behavior concern, if they are barky at other dogs, or growl at people, not many get to see their good dog qualities. These dogs are typically kept away from the things that cause the problem behavior. As a result, they may not go for a walk when people are about. They are put away when company visits. They are rushed in and out of the veterinary clinic, instead of making the rounds to say Hi!

My dog Bayou had a serious case of "stranger danger." The Bayou that visitors saw was the alarmed, barking, 120-pound dog with my hand tight on her collar. Or they saw her back end as she retreated to the bedroom that was her safe space. Visitors never got to see the snuggly couch potato. They never witnessed her smile as she snagged a forbidden treat from the kitchen counter. They never saw the huge Bayou trying to fit herself into a cat bed. That Bayou did not exist outside of her small circle of friends. But Bayou was a good dog.

As part of my initial screening with a new client, I send a lengthy questionnaire. One of the questions I ask is, what are your favorite things about your dog? This section is always filled out and usually has extra lines added. I know you love your dog and I know your dog is a good dog.

**Bayou the Great.**

# 1

# Jack

Lisa wanted a pit bull. Her sweet dog Scout had passed away and she and her husband Don and dog Ruby were ready to add another canine member to the family. Lisa knew that pit bulls or pit bull type dogs were one of the most maligned types of dogs and the type of dog that filled the shelters. It was in Lisa's heart to give a home to one of these dogs. So, she went to the local animal shelter where she met and fell in love with Jack.

Jack is a low-to-the-ground pit bull type dog, whose large black and brown patches give him a certain bovine look. Jack was about three and a half years old when he was adopted by Lisa and Don. The only background the shelter provided was that his previous owner had died, and relatives had brought unwanted Jack to the shelter.

Once he was home with Lisa and Don, they noticed right away that Jack had very poor dog-to-dog social skills. The resident dog, Ruby, would be irritated when enthusiastic Jack did not quite understand the signals she was sending him to slow down or back up a little. Jack was exuberant in his effort to make friends, but his over-the-top behavior would cause Ruby to react with snaps and growls. He was a little too eager and scuffles broke out.

Jack

## I Know Your Dog Is a Good Dog

Lisa knew that incorporating Jack into the family would require a slow integration and would need to begin with limited, controlled, interactions between Jack and Ruby. Part of this plan was to have one dog in the general living quarters, while the other dog would take breaks hanging out in a bedroom with super toys and yummy treats. Within two days Lisa knew this plan was not going to work. Jack could not tolerate being alone, not for one minute.

When left in a room by himself, Jack would bark, he would urinate on the floor, would destroy anything in the room. If he was placed in a crate, he would continually muzzle punch the sides of the crate risking injury to himself. These behaviors would stop if Jack was with Lisa or Don. Lisa and Don realized that assimilating Jack into their family was not going to be as easy as they had hoped.

In addition to the stress of being alone, Jack also showed a sensitivity to sudden loud noises, like fireworks and gunshots. As they lived in an urban area, either of these sounds could occur at any time, and around holidays would happen regularly for several consecutive days. With a background in dog training herself, Lisa knew they needed help right away. Lisa began to assemble "Team Jack."

Jack's veterinarian, a key part of the team, diagnosed Jack with separation anxiety and noise phobia. The vet prescribed medication to help lower Jack's anxiety level. Lisa and Don hired a trainer experienced in working with dogs with separation anxiety who gave them a definitive management and treatment plan. Don began working from home when he could so that Jack would not have to be alone. When he could not work from home, they hired a dog sitter to stay with Jack.

This plan created huge challenges and a complicated schedule. In the beginning, Lisa and Don were not even able to sleep in the same room. Since Jack and Ruby could not yet be together without close supervision, Lisa and Don slept in separate bedrooms, each with a dog in the room with them.

With the help of the team, Jack made slow but steady progress. Jack learned it was okay to be alone a few minutes at a time. That gradually expanded and over a period of six months or so, Jack was able to tolerate being on his own for six-hour stretches. Jack was eventually weaned off his medication. He and Ruby forged a friendship and now like to hang out together, each taking one end of the couch.

As Jack has gotten older, things have only gotten better. He has begun to lose his hearing, the ultimate cure for noise phobias. He can stay home alone for several hours at a time but is still not able

## 1. Jack

to tolerate being crated. Anything that might involve crating such as recovering from a medical procedure requires a babysitter to keep him calm, in lieu of confinement. Lisa and Don have been able to resume their favorite pastime of traveling, as long as Jack has his favorite dog sitter with him.

Jack has made great progress but the path to this success was not an easy one. Lisa emphasizes that she was lucky to have the resources needed to help Jack and pointed out that not everyone does. In the seven years, Jack has lived with them, they have spent thousands of dollars on his care. Not only did expenses include veterinary visits and medication, trainers, and dog sitters, but missing time from work for Lisa when her husband could not be home, or the dog sitter was not available. If she did not have those resources, she does not know what would have happened.

I have known Lisa for a long time, even before she adopted Jack. When we talked about life with Jack, she admitted she was divulging some of this information for the first time. I asked her why she was sharing this now as she has had Jack for quite some time. She expressed the thought that I have heard from owners repeatedly. She told me that people in this situation are tired of being judged, even by friends.

That judgment can take many forms. Lisa told me that owners of dogs like Jack are told they are not doing enough or doing too much. You can be told you are silly for spending this much time, money, and worry on a dog. You are told you could be doing more and why haven't you tried this idea or that idea. It gets to be too much when you are trying to do your best.

Separation anxiety is one of the most difficult challenges dog owners and dog trainers can face. Many trainers decline to work with these dogs as the requirements for the behavior modification plan can be overwhelming or even impossible for families to accomplish. But as evidenced by Jack it can be done successfully once you build that team. From unwanted dog to pampered pooch, Jack is a testament to success.[1]

# 2

# What Is Happening to the Dogs?

Ninety-five percent of the calls I receive inquiring about my services relate to dogs that have behavior concerns. The same is true among my dog-training colleagues. Does this mean more and more dogs have behavior issues? Is something happening in the canine world to create more and more dogs with behavior problems? I do not know. Although there are scholarly articles on the number of dogs with behavior issues, I was not able to find any research looking at the number of reported issues over time. But it is something my cohort and I discuss often. You can put a crowd of dog trainers around a table with a pitcher of margaritas and we will discuss this for hours without coming up with any answer.

Maybe the idea that there are more and more dogs with behavior problems is a false effect. After all, I am only looking at the people who are calling me and I do not know what percentage of dog owners that is. Maybe of the overall dog population, the calls I receive are only a tiny percentage of all the dogs.

Maybe it is social perception. Generally, we compare our current experience to our past experiences. Growing up in the seventies I never lived with or knew anyone that lived with a dog that had to go to a trainer or a veterinarian because they were anxious. It was never heard of. So, hearing of dozens of dogs with issues seems like a lot. When I was a child, there were good dogs and bad dogs. I do know that what qualified as a bad dog was different then than it is today.

When I was a child, we were taught dogs bite. That is what they do. And if a dog has bitten then you better avoid that dog. If a dog growled because you came close when it was chewing on a bone, then leave the dog alone! I heard that more than once. If a dog chased a child that had climbed over a fence, well then, the child should have known better.

Our expectations of the place dogs hold in society has changed.

## 2. What Is Happening to the Dogs?

That is not necessarily a bad thing. Decades ago, it was not unusual to have an "outside" dog. Now we know more about dogs' social needs and the need for a dog to be a part of its family is important.[1] We have brought dogs indoors in much larger numbers than we used to. They have become a more integrated part of our life. People often refer to dogs as their children.

Have we taken this too far? Have we crossed a line in treating dogs like accessories? Some assessments estimate the market for pet clothing to be at 50.1 billion dollars in 2020.[2] Any dog owner can throw their dog a party at the local dog bakery, complete with cake and hats for their canine and human friends. There are dog day cares with pool and spa time. Do we expect our dogs to fill a more human role and thereby have less patience for what may be normal dog behavior, so we tag it as a disorder? I do not have the answers to such questions.

What is certain, is that the field of veterinary medicine and animal behavior has grown by leaps and bounds. Our knowledge of the physical health of animals has expanded. Tools to diagnose illness and injury have kept pace with that of human medicine. Treatment for medical conditions in animals has grown equally. Thankfully, giving our dogs a much better quality of life and a longer life. But what about mental health? Is it appropriate that we are giving dogs diagnoses of mental disorders and treating them with what could be compared to psychiatric or psychological care? I think it is.

In my 2017 book *Mental Illness in Dogs: A Guide for Trainers*, I wrote about the devastating 2011 earthquake that struck off the east coast of Japan near the Fukushima region. Following the earthquake, a 15-meter tsunami disabled the nuclear power supply of three Fukushima Daiichi reactors causing an evacuation of 154,000 people from the area. The tsunami resulted not only in the death of more than 20,000 people but in 300,000 becoming unhoused.[3]

Sadly, many pets were left behind in the horrible disaster. Many of the dogs were eventually rescued and placed in shelters. Nagasawa, et al., conducted a study of the sheltered dogs and found that many of these dogs were suffering symptoms consistent with the symptoms found in humans diagnosed with post-traumatic stress disorder (PTSD). "The endocrine responses of the Fukushima dogs suggested extreme stress, which persisted even after 10 weeks of adequate care."[4]

The authors further found that the low trainability and attachment scores among these dogs warrant special attention. Impaired learning ability due to oversecretion of glucocorticoids is a core symptom in people who have experienced extreme stress, including those with PTSD. In addition, PTSD patients have been reported to show impaired ability with respect to attachment and bonding. The disaster-affected dogs in this study appeared to show signs of the same behavioral phenomenon.[5] These dogs had developed mental illness after experiencing an extremely traumatic event.

Anthropologist Brian Hare, a leader in the study of the working of the canine brain, has built his Dognition program on the study of how dogs think, learn and problem solve. Hare proposes that dogs have five core cognitive dimensions: empathy, communication, cunning, memory, and reasoning.[6]

In an apt summation of the cognitive ability of dogs, Brian Hare and Vanessa Woods point out in their book, *Genius of Dogs: How Dogs Are Smarter Than You Think*, "What we know for certain is that the cognitive world of every dog is far more complex and interesting than we thought."[7]

Dr. Karen Overall, Diplomate of the American College of Veterinary Behaviorists (DACVB) and Certified Applied Animal Behaviorist (CAAB), finds a comparative relationship between mental illness in people and dogs. "Dogs develop analogous, and possibly homologous, conditions to some human psychiatric disorders possibly including generalized anxiety disorder (GAD), attachment disorders, social phobia, obsessive-compulsive disorder (OCD), post-traumatic stress disorder (PTSD), panic disorder, Alzheimer's disease, and aggressive impulse control disorders."[8]

Overall goes on to tell us that "Psychiatric disorders—whether in humans or in domestic animals where they are called behavior disorders—are among the most complex and incapacitating of all pathological conditions."[9]

Even the military agrees that dogs can suffer from mental illness. In an article for the *New York Times*, James Dao quotes Dr. Walter Burghardt, Jr., chief of behavioral medicine at the Daniel E. Holland Military Working Dog Hospital at Lackland Air Force Base. "By some estimates, more than 5 percent of the approximately 650 military dogs deployed by American combat forces are developing canine PTSD. Of those, about half are likely to be retired from service."[10]

These medical and behavioral authorities, the experts who are on the front line of investigation, agree that dogs can suffer from mental illness. The late neuroscientist, Jaak Panksepp, a pioneer in the study of animal emotions, found that animals experience the emotions of

## 2. What Is Happening to the Dogs?

seeking, fear, rage, lust, care, panic, and play. Panksepp coined the term "affective consciousness," opining that emotion has neural or biological roots, and advocates that an emotional life is a function of the brain of all mammals.[11]

Yale University now has a facility, the Canine Cognition Center, dedicated to learning more about canine psychology. There are also scientists using functional MRI scanners to study the physical action of the brain of dogs while the dogs are interacting with their environment.[12]

If we accept, as the research supports, that dogs do possess a more advanced brain than we thought and that they are not always simply responding on instinct or repeating behaviors they have learned in the past, then we must accept that these advanced brains can also be subject to illness.

In comparing humans and other animals Dr. Nicholas Dodman, in his book, *Pets on the Couch*, tells us, "We share physical similarities and we respond to incoming sensory information in much the same ways. Under the hood, so to speak, in terms of the nervous system or other organ systems, there is not much difference in how things work."[13]

Is it possible there are more and more dogs with behavior issues? Certainly, it is also possible that the problems have always been there but now we have the science to understand the cause of behavior, diagnose the issue, and provide treatment. Decades ago, dogs that had growled or bitten or reacted to people or other dogs would have not stayed in a home or been adopted out. They would have been euthanized. That alone may be an explanation for the seemingly growing number of dogs with behavior issues.

If you are living with a dog that has a behavior problem, your dog may have a behavior disorder. It is important to remember that a diagnosis of a behavior disorder is a medical diagnosis and just like any physical diagnosis, must be given by a doctor. If a trainer gives your dog a diagnosis, they are essentially practicing medicine without a license.

The common diagnoses I have seen given to the dogs that I work with by veterinarians include:

- Generalized anxiety disorder
- Phobias of different kinds, most commonly noise and storm
- Predatory aggression
- Fear aggression
- Separation anxiety
- Canine post-traumatic stress disorder

- Panic disorder
- Territorial aggression
- Redirected aggression
- Impulse control aggression
- Confinement distress

That is an extensive but not exhaustive list. If your dog has been diagnosed with a behavior diagnosis, do not despair. There is help.

# 3

# Finding Help

When I say you are not alone, it does not just mean there are other families with a dog like yours, it also means there is professional help waiting. Navigating through the world of dog training can be overwhelming. A friend may recommend a certain trainer but then your veterinarian says, "No, use this person." You watch television and see the latest, cool looking, tattooed tough guy telling you this is how things must be done. Or you view your Instagram® page and see pop-up ads with the latest equipment to help your dog stop pulling on its leash. Then you see a video from a dog trainer showing how they can get your dog to act like their dog in just two weeks. It can be confusing to know where to turn for help.

The confusion is compounded because the dog training profession is unregulated. This means there are no requirements people must meet to call themselves a dog trainer. There is no licensing process. There are no state laws. Anyone can decide they are a dog trainer, print business cards, and open for business.[1]

Even though there are no licenses, there are certifications. A certification is a designation earned that shows a person has a minimum qualification to perform a job. Certification can be offered by a professional society, a university, a certification body, or even an individual.[2] Not all certifications are equal. I am certified by the American Heart Association to do CPR, and when I was 14 years old, I was certified by a YMCA summer program as a babysitter. These are examples of certification and show that being certified can mean many different things.

But at minimum, a certification should mean that an individual holds a certain body of knowledge and set of skills. If someone is certified as a dog trainer it means someone, somewhere decided they meet some qualifications. For example, my dog training certification is through the Certification Council for Professional Dog Trainers.[3] This is an organization that was formed specifically to offer certification.

# I Know Your Dog Is a Good Dog

My certification requires taking a test and meeting a minimum requirement of continuing education. The test the CCPDT offers is psychometrically sound.[4] This means that all the questions on the test have been validated and found reliable and test for the knowledge it is supposed to. I can tell you, that babysitting quiz I took in middle school, not so much. It is important to look for a trainer that holds or is working towards a certification. However, holding a certification does not necessarily speak to the expertise or empathy of the individual.

So, what is a dog owner who is looking for help to do? I am going to tell you. First, let's look at the types of professionals that are available.

## *Dog Trainers*

"Dog trainer" is a very general term. Typically, we think of a dog trainer as someone who will teach skills to a pet dog. Someone who will teach our dog how to walk on a leash, how to sit down on cue, or wait before rushing through a door. In the world of dog training, there is a myriad of techniques, goals, and skill levels. Because the field of dog training is unlicensed, owners looking for a dog trainer need to proceed with caution.

As a behavior consultant, I have worked with dozens of dogs whose behavior problems have been created by or made worse by bad training.[5] Dogs can be emotionally harmed or even physically injured by so-called "trainers." So first, look for a dog trainer that is working towards or holds a certification. Certification programs typically require ongoing education; this at least shows the pursuit of updated knowledge. But even certified trainers should be screened.

The Pet Professional Guild recommends asking the following questions when considering a dog trainer or any pet professional:

1. What dog training equipment do you use when training a dog or do you recommend I use?
2. What happens in your training program when the dog responds in the way you want him to?
3. What happens in your training program when the dog responds in the way you do not want him to?
4. How will you punish the dog or advise me to punish the dog if he gets something wrong or exhibits a behavior I do not like?
5. How do you ensure that my dog is not inadvertently being punished?

## 3. Finding Help

6. How do you know that the type of reinforcement you have selected to train my dog is appropriate?

7. How will you know, or how will I know, if my dog is stressed during the training?

8. Which professional dog training associations are you a member of?

9. Will you guarantee your training results?

10. How do you think a dog's behavior should be addressed if the dog is growling or snapping at people or other dogs?[6]

On their website, The Pet Professional Guild provides a detailed review of how to interpret the answers to these questions and when you should dig a little deeper. The answers will help inform you on how the trainer approaches safety for your dog, how they will engage your dog in the training process, and if they will work to make training fun for you and your dog. It will give you clues as to how tied in they are to the training community.

Any dog trainer you consider should be able to easily answer every one of these questions. If they cannot or if they do not understand some of the terms, such as reinforcement, my assumption is they do not have the experience and education needed to be working with your dog.

In addition to being able to answer the questions above, any trainer that is developing a behavior modification plan for your dog must be familiar with the principles of the Humane Hierarchy and LIMA.

The Humane Hierarchy is a term coined, and plan developed by Dr. Susan Friedman,[7] professor emeritus in the Department of Psychology at Utah State University. The humane hierarchy is used by pet professionals to guide training plans and the decision-making process in a step-by-step manner. The first steps of the hierarchy focus on the most non-aversive methods of working with an animal and proceed through to the most aversive.[8]

The first step in the hierarchy is addressing the physical health of the dog. This requires an evaluation by a veterinarian. The veterinarian will rule out any nutrition factors, illness, or disease that could be impacting behavior. Pain, allergies, or hormonal disorders are some of the common conditions that can present as a behavior issue.[9] If these conditions are found, they need to be treated. Once ruled out as the cause of the behavior concern the trainer proceeds to the next step.

The second step of the hierarchy is to look at the dog's environment and see if there are changes that can be made to positively impact behavior. We often call this the management plan. This step looks at what I can change in the home or in the yard, or anywhere my dog spends time. Can I change where the food bowl is kept or place gates to change access to certain parts of the house? These types of interventions are found in this second step.

The hierarchy continues with changing behavior utilizing positive reinforcement and/or classical conditioning. This is where you find what you may think of as the training plan. How to teach a dog to go behind me if she is frightened or how to teach a dog to come and touch my hand. From this step, the hierarchy extends into other types of reinforcement and the last step ends with the use of punishment.

When you view the hierarchy, you can see that punishment is only used when all other techniques have been exhausted. A trainer that recommends techniques or tools that punish a dog by causing pain or fear as the first line of training should be avoided.

Personally, I never continue down the hierarchy to these last steps on my own. If I am not able to effect change in behavior by using the first parts of the humane hierarchy, I will always refer the dog to a Certified Applied Animal Behaviorist or a Veterinary Behavior Specialist and will not resort to punishment. I do this to acknowledge that a dog may have issues that are beyond my skill set. Another qualified professional may be able to effect the change I could not without using punishment.

LIMA is a position statement followed by many behavior organizations.[10] LIMA stands for Least Intrusive Minimally Aversive. Following LIMA helps to ensure the training techniques will have a minimal risk of producing adverse side effects. Trainers should continually view their plans and ask themselves if they are using the most humane training technique possible.

The principles of the humane hierarchy and LIMA support humane training and the avoidance of the use of pain and punishment in training. Having knowledge of the humane hierarchy and LIMA does not guarantee your trainer is qualified, but not knowing these principles is a red flag that the trainer does not have the competence to be working with a dog with behavior issues. If the trainer cannot explain these concepts, you should look for someone else.

## *Behavior Consultants*

A behavior consultant is a dog trainer that has pursued additional education and experience in working with dogs that have behavior

## 3. Finding Help

concerns. Most behavior consultants pursue a certification specifically in behavior. Dog trainers that wish to be certified as behavior consultants must complete education and practice hours in addition to those that apply to their dog training certification. Education focused on behavior should include topics such as applied behavior analysis and how to complete a functional analysis. It should cover ethology and a knowledge of body language as well as health and physiology. Study and practicum are followed by either a statistically validated exam or the submission of case studies.

Some of the most respected certification programs for behavior consultants are offered through the Pet Professional Guild,[11] the International Association of Animal Behavior,[12] and the Certification Council for Professional Dog Trainers.[13] All of these programs require vigorous study, hours of hands-on experience, and passing a rigorous exam.

## *Behaviorists*

If there is one thing we in the animal behavior world do not agree on, it is what titles should be used by pet professionals. The one that generates the most confusion and sometimes ire is the label behaviorist. There are many dog trainers that advertise themselves as dog behaviorists without holding any certification or advanced educational degree.

To avoid confusion and as a matter of professional respect, I do not consider myself a behaviorist. And when I see someone advertise themselves as a behaviorist without the appropriate qualifications it makes me wonder just how much they really know about the animal behavior world. I am not a dog behaviorist. I am a certified behavior consultant.

So, who are the behaviorists? I was once at a professional conference listening to a noted speaker talk about dog behavior. This speaker holds a Ph.D. degree, has authored many books, teaches at the university level, and is respected as an international expert on animal behavior. An audience member asked a question that began with, "as a dog behaviorist." The speaker politely answered the question but did correct the attendee that the speaker is an animal behaviorist, not a dog behaviorist. This was food for thought for me, I realized that there is a whole world of animal behavior being studied at higher-level institutions all over the world. This made me recognize that I should probably look to those experts to really expand my understanding of dog behavior and the professional structure of animal behavior science.

## I Know Your Dog Is a Good Dog

Among animal behavior experts, a behaviorist is someone who holds an advanced degree, either a master's degree, a doctoral degree in animal behavior or a related science, or a medical degree.

All behaviorists achieve their credentials through an academic route by pursuing a master's degree or Ph.D. degree. Some behaviorists focus on research, writing, and teaching. I have had wonderful opportunities to learn from these experts by attending conferences, studying their papers, and reading their books.

And then there are animal behaviorists who work hands-on with clients. These behaviorists typically seek certification in addition to their academic degrees. The certification shows clients the standards under which the behaviorist practices and their knowledge base.

The Animal Behavior Society is the organization that provides certification for behaviorists. The behaviorist will be either a Certified Applied Animal Behaviorist (CAAB) or an Associate Certified Applied Animal Behaviorist (ACAAB). The criteria the Animal Behavior Society sets forth to qualify for certification are:

- Obtained an undergraduate degree, usually requiring 4 years at an accredited college or university.
- Gained admission to an accredited graduate school or veterinary school through a highly competitive admission process.
- Completed post-graduate education receiving a Master's (2-year full time) or Ph.D. (4-year full time) degree in a behavioral science, or DVM (or VMD) (Doctor of Veterinary Medicine) degree with a behavioral residency.
- Passed rigorous oral and written examinations given by their faculty committees.
- Published articles in scientific journals.
- Supervised hands-on experience with animals.
- Met the course work and experience requirements for certification as set forth by the Animal Behavior Society.[14]

Now you see why I do not advertise myself as a behaviorist. Those are pretty demanding requirements. Sadly, CAABs are not numerous and may not be found within easy driving distance in many parts of the country. Happily, more and more professionals are offering virtual services.

In my own opinion, one of the signs of a good dog trainer or behavior consultant is one that knows when the dog needs help from a higher-level professional. No dog's quality of life or life should be

### 3. Finding Help

sacrificed for the sake of the ego of the trainer that thinks they can fix any dog. If you feel you need the expertise of a behaviorist, your trainer or veterinarian should be able to help you locate the appropriate professional. You can also search at animalbehaviorsociety.org.

## Veterinary Behavior Specialists

A veterinarian may also become a behaviorist. Just as some veterinarians go on to specialize in orthopedics or oncology, Veterinary Behavior Specialists are veterinarians that have completed a residency or training program in the discipline of behavioral medicine. Once board certified, the veterinarian is known as a Diplomate of the American College of Veterinary Behavior (DACVB). As part of these programs, the veterinarian has studied topics including sociobiology, psychology of learning, behavioral genetics, behavioral physiology, psychopharmacology, ethology, and behavioral endocrinology and more.[15]

The advantage of the Veterinary Behavior Specialists over other professionals is that they are licensed to prescribe medication. Almost all the dogs I have worked with, have had medication as a key part of their behavior modification program. When I was a new trainer, I viewed a referral to this professional as a last resort. Now, after much experience, I have come to view the Veterinary Behavior Specialist as a key member of the team. In most cases, a dog will benefit greatly from an early referral, not only for consideration of medication but for a full medical-behavioral evaluation. It is not unusual for a dog with behavior problems to have concomitant health issues.

Unfortunately, these specialists are also not numerous and may not be easily accessible. But many do provide virtual care. This typically needs to be done in conjunction with your general practice veterinarian due to state licensing guidelines. If you feel you need to see a Veterinary Behavior Specialist, then your trainer or your general practice veterinarian should be able to guide you. You can also look at avsab.org for a directory.

## Role of the General Practice Veterinarian

Your dog's veterinarian plays an important part in caring for your dog and supporting care for behavior issues. They should always be consulted. As a rule, I will not start working with a client until they have had a thorough examination with their veterinarian to rule out any health conditions that may be contributing to, or even disguised as, behavior issues.

However, the general practice veterinarian is not a specialist. They have not had the focused education and experience the Veterinary Behavior Specialist has had. Although many are comfortable prescribing some medications at low doses that target behavior, not all do. In fact, some general practice veterinarians do not feel comfortable treating behavior diagnoses at all. Unlike dog trainers, veterinarians are licensed professionals. Their medical license may have restrictions on areas of practice and what type of diagnoses they treat. Again, your veterinarian is an important part of the team treating your dog but will not likely be the single professional you need.

## *Sitters, Walkers, and Day Cares*

There are other pet professionals that can be an important part of a dog's behavior team. Those include dog sitters, dog walkers, and dog day cares.

For example, the behavior modification plans for dogs like Jack, who have separation anxiety, typically begin with the step of never leaving the dog alone. That is not very practical for most families. There are very few families, not to mention single owners, who are never away from home some of the time. A dog sitter or dog day care can be a good option for making sure the dog has company.

A good dog walker can provide services for many types of dogs with behavior issues. Some dogs benefit from the extra exercise a dog walker can provide. But dog walkers can also be instrumental for dogs that should not go for walks. That's right, a dog walker for a dog who doesn't walk.

One of the biggest challenges of living with reactive dogs is taking them out for a walk. One of the biggest looks of relief I see in owners of reactive dogs is when I tell them they do not, or sometimes should not, be taking their dog for a walk. This is not to say that a reactive dog will never go for a walk but learning to walk calmly and enjoying a walk without being stressed is a process for a reactive dog. This process should be part of the behavior modification plan and practiced with the assistance of the trainer. Until then, it is okay for some dogs to skip walks.

## 3. Finding Help

But many dogs are alone much of the time, some of them confined in a crate or pen for the greater part of the day while the owners are away. A good dog walking company can provide non-walk activities for your dog. These activities can include at-home exercise, play, and mental enrichment. They can set up puzzles or scent trails. They may just sit with your dog, giving them company and attention. Call your local dog walker: will they do a no-walking "walk"?

## *Fear Free*™

Hiring any pet professional to work with a dog with behavior issues can be a delicate process. Every dog should be treated humanely, and with kindness, but for dogs with behavior issues this becomes more critical. Behavior issues such as fear, or anxiety can be made worse by punitive or harsh handling. A pet care provider who does not understand a dog's behavior issues can create a bite risk, putting the welfare of the humans and the dog in peril. One way to help ensure a pet professional is familiar with the needs of a dog with behavior issues is to look for those practitioners that are Fear Free™ certified.

Fear Free™ is a certification program developed by veterinarian, Dr. Marty Becker. "Founded in 2016, Fear Free provides online education to veterinary professionals, pet professionals, animal welfare communities, and pet owners."[16]

The Fear Free™ "mission is to prevent and alleviate fear, anxiety, and stress in pets by inspiring and educating the people who care for them." Veterinarians, dog trainers, dog walking companies, day cares, groomers, and pet sitters are eligible to participate in the Fear Free™ certification program. There may also be pet professionals who practice under fear free principles but may have not completed certification. If a pet professional advertises as practicing fear free, they should be able to explain what this means. Seeking fear free practitioners can help ensure the most humane treatment for your dog.

So now you know who is out there—but how do you find them? The availability of the appropriate professional may depend largely on your geographic area. Behaviorists and Veterinary Behavior Specialists can be few and far between. Certainly, talk to your friends and your veterinarian. I also refer to the websites of professional organizations that offer certifications for trainers and behavior consultants.

### I Know Your Dog Is a Good Dog

In addition to animalbehaviorsociety.org. for behaviorists and avsab.org for Veterinary Behavior Specialists try the following:

- Pet Professional Guild
- International Association for Animal Behavior Consultants
- Certification Council for Professional Dog Trainers
- Karen Pryor Academy
- Peaceable Paws Dog and Puppy Training
- GrishaStewart.com

# 4

# Maya

Maya was meant to be a show dog. She belonged to a breeder who had kept her with that intention, but at some point, changed her mind. It was never revealed why the breeder decided against keeping Maya, but Elzy, Maya's owner, suspects it was due to Maya's behavior.

Elzy had been looking for a German Shepherd Dog. She had lived with Shepherds in the past, and they are one of her favorite breeds. Elzy had heard through the GSD community that there was a three-year-old Shepherd girl in need of a home, so through a train of communication and networking, Maya came to live with Elzy.

Maya's behavior issues were evident immediately and they were severe. It is unknown what caused Maya's behavior issues. It is suspected she spent the better part of her first three years in a kennel with little attention or socialization. Information that was passed onto Elzy indicated that Maya was only removed from her kennel to be transferred by a leash from the pen to the training ring. Maya acted as if everything was strange and new and she was scared to death of everything.

Once in Elzy's home, this poor dog would cower and avoid eye contact. She

**Maya**

would shut down, unable to even take treats from Elzy. She would not play with toys; in fact, she didn't seem to understand the purpose of toys or play. She was terrified of having a collar put on and would outright panic if a leash was attached.

If outside in the yard, Maya would either freeze or try to escape back into the house. But in the house, even if she had plenty of room, Maya would literally try to climb up a wall, her fear was so great. Maya could not tolerate being in a room with the door closed but was afraid to exit any room she was in. She would balk at thresholds. Elzy found herself in a really difficult situation, but she had committed to this dog and was going to do her best to help her.

Elzy remembers thinking, "How do I even begin to communicate with this dog; how do I even start working with her?" She began by talking with her veterinarian who recommended medication and training. Elzy was hesitant to start medication, she worried about the side effects, but did decide to pursue training. That is when she contacted me.

During our initial phone call to talk about Maya's history and schedule the first in-home visit, Elzy explained there would be a process for my arrival at her home. Elzy would bring Maya outside to meet me before going into the house. It seemed to be easier for Maya to meet visitors outdoors instead of having the first meeting indoors. This was not unusual. I've had other dogs, usually working dogs, that feel more comfortable with this type of introduction.

The time came for the first visit. I stood in the driveway with my back to my car, holding my equipment bag in front of me like a shield. A medium-sized, gorgeous German Shepherd came toward me. Her body language was asking me to "not touch," and I respected that. I avoided eye contact and gently scattered some treats on the ground hoping to let her know I was a source of good things. Maya sniffed me and my bag, she looked at me with wide eyes and a low tail. "Okay," Elzy said, "we can go inside." As we entered the house, Maya remained a mix of low growls and tension. I quietly sat at the kitchen table and slowly continued to drop treats on the floor, careful to not make any sudden movements.

Elzy, it turned out, was a dream client, she was experienced with dogs, she was smart, and had a lot of common sense. We talked about the goals we would be setting for Maya and the plan to reach those goals. Elzy knew the priority was to build trust with Maya, so we focused on relaxation and having fun. Over the next few months, Maya made great strides. I loved seeing the relationship grow between Elzy and Maya. I almost cried the day Elzy called to tell me that Maya had played with a toy.

## 4. Maya

Progress was steady but it was slow. Elzy did, over time, choose to begin medication for Maya. She does feel the medication helped to calm the panic that Maya would have on occasion. We continued to adjust our goals and the behavior modification plan, Maya continued to bloom and our time for in-person visits came to an end.

Over the next few years, Elzy kept me updated on Maya's progress. Maya had begun to tolerate visitors and had even made a few human friends, especially young visitors. Maya loved kids. Who would have thought! Maya was still very nervous if she was away from home, but she and Elzy were now enjoying long walks. Maya remained generally cautious about the world outside her door, and Elzy maintained a management plan to keep Maya and those around her safe.

Now almost five years after I first met Maya, I called Elzy to ask if I could meet with her to talk about my ideas for this book. As in the old days, Elzy still brought Maya outside to meet me, she is after all a German Shepherd and she is not going to let just anyone into her home. This time I was greeted by a dog with a loose, wiggly body, a freely moving tail, and a soft face. No need to drop treats on the ground, she took them directly from my hand. And when we went inside, Maya actually hopped with happiness. She sat near me and pawed my knee for more treats. "What a change!" I told Elzy, "I can tell you have done a lot of work!" I asked Elzy to tell me about life with Maya. What things had helped her to get to this point.

Elzy tells me having an awesome veterinarian made all the difference from the beginning. The veterinarian did not judge her and was supportive of her keeping Maya when others told her she should give Maya back to the breeder.

Elzy feels the biggest catalyst in Maya's progress was helping Maya understand that she had choices and that she had some control over her environment. When she noticed Maya was afraid to go outside, Elzy began leaving the door from the kitchen into the garage open and the door from the garage to the fenced backyard open. Once Maya learned she had the freedom to go in and out she began spending short periods in the yard.

Maya grew to enjoy being outside but remained hypervigilant while there. She continually watched for activity in the other houses and yards she could see from her patch. So Elzy built a privacy fence. Blocking the view of the neighborhood helped Maya to relax and shift to being off-duty while outdoors. Now Maya enjoys playing outside, especially with one of her young visitors who stops over from time to time.

## I Know Your Dog Is a Good Dog

Maya loves to go for walks now. In the past, while walking around the neighborhood, Maya would often try to bolt back home. If Elzy drove to a park for a quieter walk, Maya would sometimes just refuse to get out of the car. Elzy employed her "power of choice" plan and when on walks, if Maya would start to pull home Elzy would stop and think, why is she anxious. She would observe the environment and start to note the routes that Maya preferred and started letting Maya choose the path.

When at the park they would play the "are we getting out of the car?" game. Sometimes they would park and sit and watch the world go by then leave, never exiting the car. Other times if Maya would leave the car, they would just get out, stand around and then get back into the car and go home. Elzy believes Maya began to understand she was not going to be forced to be somewhere she did not want to be and also was not going to be abandoned there. Elzy is a big believer in relaxed walks. She lets Maya use her nose as much as she desires. Elzy tells me, "All walks are nose walks." "All in all," Elzy explains, "I really did a lot of passive training."

Elzy and Maya still face challenges to their harmonious life. One of the biggest is the unwanted advice Elzy receives. She tells me that owners like her are put into a difficult position by too many people having too many opinions and applying too much pressure on owners to fix their dogs. That creates a needless emotional burden.

It remains very difficult for Elzy to be away from home. Maya grows very anxious when away from Elzy and if separated from Elzy in someone else's care, Maya's stress level will spike and her negative reaction to strangers will increase.

Elzy tried to board Maya once, to take a brief trip out of town. She gave careful instructions to the kennel where Maya would be staying. She explained Maya's fear issues. She explained that the supplies she brought with her were specifically chosen because they made Maya more comfortable and asked that none of the items be removed from her run.

On the last day, before Elzy picked Maya up, the kennel staff decided to launder all the items and removed everything from Maya's run. Maya was without her security toys and blankets. By the time Elzy arrived to pick her up, Maya was in full panic mode. Needless to say, Maya has not been boarded again and for the past five years, Elzy's travel has been severely limited.

Elzy does have a friend that can keep Maya on a very limited basis,

## 4. Maya

but Elzy must measure each travel opportunity to decide if it is worth the stress to her and to Maya. The sum of these experiences, Elzy tells me, is that "I trust people less, to allow me to keep my dog safe."

Because of the challenges Maya faces in life, Elzy points out that she has had to let go of the dream she held of what life would be with her new dog. As an experienced dog owner, she had envisioned she might do therapy work with her new Shepherd or participate in dog sports. She has had to say goodbye to those dreams for now.

Elzy is grateful she can be at home with Maya most of the time. She feels this was an integral part of her recovery. In the early days, if she would have had to leave Maya alone each day, she believes it would be like living in the *Groundhog Day* movie, with any step forward undone each night and each day repeating itself.

As I look at Maya sitting with her paw on my knee, I ask Elzy to tell me her favorite things about her dog. There are many things, but for Elzy, it is the small victories, and she celebrates each one. Seeing Maya play with toys was a huge triumph. Watching as Maya let go of her past trauma and play with her human friends was one of her best achievements. The dog who used to climb the wall in panic will now happily take an occasional puppy treat from the staff at the drive-up window at the local coffee house.

Maya is a happy dog, but Elzy reminds me that she has had to limit her own life to support Maya's progress. It is a journey that Elzy and Maya have made together, and Elzy is very proud of what they have accomplished, as she should be. I watch Maya and I know she is a sum of her past and the love she receives in the present.

# 5

# The Behavior Modification Plan—Part 1

Once you find the right professional and you have scheduled that first appointment, I am sure you will be wondering, what is the trainer going to do? Will we go on a pack walk? Will I have to call my neighbor out so my dog can chase him? What is the plan? Your neighbor can rest easy, we will not need him, in the beginning anyway.

What I do at the first visit with my clients is talk about developing a behavior modification plan. This is the plan that will outline how we will help your dog. Don't get too attached to the plan though, they tend to change. The purpose of the behavior modification plan is to outline the steps that will be taken to help impact your dog's behavior and improve the quality of life for the dog and the people who live with the dog.

It would be challenging to develop a behavior modification plan on your own. There is a certain body of knowledge that is needed to do this. A behavior modification plan is complex. It has many parts, often moving parts as goals will change, steps may fail, and the plan will need to be continually adapted. It requires a professional with an understanding of learning theory, functional analysis, and the principles of behavior. That is why it is important to look for a trainer who has experience in working with dogs with behavior issues, a behavior consultant, a Certified Applied Animal Behaviorist, or a Veterinary Behavior Specialist to help you in this process.

When I approach the process of developing a behavior modification plan, I think of it in parts. The first part is to complete a history and gather as much information as I can about the dog. The second part is the in-person observation. The history and observation will make up the evaluation.

The third part of the behavior modification plan is to set goals and discuss expectations. This is where a lot of discussion comes into play. Many people are not sure what their goals are and that is okay. I

## 5. The Behavior Modification Plan—Part 1

am there to help. Sometimes it takes work to put those thoughts down on paper. It is my job as the expert to review expectations and discuss what is realistic and what may not be possible. The fourth part is to talk about management. And the fifth is teaching families how their dogs communicate.

The next part is the fun stuff. What are we going to train your dog to do? These will be your survival skills. And lastly, we will plan the conditioning exercises that will focus on changing your dog's emotions and reactions to triggers. All these pieces make up the behavior modification plan. It is not always as precise as this may sound. Often goals are mixed up with management and expectations change as training progresses. But it is important for you, the owner, to see what a behavior modification plan can contain.

You may be surprised to learn that there is so much that goes into the program that is created to help a dog. You may also be surprised to learn the time I spend in a home with a family for appointments, is a small part of the time I spend on a case. I spend hours reading, talking with colleagues, and thinking about your dog.

## The History

One of the first things I do as a behavior consultant is to complete a history of your dog. The history will include almost everything you know about your dog. Don't worry if you do not have very much background. We work with what we have. I have partnered with families who found their dogs on the street and knew literally nothing about them. And I've worked with dogs that came from breeders and the owner can provide the pedigree for the dog's great, great, great, great grandparents.

As part of obtaining the history, I have my clients fill out forms and I request video of your dog and her environment. I will also talk with you by phone or in person. The history will include asking for information such as if you know where your dog came from, and information about the dog's parents and siblings. It will include a health history, nutrition information, and even the food your dog eats.

I will sometimes ask for medical records or ask permission to talk with your veterinarian. I may even ask to talk with people outside of your home who interact with the dog regularly. This may be grandparents who visit frequently, dog sitters, and even groomers. This can give me a more complete picture of your dog. A history form is typically many pages long and it is a chance for you to express your concerns.

## *The Observation*

After the history, I proceed with an observation. This is when I will meet you as a family, along with your dog. I place a lot of importance on all family members being present at the observation. This is important for more than one reason. Not only does this give me the opportunity to see the dog's relationship with each family member, it also tells me how interested and dedicated each family member is to helping the dog. A dog that lives in a two-adult home with three kids is not likely to improve if only one adult is working the plan. The observation allows me to see how the dog acts towards me as a visitor and to other things in her environment. It gives me a chance to watch body language, make notes and take lots of videos.

If your dog spends a significant amount of time out of the house such as at your workplace or at a day care, I will likely ask to observe your dog in those areas as well. It is important to gather a lot of information and accurate information. The observation helps me to understand the number of issues your dog has and the severity of the issues.

During the observation, I will be paying close attention to your dog's body language. I want to see how your dog communicates and the signals it gives in response to different stimuli. This is where video comes in handy as these signals can be so subtle or so fast that sometimes it may be hard to catch everything by just watching. Important signals may be something as quiet as a tongue flick or eye movement. I will almost always see something on the video that I missed with my eyes.

What I will not do and what no consultant should do is trigger the problem behavior to see what it looks like. Many owners will ask, "Don't you want to see how she tries to bite me?" I do not. If I did a good job with the history and observation, I do not need to trigger the behavior in question. I believe what you have told me. And my experience and education will help guide me. To unnecessarily trigger the behavior would upset the dog and could be unethical and possibly dangerous.

Once I have completed the evaluation I will discuss with clients if I am the right professional to help. There may be reasons I am not.

## 5. The Behavior Modification Plan—Part 1

Sometimes I tell families the good news that they do not need me. I do, on occasion, meet dogs whose perceived behavior problem is a normal developmental stage or common hiccups. I may refer them to a trainer for basic obedience or a puppy class or just offer a few survival tips.

Another reason I may not accept a client is that the dog's concerns need a higher level of professional. I am always honest with my clients. If I think we are going to spend weeks working together only to find out they need someone more knowledgeable than me, I will tell them at the beginning. But most of the time I can work with families and their dogs. And when we come to that agreement, it is time to talk about goals and expectations.

## The Goals

Living with a dog that has behavior issues can be overwhelming. The process of obtaining help for the dog can be mind-boggling. It is the job of the trainer or behavior consultant to sort through the information overload and help you to develop the best plan for your dog. A good place to start is with your goals. Here are some examples of goals my clients have in mind when we first meet:

- Safety with people
- Control of situations
- Help with anxiety
- Stop lunging at dogs
- Go for a walk
- Stop growling and lunging at people
- Stop biting
- Reduce friction between dogs
- Be friendly to people coming into the home
- Stop aggressive behavior

All good goals, but most focus on what we do NOT want our dog to do. Do not react, do not bite, do not growl. To effect change and to assess progress we need to set goals centered around what we want our dogs TO do. So, the first thing I do is take the goals and run them through the positive spin machine. The goals may become:

- When out on a walk and we pass a stranger, my dog will look at me for direction.
- My dog will turn to look at me when given the cue, "watch."

## I Know Your Dog Is a Good Dog

- My dog will play with a toy and nap when I am away from home.
- My dogs will each sit on their mats when I am preparing their food.

By focusing on what we want our dogs to do, we can develop a plan to teach them to do those things.

A positive action plan accomplishes several things. It changes the narrative that this is a bad dog or problem dog and focuses on what a dog and owner can accomplish together as a team. It creates a scaffold to build an action plan. And it should remove some of the frustration an owner feels when problem behaviors occur.

Once we have our positive goals set, we need to make those goals specific. This is important because progress in changing behavior must be measurable. If the goal is being friendly to people who come into the home, we can work on skills toward that. But when six weeks go by and I ask, is your dog friendlier, it may be hard to describe the progress. They seem friendlier, they haven't bitten anyone, is wonderful to hear. But if we can have a specific plan and know how we are going to measure progress then we will know if the plan is or is not working. We will know if we should continue the plan or change it up. Examples of specific goals are:

- My dog will stop lunging at strangers when out for a walk becomes: when out for a walk and we pass a person who is more than ten feet away, my dog will look at me as we pass that person.
- My dog will stop barking at other dogs that walk past our house, becomes: when my dog is barking at a passing dog and I give the cue, "thank you" my dog will leave the window and find me.
- My dog will stop lunging at other dogs becomes: my dog will walk along the edge of the park and take treats from me when she sees another dog.
- My dog will not bite me when I put on her harness becomes: my dog will eat treats from my hand while I am putting on her harness.

Having a specific, measurable goal allows us to continually tailor the plan to the dog's needs. If our goal is, my dog will rest calmly in his crate while I am away from home for one hour, we can assess the effectiveness of the plan. If the dog reaches one hour pretty easily, we know we are on the right track and can increase our goal. The new goal may be my dog can rest calmly in its crate while I am away from home for

## 5. The Behavior Modification Plan—Part 1

90 minutes. If we work on the plan for several weeks and we have only reached 30 minutes of the one-hour goal, then we need to review and probably change the plan.

But what if I told you that all the above goals were for one dog? It is important to prioritize goals. This happens by discussion between the family and the trainer. You know what is important to you. Once we prioritize the goals, we will pick the top two or three to work towards. Families with dogs with behavior issues are already under a great amount of stress. Setting two or three goals can allow work to begin at a manageable pace. When we do that, a wonderful thing will happen. I call it the "spillover effect." When a dog makes progress on specific goals, we always see an improvement in the other areas. The progress "spills over." I am not sure why, but I think as a dog builds confidence and fear and anxiety reduce it affects all parts of the dog's life.

## *The Expectations aka Reality Check*

An important part of goal setting is to have realistic expectations. I have had to tell more than one owner that the dog that is growling and snarling at me is probably not going to become a therapy dog working in a pediatric hospital. And the retriever that spends 18 hours napping and stretches for 15 minutes before finally moving, nope, that is not your future hunting dog. On a more serious note, many factors contribute to a dog's behavior. Some of these we may be able to impact and some not.

Even though, "The etiology behind the development of reactivity is unknown,"[1] it is well-accepted that genetics play a strong role in behavior and temperament. "In mice, cats and dogs, there appear to be genetic lines or strains that are 'more reactive than others.'"[2]

Genetic material is passed from parent to offspring via DNA. "There may also be in utero and epigenetic effects that contribute to overall reactivity of dogs in the same way that we know affect rodents and humans."[3] Epigenetics is the study of how genes are expressed. So, the DNA is passed on, but the environment may impact the way those genes are expressed or show themselves.

I was once called to evaluate a young, male Great Dane that had been rescued from a puppy broker. The rescue had placed the dog into a foster home so that they could assess his temperament and see what help he needed before being placed for adoption. When I entered the foster home, the large dog cowered, he tucked his tail, and he stood behind the foster parent. If I moved closer, he would "react" by growling and barking. Is it possible that this dog carried a gene for fear?

There were also several of this dog's puppies who had come into rescue with him. The puppies were about 9–10 weeks old at the time. Each puppy displayed varying degrees of fearful behavior. One of the puppies, on seeing a toddler from about six feet away, jumped, yelped, and tried to run away. Kids can be scary, but that reaction was a bit out of the ordinary. Had the puppies inherited a gene making them prone to fear? Possibly.

The Great Danes had come from a hoarding situation. They had been kept in a drafty barn with only partial doors and a dirt floor. They had been underfed and were infected with a variety of parasites. The mother of the puppies was not on-site at the time of rescue. But assuming the mother had been in the same deficient location, it is possible that the poor environment impacted the development of the puppies before they were even born.

It is possible that the puppies had inherited DNA making them prone to fear and possible that the undesirable environment impacted how those genes would be expressed. A dog's genetic makeup can impact how much change a behavior modification plan can affect.

I should tell you, reader, that one of those shy Great Dane puppies, the one who acted like toddlers were akin to monsters, caught my eye and came home to live with me. And I can also tell you that I did an excellent job of socializing and training this dog I named Blue Bayou, if I say so myself. Still, she remained on the shy side all her life. Out of curiosity, when Bayou was about two years old, I contacted several of the families that adopted her siblings. I learned that all the puppies had continued to display varying degrees of shyness in those first two years.

Social deprivation can also impact the development of behavior. A study done by Pierantoni, Albertine, & Pirrone, compared 70 adult dogs, who as puppies had been separated from their dam and litter at 30–40 days with 70 adult dogs who as puppies were not separated until after 8 weeks. "Early Age of Separation Was a Significant Predictor for Excessive Barking, Fearfulness on Walks, Reactivity to Noises, Toy Possessiveness, Food Possessiveness and Attention Seeking Behavior."[4]

History of stress can impact behavior. In their paper, "Chronic Treatment with the Antidepressant Amitriptyline Prevents Impairments in Water Maze Learning in Aging Rats," Yau et al., state, "There are few data on effects of anxiety on learning in dogs, but we know from studies on rodents and human children that chronic glucocorticoid

## 5. The Behavior Modification Plan—Part 1

excess—at any time, including pre- and peri-natally—interferes with learning at a cellular level."[5]

Stress can lead to increased levels of the hormone cortisol. "Cortisol adversely affects neuromolecular and neurochemical aspects of learning leading to apoptosis (cellular death)."[6]

Some learned behavior is maintained by reinforcement. It is hard to change heavily reinforced behavior. Just talk to anyone that has tried to quit smoking or lose weight with multiple starts and stops. If a dog bites a stranger and the stranger runs away, the dog has learned that technique works to get that person to go away. If the dog continues to repeat the behavior, the behavior is reinforced, and it becomes stronger.

Dogs can also sustain organic changes in the parts of the brain that control certain types of behavior. Brain injuries can be due to illness or injury, they can be sudden or chronic. A traumatic injury, either intentional such as abuse, or unintentional such as being hit by a car, can not only cause damage to the brain but can also create associated mental trauma such as post-traumatic stress.

It is important to understand that there are many factors that go into creating a reactive, fearful, or anxious dog. Understanding this helps us to realize that not all behavior can be changed or can be changed to a great extent. It would be almost impossible to take a dog that has a strong fear reaction to unknown people and after a behavior modification program expect them to happily go along to the little league baseball game, allowing all the children to pet him. But it might be a reasonable goal to take that dog to a little league baseball game, find a spot on a hill several yards away, and have the dog calmly rest next to you while you watch the game.

It is the job of the trainer or behavior consultant to help owners develop reasonable goals and realistic expectations. And sometimes we need to think of expectations and progress in a whole new way.

I was discussing the topic of measuring progress with my friend and colleague, Susan Fishbein. Susan has a long history of working with dogs with behavior concerns as well as years of experience working within rescue groups. She reminded me that there is no certificate of completion or blue ribbon at the end of a behavior modification plan. Progress in dogs that have been traumatized, who are severely anxious or depressed, can look very different. But there are certainly moments to celebrate.

Here are some of the benchmarks that Susan looks for when working with severely anxious or depressed dogs:

- Snoring. A dog needs to feel safe to relax enough to fall into a deep sleep.
- Having a happy dream. Most dog owners are familiar with the joy of seeing our dog yipping and running in their sleep.
- Playing with toys.
- Holding space even when we move. Some fearful dogs will scurry or bolt when the humans around them move or walk. Noticing a dog staying put is a point of progress.
- Being naughty! A dog needs to feel secure in their environment to get on the couch for the first time or dig in the trash.
- Rolling. Dogs that do not feel safe do not roll in the grass or sleep on their backs.
- Zoomies. Those sudden, fast circles around the yard.
- Sniffing. In her book, *Animals in Translation: Using the Mysteries of Autism to Decode Animal Behavior*, author and behaviorist Temple Grandin describes curiosity/interest/anticipation, or seeking, as a positive emotion.[7] If a dog is sniffing and exploring, its fear is abating, at least at that moment.
- Approaching without being lured. The dog that slouches and hides and will come to a human only for food will be able to approach a human for companionship. Even if the dog does not desire to be touched, being close can be a great goal.
- Moving more upright. The dog that would only scurry and stay low to the ground begins to have an improved posture.

I hope this gives you food for thought because after goals are set and expectations reviewed, it is time to get to work on management!

# 6

# Maizy

Maizy was meant to be a temporary dog. David and Beth's daughter volunteered at a local shelter and brought this tiny puppy home as a foster dog. Fostering is a program used by rescues and shelters that allows animals to recover and heal in a home setting while they are waiting to be adopted. Maizy and another puppy, likely a litter mate, had been found wandering the streets as strays. At only eight weeks old when found, Maizy needed time in foster care to grow old enough and healthy enough to be adopted into her forever home.

However, David and Beth's family fell in love with this pup at once. They knew it would be hard to say goodbye. It did not take too long for them to decide to adopt Maizy, she became a permanent part of the family.

David and Beth remember Maizy as a sweet puppy. In fact, Beth remembers having a book club meeting at her house and little Maizy taking turns sitting on everyone's lap. But as Maizy began to grow from a puppy to an adolescent her owners grew concerned when they began noticing changes in her behavior. And they were surprised when one day, one of the book club members, who had met Maizy in the past, came to the house, and Maizy "attacked" her at the door.

They saw other concerning changes in Maizy's behavior as she grew older. Beth and David had started kennel training Maizy which had been going well. But suddenly, if placed in the kennel Maizy would grow so upset, she would have bouts of diarrhea. This became so severe that she eventually developed stress-related colitis, a serious gastrointestinal disorder. Even though she eventually learned to tolerate being in a crate if her people were nearby, it was a long road to get there.

Away from home things were not going well either. While on walks, Maizy would bark and growl and lunge at passing people and dogs. The family tried a training class to see if that would help, but when Maizy saw the other dogs, she would "go ballistic" and try to "attack" the other puppies. During class time, Maizy and her owners were put in a corner behind a barrier. It was embarrassing and in the long run did not help Maizy's behavior.

As Maizy grew into an adult, things became worse. No visitor could enter the home without Maizy charging them. There were some close calls and Maizy's family was really worried she would bite someone. To make things more complicated, David and Beth were in the process of moving to a new state. This period of transition, moving to a new city and a new house just compounded the stress on Maizy and her family. The problematic behaviors multiplied.

Where before, walks were a challenge, now they became almost impossible. Maizy was fearful of any person or dog she encountered and would react with loud barking, snapping and growling even from a distance. Her behavior around visitors to the home continued to worsen and her owners felt she was a real safety risk. Maizy was less and less able to relax when there were changes in her environment. She became more and more stressed and clingy. David and Beth began to seek help and were referred to a Veterinary Behavior Specialist and I became their trainer.

At my first appointment with Maizy, I met a medium-sized, beautiful white dog with large spots and piercing blue eyes. Although she would likely be listed as a bully breed mix in a shelter, I saw shades of a herding breed. She had the intense gaze and lithe movements of a Border Collie. I could see her intelligence. Maizy let me know that she did not care for the looks of me, however, and at a distance, safely on a leash, used her body and voice to express her preference that I get out.

One of the biggest challenges in living with Maizy was having people in the home, but this was an important goal for her owners. David and Beth were social, outgoing people, they were living in a new city. Because of Maizy's behavior, they were not able to invite any new acquaintances to their home and were becoming isolated.

Their new home was situated next to a beautiful park that they wanted to enjoy with Maizy. But Maizy's behavior made that impossible. As the Veterinary Behavior Specialist addressed Maizy's underlying behavior issues with medication and a behavior modification plan, it was hoped I could assist in putting this plan into place and moving toward the goals of a happier home and life.

To address visitors in the home, we focused on finding a spot that could be Maizy's safe space. A place where she could hang out while visitors were present. There was a lot of trial and error as there were differences between where the humans thought Maizy should be and

## 6. Maizy

where Maizy thought she should be. In the beginning, we discovered that being out of sight of her owner was stressful for Maizy. Being closed away created a lot of crying, panting, and scratching at doors. But being within sight was stressful for visitors as Maizy barked and growled. It was a complex goal that required a lot of experimentation and gradual steps.

At the same time, we worked on taking a walk in the park next door. This started with some controlled circumstances. At first, the street between home and the park had to be clear. Walks happened at a time of day when there was minimal activity. Then Maizy's family gradually began practicing at busier times of the day. Over months, by instituting medication, training, behavior modification, and lots of patience and practice, Maizy learned walks were not a bad thing. The walks at the park grew into walks and bike rides to new locations. Maizy continued to accomplish goals and Maizy and her family was able to experience a greatly improved quality of life.

Now almost 18 months after that first meeting I sit comfortably talking with David and Beth, while Maizy hangs out in another room with no barking, crying, or growling, a triumph!

I asked David and Beth to look back and tell me about the things that were helpful in their journey with Maizy. They point out that having a supportive veterinarian makes all the difference. That includes a veterinarian who recognizes when a specialist is needed. The specialist, a veterinarian that is board certified in behavior, has made a huge contribution to Maizy's improvement. Medication has helped Maizy deal with the challenges and fears in her life. The medication helped Maizy to be calm enough to be able to learn new skills.

Understanding how important routine is to Maizy and that changing her routine can lead to an uptick in problem behaviors is something they always keep in mind. As Maizy is so uncomfortable with people being present in her home, having a day care and boarding facility that understands her needs is key. Being able to stay at the boarding facility keeps Maizy safe while allowing David and Beth to celebrate holidays and important occasions with their extended family.

David and Beth express that having a trainer that would come to their home was beneficial. As a trainer, I know that being able to assess the environment and help set up management plans is a key piece of helping dogs like Maizy feel safe and more confident.

Beth and David greatly appreciated a trainer's help in choosing two priorities from the long list of Maizy's concerns. Focusing on a couple of the high-priority obstacles helped reduce their own stress and helped lessen the feeling of being overwhelmed. As a force free trainer, I know that learning never takes place in a vacuum and working on singular items will always allow learning to leak over to other issues. It also helps that Maizy is food motivated.

It has been helpful for Maizy's owners to master the way in which dogs think and communicate, and how they learn. Understanding how dogs use their body language to express their emotional state has been fundamental. David and Beth are now able to observe Maizy and recognize if her stress level is rising. If on a walk, Maizy's body language will tell them if they need to steer clear or retreat when triggers enter her environment.

In fact, David and Beth, both skiers, talk about going "off piste" with Maizy or leaving the path when triggers are approaching. They've become very good at this even though they worry they look rude when they suddenly avoid a neighbor. In fact, they have gotten so good at reading dog body language that they recognize the signs of stress in other dogs. They reflect that now, out on a walk, they can spot reactivity in a dog, even if the dog's owner has not realized it is happening.

I ask what has not been helpful and Beth and David are not sure. They tell me they do not look at things as not working. They look at behavior modification as a trial-and-error process. Beth points out, you must accept this and be willing to try different things to learn what does and what does not work. You must give yourself the freedom to explore.

Our process for teaching Maizy to go to a safe place when visitors come to the house is a wonderful example of this. Leaving the area of activity and going to a safe space is one of the skills I use for dogs that are not comfortable with strangers entering their home and may become reactive or put the person at risk for biting. The dog is taught that the doorbell or knock on the door is a cue to run to their safe place, where they will have treats and toys and all manner of wonderful things and where no stranger will bother them.

Because Maizy was highly reactive, we first chose a bedroom behind a closed door as her safe space. But, found that she would bite and chew at the door. So, we then placed an exercise pen in the room behind the closed door. At the same time, we worked on helping her learn to relax and be comfortable in the pen. But we found when separated from her human family members that her anxiety increased, and she became more upset. Maizy was able to climb over the top of the five-foot pen and again would bite and scratch at the door.

## 6. *Maizy*

So, we changed the plan. Beth and David started having Maizy run to her crate in one of the central rooms where she could see the visitors but still be at a safe distance and contained. While in her crate one of her owners would sit nearby, capturing any calm behavior with reinforcements. This worked much better. David and Beth began making this the routine and Maizy soon had several successful periods of quiet time in her crate when strangers were in the house. Once she accomplished this, they were able to grow the behavior and have Maizy relax calmly in other parts of the house. This plan took time and required a lot of flexibility and not giving up.

I asked Beth and David how living with Maizy impacts getting a future dog. They admit they may not get another dog. Not all of that is due to Maizy, it is also due to their stage of life. David and Beth love Maizy. However, they know that if in the future they are blessed with grandchildren that life will become much more complicated.

Now the work they have done has allowed those walks in the park they always dreamed of. They love walking Maizy, and do so daily, but Beth reminds me, every walk is a training walk. You do not let your guard down and you are always aware of what is around you. They both agree that this is how life with Maizy is going to be. They do believe in rescue and would like to think that if they did get another dog, it would be a rescue dog.

For now, they continue to focus on and enjoy Maizy. In the last year or so she has made many improvements. Due to Beth and David's hard work and diligence, Maizy is even able to join in on weekend bike rides, sitting calmly in her own doggy trailer. Maizy will now lie quietly under a table at cafes along the way if she is at a comfortable distance from people and other dogs.

Maizy has made tremendous progress, in fact, when I arrived to talk with Beth and David, Maizy knew the knock on the door was the cue to retreat. The dog who in the past would scratch at the bedroom door and bark continuously now remained relaxed and entertained herself the entirety of my visit. David and Beth celebrate these improvements and are now able to enjoy short periods of entertaining a few friends in their home, helping to end their isolation. A huge milestone!

Maizy's family loves all her wonderful traits, qualities that are not often visible to others. She is sweet, she returns tenfold all the love she receives from her humans. She likes to talk, and each day when David arrives home from work, she will use her howls and wails to give him a report on all the day's happenings.

### I Know Your Dog Is a Good Dog

Maizy is smart and loves to learn. Amazingly, Maizy has learned to ask for help and her humans have learned how to respond. One of Maizy's reinforcements during training is to play tug. Now when going for a walk a couple of her favorite toys will go with her. Maizy knows that when a trigger such as a dog or a person appears it is her job to let her humans know, she has learned the routine is to move away, to look at her humans and that they will play tug.

David and Beth know Maizy is a remarkable dog and was meant to be theirs.

# 7

# The Behavior Modification Plan—Part 2

You will notice the first part of the behavior modification plan involves a lot of talking and planning. Those plans are necessary, but it will not be long before you are ready for the hands-on active part of your plan. There is much you can do early on to start improving the life of your dog and yours!

## *Management*

I was contacted by an owner whose dog had some habits the family found annoying. The dog would sit at the window and bark at any passing person, dog, cat, butterfly, or cloud. When visitors came in the door, the dog would start running and enthusiastically jump into the arms of the hapless guest. The dog was happy and friendly, but his gusto for life was wearing on the humans living with him. I suggested the family begin with some management techniques while we worked on training some better manners.

I suggested covering the bottom of the large windows with an opaque, decorative window cling to obstruct the dog's view through the front windows. I suggested having the dog in another room or behind a gate when visitors arrived to prevent jumping. We talked about the training plan and scheduled the next visit.

Prior to the next session, I received a call from the owner telling me they did not think they needed further meetings because the management plan was working great. The dog could not see what was going on outside so the barking had been greatly reduced. Having the dog behind a gate when visitors arrived, gave the dog a chance to calm down before he greeted company and now the jumping rarely happened. The family was happy with the results and did not feel they needed further help.

## I Know Your Dog Is a Good Dog

All they had needed were a few ideas to manage the dog's behavior. Easy case for me!

Management, in simple terms, means arranging the environment to prevent the problem behavior from occurring. If we can reduce the problem behavior from being practiced, we are interrupting the reinforcement of that behavior. Not only is management useful for dogs with mild, annoying, behaviors, but is essential for dogs with larger behavior concerns.

Any behavior that occurs over and over is likely being reinforced. Any behavior that is reinforced will become stronger and more frequent. It is worth repeating: any behavior that is reinforced will become stronger and more frequent.

Let's dissect that statement because it is important. Reinforcement is anything that follows a behavior that makes the behavior likely to happen again. That reinforcement can come from within or without. I work hard, I receive a yearly bonus, and I work hard the next year. Working hard is reinforced by an external reward, money. My kitchen faucet breaks, so I decide to fix it myself. It begins working, I feel really proud of myself and decide to take on another home project. My behavior of home repair is reinforced internally.

Now, how about this. I am driving in traffic; another car cuts me off and drives away at a fast speed. I scream at the driver, even though he is now miles down the road and cannot hear me. The screaming relieves the stress of a near crash. The stress relief feels good. I'm likely to scream at the next car that cuts me off.

I once had a little Shih Tzu named Max. Max was a barker; he would sit by the front door and bark his high-pitched bark at anything that moved. He once barked at a leaf that was blowing across the lawn. One day I had just had enough, I yelled at my little dog, "shut up"!!!! Whew, that felt good. Luckily, I knew that instant feeling of stress relief could reinforce my yelling, and I recognized this might feel good to me at the moment but was not good for my dog. I needed to address his barking in a different manner.

In order to arrange a management plan and prevent this unintentional reinforcement, we need to know what stimuli are triggering the problem behavior. The plan will work best if we are very specific about those triggers. It can help to sit down and think about this in a detailed way and to write down your thoughts.

Maybe one of those triggers is other dogs. The appearance of another dog causes your dog to bark and lunge. Is it all dogs? Is it big

## 7. The Behavior Modification Plan—Part 2

and little dogs, or fluffy dogs, or dogs with hair over their eyes? Is it dogs who are across the street, forty feet away, fifty?

Maybe your dog barks at people while out on walks. All people? People on bikes, people carrying packages. Does it happen everywhere? Away from home, at home, while inside the house? Out the front window or all windows? In the yard? Does it happen at all times of the day? Does it happen at mealtimes? Is it only after dark?

A management statement may look like this; my dog barks at children carrying backpacks when they get off the school bus in the afternoon and walk down my side of the street. Management for this trigger may be to remove the dog from the front of the house during the time the school bus arrives. Being specific helps us identify the behavior that needs to be managed and helps us create a specific management plan. Trust me, I know how annoying it can be when the trainer, me!, works on getting those specifics. But it is worth the time and effort.

Here are a few of the common situations that can benefit from management and some management suggestions:

- While I am standing in the kitchen preparing my dogs' meals, my dogs start to bark and snap at each other.
- One of my dogs finishes his meal fast and starts to crowd my other dog who is still eating, causing the dogs to start growling at each other.

MANAGEMENT TIP: Separate dogs in different areas or by a barrier before preparing meals and keep them separated until they are both finished eating.

- My dog barks at me incessantly while I am preparing his food.

MANAGEMENT TIP: Place the dog in another area of the house while preparing food. Or prepare multiple meals ahead of time.

- My dog paws at me while I am eating.

MANAGEMENT TIP: Place the dog in a crate or behind a barrier and provide a high-value chew toy/bone during mealtimes.

- My dog snaps at anyone who comes near when he is chewing on a high-value toy/treat/bone.

MANAGEMENT TIP: The dog is only allowed to have high-value chews when crated or tethered.

- My dog chews on shoes.

## I Know Your Dog Is a Good Dog

MANAGEMENT TIP: Keep shoes in places they cannot be accessed.

- My dog pulls so hard while walking he chokes himself on his collar.

MANAGEMENT TIP: Switch to using a harness.

- My dog climbs on the furniture when I am not home.

MANAGEMENT TIP: Place empty boxes on furniture.

- My dog pulls and lunges at other dogs while we are on a walk.
- My dog lunges/growls/barks at people we see while on a walk.

MANAGEMENT TIP: Walk dogs at hours when other dogs and people are not likely to be around.

- My dog steals food from the kitchen counter.

MANAGEMENT TIP: Do not leave food on the counter.

- My dog jumps on visitors that come into the house.
- My dog knocks down my young child.
- My dog nips at visitors' feet when they are leaving the house.

MANAGEMENT TIP: Keep the dog on a leash.

You get the idea. Some of these management tips are obvious and you have probably tried some of them already. What is important to know is that using management is okay! It is a valid solution to many behavior concerns. It is not cheating or a shortcut. Further, it is an important part of the behavior modification plan as it prevents the dog from practicing the problem behavior.

However... One thing trainers and behavior consultants like to say is, "management is wonderful, until it fails, and management will almost always fail." If management is directed toward nuisance behaviors, it may not be a great concern. If a dog steals food from the counter, you may have decided to manage this by never leaving food on the counter. But one morning your alarm does not go off, you are late for work, and you barely remember to grab your purse. You forgot to put the roast that was thawing on the counter back into the refrigerator. You arrive home at the end of the day to find the remains of the roast on the floor. Dinner is ruined. Not a huge tragedy.

But sometimes management is directed towards dangerous behavior. Your dog has bitten visitors and you are managing this by always having two closed gates between the dog and company. Your eight-year-old child has friends over and is very excited to show his friends his newest toy. He runs to retrieve the toy from his room. In his excitement, he rushes through the gate but does not confirm it is latched. The dog escapes and bites a child. This is a huge problem with a lot of potential hazardous fallout. As much as we try, we are human, and humans make mistakes.

For some cases, management may be all that is needed, but for other cases, it is only the beginning of a plan to change behavior. Management is something you can begin right away, on your own, while you are waiting to begin your dog's full behavior modification plan.

# What to Do Right Now

Along with management, while you are waiting to work with your trainer, there are a few more things I recommend starting as soon as you can:

## Stop All Punishment

This is the cardinal rule of living with and working with dogs that have behavior concerns. Dogs who have anxiety, aggression, reactivity, or depression are already living under stress. These dogs are not being belligerent, disobedient, or stubborn. In fact, most of these dogs spend their days trying really hard to navigate through life with the minimum amount of trouble.

Punishing or treating a dog harshly will only worsen the issues. So, what does this mean? It does not mean letting your dog do whatever it wants; remember, management can go a long way in structuring your dog's day and decreasing problem behavior. What it does mean is to stop using any equipment that causes pain or fear. This includes shock collars, electric fences, choke collars, or prong collars. It means not yelling at your dog, shoving, manhandling, or hitting your dog.

## Reinforce the Behavior You Want

Catch your dog being good. This is harder than it sounds, as we usually don't notice our dog if they are, for example, resting quietly. When you do see your dog displaying behavior you like, reinforce it! You can reinforce behavior with what is rewarding to your dog, it may be praise, play, or food. Reinforcement doesn't always have to be food, but food works well. I know a Veterinary Behavior Specialist who has said, "If you like it, throw food at it!"

## *Practice Safety*

Trainers like to say past behavior is the best predictor of future behavior. If your dog has shown aggression in any certain situation, she is likely to do it again. Prevent your dog from being in that situation until you can work with your trainer.

## *Take a Walk*

That may sound like funny advice for a dog owner. Especially when I've said you do not have to take your dog for a walk. But if you do, it needs to be a restorative walk, for you and your dog. It makes me so sad when I see a dog on a short leash trotting along a busy road next to its owner. I always wonder if the dog is enjoying that walk. I have a friend who has called walks like this "forced marches." After a walk, a dog should be calm, rested, and relaxed. They should not be wound up or so exhausted they cannot stand. If they are, you need to review your walking plan.

Think of experiencing a walk through your dog's brain, her eyes, ears, and nose. I always put my dogs in the car and take them to a park for a walk instead of walking through my busy neighborhood. It takes more work. It involves different shoes and equipment that I must find and keep organized. But it is worth it.

When I and my dog walk, we prefer a spot with few people. My current dog likes people but being somewhere that is not crowded gives him the opportunity to unwind. I look for shade. I look for grass and hills and creeks. I use 30-foot leashes when walking my dogs. I find they actually pull much less when they have the space to explore. I let my dogs choose the route. They will usually follow their nose.

And guess what I do? I do a lot of standing around. Instead of a full-out run from point A to point B, my dogs are busy being dogs. They search through brush, they dig holes, they track scents. And while they are enjoying their walk, I enjoy mine. I listen to the birds, I watch the clouds, I smell the flowers. Both my dogs and I go home relaxed. That is what a walk should be.

If you have a dog that is reactive on walks or a dog that pulls like a freight train, I ask you to just give this a try. If you do not feel confident

# 7. The Behavior Modification Plan—Part 2

having your dog on a long line you can add ways to keep your dog secure. Many people use two leashes, one attached to a collar and one attached to a harness. That way if one leash becomes disconnected you still have one.

If you feel that a long line gives your dog extra room to take off and may increase the likelihood of pulling you down, check out leashes that have built-in handles, often called traffic handles. This can allow you to let out the leash a little at a time to avoid rope burn. I have also known people who tie large knots in their long line every ten feet or so. It serves the same purpose. One type of leash I strongly recommend not using are the leashes that automatically unwind from a cartridge within the handle. Every one I have tried eventually wears out and breaks. You end up with a loose dog and a wire flinging back at you under force. I've also seen these cause injury to fingers and hands.

## *How Dogs Communicate*

Once goals are established and the management plan is in place, it is time to involve the important part of the behavior equation, your dog! It is time for you and your dog to start on your first homework assignment. That is, to learn how your dog communicates or at least tries to communicate with you. You and your dog are embarking on a journey called a behavior modification plan. You will work together as a team. You are going to be asking your dog to tell you how it is feeling in different situations. You are going to be asking your dog to listen to you for instructions. It is impossible to do this if you cannot communicate.

Communication, in the broadest sense, is the exchange of ideas, thoughts, feelings, or intentions using speech, signals, or writing. Brenda Aloff offers a fantastic photo guide to dog body language in her book, *Canine Body Language: A Photographic Guide Interpreting the Native Language of the Domestic Dog*. "For dogs, communicating is primarily about intentions, especially intentions about what is 'safe vs dangerous' or about predation. 'Come closer, let's do some mutual grooming.' Or 'this bone is mine and if you come closer, you'll be very sorry.' Or 'Let's go get that deer!' Dogs communicate these messages largely through their body language. They don't write, of course, and their vocalizations are actually a minor part of their language. If you want to know a dog's intentions, look at the signals he is giving with his body."[1]

# I Know Your Dog Is a Good Dog

Dogs have so much to tell us. But we speak two different languages. If we are going to set about changing our dog's emotions and modifying their behavior, we first must learn how to interpret their communication. Noted canine behavior consultant, Sarah Kalnajs, CDBC, CPDT has produced a very popular set of DVDs with hours of viewing and interpreting dog body language. Kalnajs describes canine body language as distance increasing (go away) and distance decreasing (come closer).[2] I highly recommend viewing these DVDs to see wonderful examples of canine body language along with Kalnajs' interpretations. You will learn a lot and discover so much about how your dog is communicating.

Your trainer should be spending time dedicated to helping you understand what your dog is telling you. Understanding your dog's body language is the very first key to unlocking the door to success. Your dog's body language is going to help you know how your dog feels at any given time during the behavior modification process. What your dog is telling you is going to regulate everything you do in the process; it will determine each next step.

In the process of changing behavior, you, your trainer, and your dog will at some point, be working in the presence of the dog's triggers. This may be triggers such as dogs or people that cause your dog to react, it may be your absence from a dog that has separation anxiety. During the modification process, we must know how our dog feels about the situation. We need to know if we are asking too much or if we can ask more. Our dogs will attempt to communicate to us that I'm nervous or I feel great! They will tell us I might bite, please go away, or okay I think I can give it a try. They will tell us about these things through their body language.

Learning how to interpret what your dog is telling you is not important only because we love them and want a deeper relationship or because it is fun. This is important because their language will tell you if the behavior plan is helping or not. It is important because it will help keep your dog and those around them safe. It is important because it may save your dog's life.

## *Stress Signals*

One tip that I give to my clients is that in general, "come closer" language tends to be loose, curvy, and floppy. "Go away language" tends to be stiff, straight, and still. In addition to general body language there is a type of vocabulary we call stress signals. These signals are a group of

## 7. The Behavior Modification Plan—Part 2

behaviors that we believe are an early indication that something in the environment is causing an uptick in the dog's stress level.

All organisms show signs of stress, even humans who get nervous may develop sweaty palms or start to breathe faster. If we can recognize the early signs of rising stress in our dog, we will be able to help lower that stress level. Stress signals allow us to pause, observe the surroundings, and intervene or exit that environment. A stress signal can be an early warning as to what will happen next. "They are often shown by a dog if he feels insecure, stressed or overburdened."[3]

There are many of these signals, you will not see all of them in all dogs. In my experience, most dogs will have two or three "go-to" stress signals that they will exhibit. Some common stress signals are:

- Yawning
- Sneezing
- Scratching
- Sniffing the ground
- Lip licks or tongue flicks
- Raising one front paw

One thing to remember about stress signals is that many of them are common, normal behaviors. It is when they happen out of context that we need to pay attention to them. I worked with a dog several years ago that would sneeze toward the end of our training sessions. There was nothing around that should be causing a sneeze such as dust or pollen. So, when I heard the sneeze, I took this as a cue that the dog was becoming overwhelmed. I was likely asking too much of the dog or had gone on too long with training. If I heard a sneeze, I knew that I needed to end the training session, even if time was not up.

But sometimes a yawn is just a yawn. For example, drooling is a common sign of stress in dogs. It is not unusual for a dog that is distressed at being confined, to drool when enclosed in a crate. Sometimes the drooling may be so excessive that the dog's neck and chest will become wet. However, I live with a Golden Retriever that LOVES food. When he watches people eat, he will have ropes of drool coming from his mouth. He may be stressed at not getting some yummy people food, but not quite the same thing as a stress signal. It is all about the context.

It is important to learn what signals your own dog exhibits. I ask my clients to observe their dogs in several different environments and to watch for stress signals. Once they discover the stress signals their dog uses, I ask them to choose the one they see most often, then spend thirty minutes observing their dog and count how many times the signal occurs.

Try this in different areas. This will give you a good opportunity to start learning your dog's communication style. If you are in the front yard and you see eight tongue flicks, for example, in a half hour, and then are at the park and see 15 tongue flicks in a half hour you have learned something about your dog.

Once you are familiar with how your dog expresses stress you can better know what makes them uncomfortable. Learning how your dog communicates will help you clearly identify your dog's triggers, those things in the environment that cause stress or reactivity. This will be part of the foundation for building the next steps of the behavior modification plan.

All this tracking and logging is the beginning of a better communication system you will have with your canine companion. And the information you gather will be of great use to your trainer. Before long noticing that your dog is saying something, understanding the communication, and acting on the conversation with your dog will become automatic.

Understanding canine body language keeps us and our dogs safe. I don't want to be bitten and I do not want my dog to bite. If I can "hear" what my dog is saying by observing her body language I can avoid altercations. If I am not willing to listen, my dog will need to get louder.

I had a call from an owner whose dog had bitten a child that was visiting their home. The owner explained that her dog had been resting quietly on the floor when the child sat next to the dog and leaned on the top of the dog. The dog got up and walked away (please go away, you are making me uncomfortable). The child followed the dog and was stroking the dog's ears, and the dog growled. (I really mean it; you really need to go away because you are scaring me.) The dog left the room, and the child ran after the dog, the dog turned and barked at the child (I'VE TOLD YOU TWICE NOW, LEAVE ME ALONE!). The dog went behind a couch, the child followed, and the dog bit the child.

If the owner had been familiar with canine body language, the bite probably could have been avoided. I guarantee that if this interaction had been on video we would see a huge amount of canine body language from the dog, likely with many stress signals at the beginning of the interaction. That dog tried very hard to be heard. But no one was speaking his language.

# 7. The Behavior Modification Plan—Part 2

## *Growling*

A note about growling. When I was early in my training career, I had a dog named Thelma. Thelma was a dog that was very nervous around people she did not know. I was talking to my training mentor, describing an incident when Thelma had growled at a visitor to my home. "I scolded her right away," I explained with a tinge of pride in my voice. "Oh," my mentor said, "you should not have done that." This very experienced trainer explained that growling is simply communication. The dog is expressing that there is something wrong, that it is concerned or scared.

Punishing a growl, and most dogs do find scolding punishing, will teach a dog that growling is unacceptable. By punishing the growl, we will take away an early warning signal. A dog who would have growled as a warning to a bite may just eliminate the growl and go for the bite. My embarrassment at what I felt was a huge faux pas cemented my mentor's advice in my mind. I have never forgotten those words of wisdom. I believe it is part of the reason I have not yet been bitten by a client dog (that sound you hear is me knocking on wood).

Dogs largely communicate with their body language, but they do have a repertoire of vocalizations. Growling is one. Growling means I am uncomfortable, I need space. After several years of experience, I have learned that if I am working with a dog that growls at me, I say, "thank you!" I step back, I look at the environment and my interaction with the dog, and think, what can I do to lower this dog's stress level.

The study of how dogs communicate is ongoing. I know there will be many exciting discoveries ahead. For now, we look, and we listen. What is your dog saying to you? If you would like to dive deeper into the science of all the ways dogs learn and communicate, check out the website for the Family Dog Project[4] and take a look at their publications. There are pretty exciting things on the horizon for canine communication.

## *Positive Reinforcement Training*

Management and understanding canine communication are both parts of the foundation of a behavior modification plan. An additional part is training your dog to offer certain behaviors or skills on cue. How we teach a dog these skills is of utmost importance. Not all training methods are alike.

## I Know Your Dog Is a Good Dog

Dog training, as we know it, developed from methods used in the early twentieth century. One of the earliest books on dog training was published in 1910 by Colonel Konrad Most.[5] Most is considered by many to be the father of modern, traditional, training. Most's approach to dog training was largely based on the way military dogs were trained for World War I and World War II. It was these principles of military training that grew into obedience training for the family dog.

Through the 1950s and 1960s, several books were published that influenced traditional dog training. Blanche Saunders became a nationally known dog trainer and traveled through the United States in the late 1950s and early 1960s promoting her style of obedience training. Saunders describes teaching a dog to not jump on people by first shouting NO and if that does not work to bump the dog's nose once to make her get down. To get dogs off furniture, Saunders instructed, to push them.

Saunders was very much in favor of the use of a leash and collar to jerk a dog and using the leash to pull the dog. In fact, one of her books, *The Complete Novice Obedience Course*, has as the front cover illustration, a woman standing on a dog's leash pulling them into a down position.[6]

In the later part of the twentieth century, a few scientists began to take a deeper look into canine behavior and how dogs developed as a species. Almost every certified dog trainer has a copy of *Genetics and the Social Behavior of the Dog* by John Paul Scott and John Fuller, first published in 1965. Scott and Fuller took an in-depth look at how genetics impacts behavior through all the developmental stages of dogs, from birth through puppyhood, adolescence, adult, and senior years.[7]

I can remember seeing British dog trainer, Barbara Woodhouse, on the *Tonight Show* in the 1980s. The host, Johnny Carson would feign amazement as Woodhouse demonstrated teaching a dog to walk on a leash with her high-pitched "walkies!" She touted her series of leash jerks as the way to teach any dog to walk nicely on a leash.

Then, in 1999, came a book called, *Don't Shoot the Dog!* by Karen Pryor. Pryor writes about her experience of using positive reinforcement training when she worked in Hawaii as a head dolphin trainer.

"I had trained dogs and horses by traditional methods, but dolphins were a different proposition; you cannot use a leash or a bridle or even your fist on an animal that just swims away. Positive reinforcers-primarily a bucket of fish-were the only tools we had."[8]

Pryor began applying the principles of positive reinforcement training she used with sea mammals to other species and began writing about her success. It is not an understatement to say that her book,

# 7. The Behavior Modification Plan—Part 2

*Don't Shoot the Dog!* cracked open the dog training world, shook it up, and dumped it on its head. Thousands of modern-day dog trainers, myself included, have been influenced by this book and subsequent books by Karen Pryor.

While traditional training depended on domination and coercion, positive reinforcement training supports humane treatment, building trust, developing clear communication, and establishing a relationship with our dogs. This is not just a feel-good, lazy, or permissive way of training. Positive reinforcement training is based on the scientific principles of how an animal, any animal, learns.

In learning theory, positive reinforcement means that when a behavior results in something happening that I like, I will tend to repeat that behavior. I go to work, and at the end of the week, I get a paycheck. Getting that paycheck increases the likelihood that I will continue going to work. Because money is something I like, the paycheck reinforces my behavior.

I can certainly tell you that if I went to work, and at the end of the week instead of money my boss gave me a pat on the back and said, "Good job! See you next week!" that would not be very reinforcing for me. That is probably the last time that boss would see me, and I would not be very likely to keep coming back.

So, a reinforcer is something important or rewarding to the learner. For dogs, food is very reinforcing, and so food is often used in training. Playing games, like tug, can be a reinforcer. Even the chance to smell the ground can be a reinforcer. The dog is the one that decides what is rewarding enough to be a reinforcement. It is up to the owner, with the assistance of the trainer, to figure that out.

"Scientifically speaking, reinforcement is an event that (a) occurs during or upon completion of a behavior; and (b) increases the likelihood of that behavior occurring in the future."[9] "Reinforcement training is not a system of reward and punishment—by and large modern trainers don't even use those words."[10]

Along with teaching our dogs new skills, positive reinforcement training does many wonderful things for the human. It removes the burden on the human that you must hurt your dog to help your dog. It takes away the idea that you must dominate your dog for your dog to learn. It provides the owner the opportunity to think and to learn. Instead of approaching training with the construct of, how can I stop my dog from doing ... (fill in the blank here, with whatever problem behavior you can think of). It helps us change our thinking to, how can I get my dog to ... (fill in the blank with the wonderful things your dog can do).

### I Know Your Dog Is a Good Dog

Positive reinforcement training builds confidence in our dog. I love seeing an "Ah! Look what I did!" expression on a dog's face. Positive reinforcement training can add structure to a dog's world. They learn there is cause and effect. If I do this, that will happen. This helps to set boundaries and improve impulse control. And best of all, positive reinforcement training teaches a dog how to learn.

When I first started training, it was common to physically move or force our dogs to do what we wanted. If I wanted the dog to sit, I may pull up on the collar and push down on their rear. With positive reinforcement training, I will help my dog to figure out what behavior will be reinforced. We will work as a team.

When I was young and learning to read, I loved the Nancy Drew girl detective series. I can still remember coming across a new word, sleuth. I had no idea what that was and asked my mother for a definition. Of course, I knew her answer would be to look it up in the dictionary. But I thought I would try anyway. It would have been much easier on me if she just told me. It didn't work and I hunkered down by our set of red-bound dictionaries to find the definition.

By being an active learner, by acting and exploring and searching for the answer, my brain was working and once I found the answer, I never forgot it. If my mother had quickly told me the definition, I would have it at that moment, but may not have remembered the next time I came across the word. It would have also encouraged my behavior of asking instead of doing it for myself. By requiring me to use my own brain, my mother taught me not only the meaning of the word but how to find out the meaning of words. She gave me tools to learn. With positive reinforcement training our dogs learn the process of learning and that impacts every future learning task.

What does positive reinforcement training look like? Most modern trainers use a process called marker training. In marker training, the trainer will get a behavior, then mark the behavior and then reinforce the behavior. With this process, the behavior will happen more often and will become stronger. It is reinforced. By the way, I just gave you the formula to teach your dog almost anything. The secret is out.

## *Using a Marker*

What is a marker? A marker is a signal that tells the dog that what you were doing when you heard or saw the marker is the behavior that earned the reinforcer. Picture this: You are learning how to dive into

## 7. The Behavior Modification Plan—Part 2

water. You dive, then get out of the water and your coach says, that was perfect, do that again. But imagine if with the next dive, you are in the perfect position and you hear a whistle. You know that at the moment, of that whistle, where your body is in space, the position of your body, and the muscles you are using. That is a much clearer signal to you that this dive is what you need to do again.

For most dogs, an auditory marker is used. I typically use the word, "yes." Some trainers will also use a mechanical clicker, a small plastic box that makes a click sound when a piece of metal or button in the box is pushed. For dogs that are deaf, a visual marker can be used, a flashing light or a waving of the fingers for example. For dogs that are deaf and blind a tap on the shoulder has been used with great success as a marker.

### *Timing*

An important point to remember about marker training is the timing of the marker. The marker, whether it is a verbal "yes" or a click, must happen at the moment the behavior happens. Think of marking as taking a picture of the behavior. This is clear communication for the dog to tell him which behavior was reinforced. And then, once the behavior is marked the reinforcer must be delivered within seconds. Here is a pro tip: video your training sessions with your dog. I do, most professionals do. You will be amazed at the things you see that can be improved. This is how I learned that I tend to mark late, so I was able to correct that.

How do you get the behavior so you can mark it? With traditional training, dogs were coerced or physically placed into a behavior. To get a dog to stop pulling on a leash the trainer may jerk hard on the collar. To get a dog to lie down, a trainer may pull down on the leash, forcing the dog's head to the floor. Because positive reinforcement training focuses on bonding and trust building, those methods are not used. Instead, modern trainers will use capturing, luring, and shaping.

### *Capturing*

Capturing means marking a behavior when it happens naturally. If I want to reinforce my dog lying on his bed, I will keep treats handy and any time he chooses to lie on his bed, I will say "yes" or click the clicker and toss him a treat. My dog will soon figure out that if I go lie on that bed, she is likely to make that noise and give me food so that might be fun to do. Once the behavior is happening consistently you can think of a cue for the behavior, such as "bed." Your trainer can help with that process.

Capturing requires attention and preparedness. Treats need to be readily within reach in a variety of locations. The number of times the behavior is marked needs to outweigh the number of times it is not. Let me expand on that by using the example above of capturing your dog lying on a bed. If your dog lies on its bed 20 times a day and you only notice and mark four times, that may not be meaningful enough to your dog for learning to take place. That means that the 16 other times your dog lay on her bed, nothing happened. That will weaken learning.

## *Luring*

Luring is using food or some other attractive item to get the dog to do the behavior. If I want to teach my dog to sit, I may hold a treat in front of his nose, bring it up over his forehead which causes his head to go up and his rear to go down. I have lured him into a sit. That gives me the opportunity to mark the sit and then reinforce the sit.

If I am teaching my dog to touch my fingers with his nose I may wiggle my fingers, the dog is curious and puts his nose close to my hand. I can mark and reinforce that behavior.

## *Shaping*

Shaping means breaking a large behavior into small pieces and teaching each piece separately. All the dogs you see on television doing fancy stuff, have most likely been shaped. I once taught my boxer, Lola, to grab a tissue out of the tissue box when I sneezed. I did this by shaping each step. I used capturing to teach her to walk to the tissue box as a stand-alone behavior. Then I used luring to teach her to touch the box with her nose as a separate behavior. I taught her to pull a tissue from the box on its own. Then touching the tissue to my hand was yet another piece. Then we worked on chaining all the steps together and added the sneeze as the cue. Shaping is great fun!

These basic methods can be combined and often we are doing that without realizing it. Internationally known dog trainer and behavior consultant Pat Miller describes lure-shaping as using a combination of luring to shape the small pieces of a behavior. Miller has also done quite a bit of study on dogs learning a behavior by imitating people or other dogs.[11] I had the pleasure of attending a workshop with Miller

## 7. The Behavior Modification Plan—Part 2

and watched a trainer teach a dog to touch a chair just by the human demonstrating the behavior and having the dog imitate it.

### Am I Doing This Right?

Everyone that has tried to train a dog will reach a point when training doesn't seem to be working. I know this has happened to me. There can be numerous reasons for training to stall. One of the first things I do when this happens is to look at myself, not the dog. Most of the time when my dog is not learning it is because I am being a sloppy trainer. It is not because the dog is stubborn or stupid, it is because I am confusing the dog. Here are some of the mistakes I commonly make.

Am I marking the behavior on time? Am I saying "yes" too early or too late? If I am, my dog is probably confused about exactly what behavior I want.

Am I delivering the treat or other reinforcer quickly? I've been known to keep treats in my pocket and then must search them out. By the time I get the treat to my dog he has forgotten what we were even doing.

Am I ignoring my dog by being distracted or talking to other people? I have been guilty of asking for a behavior, like waiting at the door, and then checking the mailbox and not noticing that my dog is offering the behavior I just asked for! The behavior has gone unreinforced.

Am I trying to progress a behavior too fast? It is hard to stop a training session when your dog is doing great! When you've been working hard on teaching your dog a new skill and she finally does it, it is exciting and you are so proud of her, you want to do it again. But I have ruined a good training session by asking for a behavior just once more. I have caused my dog to get bored or frustrated. When I get that "just one more" feeling, I know it is time to stop.

Am I giving a hand cue and a verbal cue at the same time? This is also confusing to dogs. A hand cue will outweigh the verbal every time and I'm left wondering why my dog is not learning the word I am using.

Am I waving my hands around? I'm guilty! My dog is trying to figure out if I am giving a hand cue or handing her a treat or just what the heck I am doing.

Am I frustrating or boring my dog? This happens when I make training sessions too long.

Did I forget to consider other factors? Am I trying to use food to motivate a dog that just ate? Am I trying to teach loose leash walking to a dog that just had a walk in the hot sun or in the reverse, am I teaching loose leash walking to an adolescent who had no exercise that day?

Almost every time the plan does not seem to be working, a good trainer can reach success by changing and improving what they are doing. It's almost always me and not the dog that is putting up the obstacles.

I loved to do training games with my dog Lola. She loved to learn, and it was a fun bonding experience for both of us. Just for grins, I decided to teach Lola to put her front feet on a platform. I took an old textbook and covered it with duct tape. That was our platform.

Lola always knew that when I came into the room with my clicker and the treat bag the game was afoot! I placed the platform on the floor in the middle of the room. Lola knew I wanted something from her. She knew when she figured it out that I would click, and she would get that treat. Lola tried various things, some things she knew like offering a sit or trying to shake hands. Then she tried things she didn't know like nudging a table, but she never approached the platform. It was like the platform was invisible. I could feel myself becoming frustrated and I knew that was a big red flag for me to stop the training session and think.

I had to ponder; how can I help my dog succeed? How can I set up the environment for the behavior to happen? I thought for a minute then I had an idea. I gathered nine or ten more books. I put them together on the floor in a large rectangle. The books filled up so much of the floor that Lola could barely turn around without touching a foot to a book. When her foot accidentally touched the "platform" I captured that moment and clicked. Aha! Her eyes lit up. I could see her brain working, she was thinking, "Ohhhh, you want me to put my foot on the book, okay!" She started to do this easily. After a few repetitions, I took two or three books away from the collection. After a few more successful tries, I removed a few more. Finally, only our original platform book was left.

Lola had learned that putting her foot on the platform was the game. She learned this without me punishing her, forcing her, or scaring her. Because this is the way I trained Lola, she loved to learn, and she was an engaged and happy student. It was my job to help Lola accomplish the task I wanted. I cannot understate how much looking at yourself first, will improve any training session.

## *The FAQs on Marker Training*

Here are some common questions I hear from clients about marker training.

# 7. The Behavior Modification Plan—Part 2

How do I introduce a marker to my dog?

We start by doing something we call charging the marker. If you are using a mechanical clicker, click once and drop a treat on the floor. Make sure your dog sees the treat. Repeat this several times in a row. When you click and your dog looks at the floor waiting for the treat to drop, you know you have them. If you are using a verbal marker, use the same process, say your marker word, and drop a treat.

Once your dog understands the marker means a treat is coming be prepared to deliver that treat every single time. Even if you make a mistake. I have kept clickers in my back pocket at times causing them to click when I sit down. If I click, I treat. The dog will not be confused. They will be learning click means treat. Although I try really hard not to have accidental clicks.

If I am using a clicker, do I have to have one with me all the time?

If you are working on capturing a new behavior, you will want to have a clicker handy. I tend to have them all over, in the house, in the car, and in my pocket. If you truly want to capture, you will not want to miss opportunities to mark the behavior.

Will I have to keep using a marker forever?

No, the marker is used to teach a new behavior. Once a dog understands a behavior you will put that behavior on cue. Once a behavior is on cue you do not have to continue to use the marker. However, if you are practicing the behavior in a new environment or working on solidifying the behavior you can always bring back your maker to help with the learning.

My dog has a noise phobia, will a clicker scare her?

It might. If it does try using a verbal marker. Or you can slowly introduce the clicker by making it very quiet. You can do this by enfolding the clicker in your hand or wrapping it in a cloth.

Can I use a clicker sometimes and a verbal marker at other times?

Yes, you can, there is no reason a dog cannot learn more than one marker. My students would laugh at me at moments I wanted to capture a behavior and couldn't reach my clicker, so would instead yell, "click!" But for the sake of clean learning instead of messy learning choosing what you will use and sticking with it, will work better.

# I Know Your Dog Is a Good Dog

WILL MY DOG GET FAT FROM CONSTANT TREATS?

Hopefully not. Here are some suggestions I've used for dogs that need to cut calories.

Use your dog's daily ration of food if it is rewarding for them. Remember the dog chooses what is reinforcing. If they have low interest in their kibble, it may not be reinforcing enough.

Find new treat ideas for your dog. I have had dogs that work for blueberries, green beans, yogurt bites, and all kinds of things.

Mix a small portion of the desired treat with something low-calorie. I learned a neat trick from a dog day care owner. When she had dogs that did not want to eat while boarding, she would take small amounts of freeze-dried liver, pulverize it in a coffee grinder and sprinkle it on the dog's food. You can try this by mixing a high value reward, like small pieces of hot dog with kibble, or a low-calorie treat, or low-calorie cereal.

Think small. A treat only needs to be the size of a kernel of corn. I can cut one cheese stick into at least 50 treats. I have also used cat treats; they tend to be very small with a strong smell. In the big scheme of things, if you have a dog with serious behavior issues, they are more likely to be euthanized because of their behavior long before they would die due to obesity-related issues.

If you would like to learn more about marker training, the book *Clicking with Your Dog: Step-By-Step in Pictures* by Peggy Tillman is a great place to start.

## *Why Method Matters*

Positive Reinforcement Training is the most appropriate method of training for dogs that have behavior concerns. Such dogs are already dealing with fear and anxiety. Training methods used for dogs that have behavior concerns MUST NOT use punishment, MUST NOT frighten the dog, and MUST NOT cause pain.

In her book *Click to Calm: Healing the Aggressive Dog*, Emma Parsons writes about her journey with her Golden Retriever, Ben. Ben was dog reactive and had attacked other dogs. Parson describes Ben's reactivity as so severe that it "had caused me so much grief in my life, both personally and professionally. It had become a source of tension in my marriage and almost caused me to lose several friendships."[12] Parsons describes a seminal moment in her journey with Ben while in a class with behaviorist Karen Pryor, "She was the one, who during one of

## 7. The Behavior Modification Plan—Part 2

Ben's fits in class, came over, gently put her hand on my arm and calmly said, Emma it is only behavior."[13]

As they were to Emma Parsons, those words are a great comfort. We do not have to use harsh training to help dogs with behavior issues. Parsons writes, "With a clicker and the principles of operant conditioning, you can shape the emotional state of an animal just as you can shape any other behavior."[14] For a dog that is struggling with mental health issues such as fear, anxiety, panic, depression, and reactivity, positive reinforcement is the only training method that should be used.

You will encounter training methods that spout the necessity of being your dog's pack leader or the alpha. These are meaningless terms in the training world.

Even before I was a trainer myself, I enjoyed taking my dogs to training classes. My beautiful Boxer Lola was one of the smartest dogs I have ever lived with. Lola and I enjoyed taking classes together and did so for most of her life. Lola was one of the kindest, most loving, eager-to-please dogs you could meet. She went with me everywhere and was a favorite of everyone she met.

When Lola was a puppy, I attended a class with an old-fashioned traditional trainer. The trainer explained that our dogs need to understand we are their leader. One technique to prove this to your dog is to never step around or over them. If your dog is in your path, make him get up and move. This was important to do so your dog would understand you are the boss.

Even before I learned about modern training, I rarely followed some of the instructions from this traditional trainer. Lola was so compliant I rarely had to ask her to do anything. She was highly intuitive and usually knew what was wanted without being asked. Besides, one look into those droopy, dark brown eyes and it was impossible to be harsh.

In her old age, Lola developed severe arthritis. She had difficulty moving, especially going from lying down to standing up. There were many times, as I stepped over Lola while she was napping in the sun, that I would remember that trainer's advice. What if I had followed those instructions? I never failed to feel a wave of sadness at the thought of making my lovely, old dog move out of my way only to make the point that I was in charge. I'm glad my instinct told me this was not necessary and so happy that I ended up in a time and place where I learned about modern, force-free training.

These theories about dominance-based training grew out of early military training and were supported by a flurry of studies of captive

### I Know Your Dog Is a Good Dog

**Lola the Great**

wolves that took place in the 1960s. Those studies are outdated. Even the scientists that conducted that early research, such as David Mech, have updated their body of work to show that captive wolves do not behave the same way as wolves in the wild. We cannot observe unnatural behavior in captive animals and extrapolate that to our domestic dogs. We know better now.

The American Veterinary Society of Animal Behavior is the professional association for Veterinary Behavior Specialists, one could say this group is the highest authority on treating canine behavior disorders. The AVSAB provides a position paper on the topic of dominance and punishment-based training.

The position paper states, "In the last several decades, our understanding of dominance theory and of the behavior of domesticated animals and their wild counterparts has grown considerably, leading to updated views.[15] Dominance is defined as a relationship between individual animals that is established by force/aggression and submission to

## 7. The Behavior Modification Plan—Part 2

determine who has priority access to multiple resources such as food, preferred resting spots and mates."[16]

We are not in competition with our dogs for resources. Further, our dogs know we are not dogs. Dogs do not disobey, urinate on our stuff, jump on us, or show aggression toward us because they want to be in charge.

This incorrect understanding of dominance has leaked into training and created training methods that are based on scaring, hurting, and punishing our dogs. This is a problem because these training methods can scare an already fearful dog, punish a depressed dog, or inflict pain on an anxious dog. The real danger of punishment-based or dominance-based training is it has no endpoint. If I must ramp up the punishment to get the result I want, where do I stop? What do I do if the dog does not do what I want? How far do I go with punishment?

Again, from AVSAB, "In observational studies, dogs trained with aversive methods or tools showed stress-related behaviors. Survey studies have shown an association between the use of aversive training methods and long-term behavior problems including aggressive behavior towards people and other dogs, and anxiety-related behaviors."[17]

Be aware of training programs that promise to "fix your dog." Often these programs are punishing dogs to the point they will stop the problem behavior, but the dog is likely only suppressing the behavior. As an adult, if I walk into a room with a 5-year-old boy sitting in a small chair and tell him to stop talking and wiggling, well he probably will not. But if I stand over the child, glare at the child, or make a threatening noise at the child he might stop the problem behavior. If he does not, maybe I will grab the skin around his neck and shake him. (Just for the record, I would never, never do this.) If I did, the child would likely stop the problem behavior. But how would he feel about me? I am guessing he would not like me very much. And what happens after I leave the room and he knows he will never see me again? The problem behavior will likely come back sooner or later. Punishment can interrupt a behavior; it can suppress a behavior, but it does not improve the underlying emotion that causes a behavior.

I was contacted by a wonderful woman who had recently adopted two large black Labradors. She had intended on only adopting one dog but when she arrived at the rescue to pick up her dog, she learned that she would be splitting up a bonded pair. So, she came home with two dogs. The dogs were among the sweetest, gentlest, most good-natured

## I Know Your Dog Is a Good Dog

dogs I had ever met. They were happy! They loved their new home and everyone they met.

The dogs were big; the male was well over 100 pounds. Neither dog had any apparent skills that would be used in living in a home. They did not know how to sit, one of the first things most people teach a dog, and always a clue a dog has probably lived in a home. They did not know how to wait at a door or walk on a leash. In fact, when the petite owner was walking the almost 200 pounds of dog together, she had to work to stay on her feet and not get pulled down to the ground.

The owner and I started with some basic skills; getting the dog's attention, keep all of your feet on the ground when meeting people, keep slack on the leash when out walking. The female dog learned fast. But the male dog seemed to be inattentive. When I would enter the room with treats and a clicker in my hand, he would take a treat but when I tried to lure a behavior, he would start to look out the window. If I moved toward him to work on having him touch my hand as a target he would walk away. The dog was so easygoing and loved getting treats that I truly did not think the training was stressful. Was he just a big goof? I began to wonder if he could hear. He had arrived at the rescue in less than optimal physical condition. He was grossly overweight and had greasy skin and dirty ears. Could he have had a history of ear infections that damaged his hearing?

I called on one of my colleagues to come and observe a training session. My friend was able to get the dog's attention, even if standing behind him. He did not seem to have any hearing deficits. She didn't see any overt signs of stress either. We wondered if he just enjoyed looking out the window and preferred that over training?

Then, a light bulb went off over my head. I had seen this before. Several years prior, I had been called by a Brittany breed rescue to work with a dog that was in foster care. The quiet, gentle dog had developed separation anxiety when separated from her foster mom. Part of my plan to address the anxiety was to teach the dog a few skills to help build her confidence. But whenever we began a training session, the little Brittany would show multiple stress signals, she would salivate and pant, even when we proceeded slowly and carefully.

We did have this dog's history. We knew the Brittany had been a former hunting dog and had been trained with an electric collar, a punitive training method. We knew she had been dumped when she failed to hunt. I believed that since this gentle, little, dog had been trained with a painful shock collar that to her, any training session predicted

## 7. The Behavior Modification Plan—Part 2

bad things were about to happen. Her method of dealing with the stress of training was to shut down and pretend she was somewhere else. She would completely disengage from me when we tried to train simple skills.

It made me wonder if the big lab had a similar history. We would never know. He couldn't tell us. But he was a hunting breed, from a rural area and did not have a strong work ethic. Was he a discarded hunting dog? Had he been trained with an electric collar? I don't know but based on my past experience I changed my whole approach to training with this dog. We worked to develop a plan in which training did not look like training. Instead of worrying about teaching this dog to sit, the owner and I taught him tricks! We taught him how to shake hands and push a toy with his nose.

Why tricks? Some dogs with a history of punitive, painful training have an aversion to anything that may look or smell or has shades of being a training situation. Understandably, some of these dogs let me know this right away by growling or stiffening and giving me a warning stare. But I think there are some dogs, like this lab, that are by nature so soft and gentle that growling is not their go-to behavior. I think the thought of being in a training situation did upset him and he showed this by disengaging with me, by looking out the window.

By teaching him tricks, we removed all pressure from the training process, including from the owner. This dog learned that training could be fun, it opened the door to a new world. Once he learned the marker training "game" he went on to learn a host of new things. Soon the owner was walking both dogs together for miles without being dragged behind.

Punitive training tells dogs what they are doing wrong. It does not tell them what they should be doing. Punitive training can instill fear in dogs. Fear of doing the wrong thing, fear of being punished or hurt for doing the wrong thing. Because of this, some dogs will just refuse to do anything. Training with rewards or as we can call it, positive reinforcement training, allows dogs to fail. That is of utmost importance. How many of us ever become skilled at anything without a period of trial and error? We learn from our mistakes. We learn to try new things. Why would we not want to give our dogs that same opportunity?

When I am working with a dog that is anxious or fearful or reactive, I want them to feel the freedom to make a mistake. I want them to know that if they make the wrong choice, nothing bad is going to happen. Because if I do not allow them to make the wrong choice, I am taking away the motivation to make the right choice. If a dog is punished over and over, it will simply stop trying. I want to teach a dog to pause, to think, to choose, and to trust if the choice is not the right one that it is okay to choose something else. And when the right choice is made, they are rewarded. This is not because I want to always be warm and fuzzy with my dog. I do this because science shows me this is the most effective, most humane way to train any animal.

## *Survival Skills*

I do teach some specific skills, or cued behaviors, as part of an overall behavior modification plan. Which skills I train, depends on the individual dog. I consider these survival skills because they will allow you, the human, to remain calm in a stressful situation. They will help give you control over what happens next. And these skills will give you a way to quickly communicate with your dog. Teaching survival skills creates predictability which can help you relax and allows your dog to relax with you.

Think of these skills as tools in your tool kit. If you are working on a project and need to tighten a screw, you pull out your Philips screwdriver. Then you realize what you really need is a flathead, you don't panic, you just put the Philips away and take out the flathead. You may need your dog to move away from a person and closer to you so you pull out your recall, then realize a hand target would work better. Tools in your toolkit! For most dogs, I typically start with some of the following skills:

**Leave It**. Leave it means I know you are thinking about it, but you cannot have it. Let's think about something else I have for you.
**Drop It.** Drop it means let go of what is in your mouth.
**Wait**. Wait means stop forward motion, that is all, it does not mean you have to sit or lie down, just stop moving forward.
**Targeting.** Targeting means touching something I am indicating. Usually, it means touch my hand with your nose.
**U-Turn**. Just as it sounds, turn, and go in the opposite direction.
**Safe Space**. Go from where you are to a designated space. This may be to a bed or to a room or even into a crate.

There are many different skills we can teach a dog; again, which skills are needed depend on the dog.

# 8

# Freckles

In the world of animal rescue, the foster home is one of the most healing places an animal can land. A foster home is meant to be temporary, a place for an animal to rest, decompress, recover, and rehabilitate. The goal is that the animal will eventually leave the foster home to be adopted into a permanent home.

My friend Kaitlin has had years of experience as a foster home for dogs. If you ask her how many dogs she has fostered over the years, she will need to ruminate and count. She has had foster dogs that needed a short-term place to rest before they went on to their next stop, dogs that had to recover from illness or medical procedures, and dogs that needed to be evaluated to see what type of home would be their best fit.

Freckles is by far the foster dog that has been with her the longest. When I talked with Kaitlin and her husband Chris, Freckles had been in their home as a foster for 18 months.

Kaitlin and Chris volunteer at a large, no-kill shelter that focuses on the rehabilitation of dogs. Their volunteer duties typically include taking dogs for walks, doing some training with the dogs, and taking them on car rides. Chris had met Freckles during his volunteer hours and had fallen for the sweet looking beagle mix. When Chris and Kaitlin learned that Freckles needed knee surgery, but it would only be done if she had a foster home to go to following the surgery, they volunteered.

They knew that fostering Freckles would not be easy. Freckles had been at the shelter for four years and her history was tragic. She had been part of a large rescue operation. Dozens of dogs had been found living in a hoarding situation. The first rescuers found Freckles living in a crate with another dog they believed to be her sister. They estimated her age at about two years. The physical status of the rescued dogs was critically impaired. Today, Freckles' bowed legs are a testament to the lack of nutrition and exercise she received before her rescue. This small dog had most likely spent the better part of her first two years of life in the crate in which she was found.

## I Know Your Dog Is a Good Dog

Freckles' behavior challenges were apparent as soon as she arrived at the shelter. She was very protective of her sister. Certainly, in Freckles' experience, humans only brought harm. When the shelter staff approached the two dogs, Freckles would lie on top of her sister and threaten to bite anyone that came near. Even with precautions taken at the intake exam, a terrified Freckles was able to bite through the heavy, leather gloves rescuers term "bite gloves."

Freckles had improved in her four years at the shelter but still needed to be handled with care. Kaitlin, a certified professional dog trainer, and Chris were uniquely equipped to give Freckles the quiet, low energy space she needed to heal, so they prepared to bring her home.

Part of that preparation was learning the method for leashing Freckles. As Chris had volunteered in the building where Freckles was housed, he had already become proficient at this process. The procedure for leashing Freckles began with Freckles in her crate. The D ring of the collar needed to be hanging below her chin. When the leash was clipped on, the handler's hand must be kept below Freckles' face, otherwise, the handler risked being bitten.

Kaitlin and Chris also knew that Freckles' default when scared was to seek to escape. They knew it was important that her environment was secure. Kaitlin and Chris have a six-foot privacy fence that extends two feet underground. They felt this, along with weekly checks of the perimeter of their yard to make sure there are no new openings, would keep Freckles safe. Kaitlin and Chris had crates and beds and pens, and treats! They were ready and Freckles came home.

As Freckles' leg healed Kaitlin and Chris watched and learned more about her. In addition to her knee, they began to see she had a much more significant injury to her soul. They suspected the first two years of her life had been hell and that she was still dealing with that experience. Freckles exhibited what is commonly accepted as signs of post-traumatic stress in a dog.

Dr. Karen Overall, DACVB, describes post-traumatic stress disorder in dogs (CPTSD), as a "Profound, non-graded, extreme response manifest as intense avoidance, escape, or anxiety and associated with the sympathetic branch of the autonomic nervous system in response to exposure to an identifiable, untenable (from the patient's perspective) stimulus or situation that the individual was unable to avoid or from which escape was impossible when these behavior and physical signs were first felt."[1]

Kaitlin observed many of the signs described by Dr. Overall in

## 8. Freckles

Freckles. Kaitlin would occasionally see Freckles doing something as ordinary as getting a drink of water, when she would suddenly startle, stop and back up, once even trying to retreat so quickly she fell over. When that would happen Kaitlin tried hard to look for any other environmental change that would cause such panic. She could not find any, no light reflecting or a tag hitting a bowl, not even an animal moving in her peripheral vision. Based on her background, it is possible Freckles was having a flashback to her previous life, a cardinal symptom of post-traumatic stress in humans and likely in dogs. As Dr. Nicholas Dodman states in his book, *Pets on the Couch*, "Yes, indeed, I teach about canine PTSD in my course to veterinary students. I would consider myself remiss if I didn't."[2]

Once Freckles' knee healed it became obvious that she would need time for her heart to heal as well. Kaitlin and Chris decided that instead of returning a now physically healed Freckles to the shelter, they would become her permanent foster home while she waited to be adopted.

Though their hearts were dedicated, this was a challenging foster assignment. For the first three months, Freckles was in their home, she would not leave her crate. Kaitlin and Chris came up with a creative solution for bathroom breaks. They set up an exercise pen in their backyard. When it was time for Freckles to go "outside," they would open their sliding door and then open the exercise pen. Then back into the house, they would each grab a side of the crate, heft the crate up, carry it outside to the pen, and carefully open the door of the crate. They would quickly close the opening to the pen and then Kaitlin and Chris would go back inside.

From a distance, Chris and Kaitlin would watch and wait for Freckles to exit the crate and potty. Freckles would always dash back into the crate when she saw Kaitlin or Chris. When she was done with her potty business, Kaitlin and Chris would reverse the whole process of carrying Freckles back into the house. Genius!

After months of this process combined with frequently sitting next to her crate to offer her yummy treats, they were eventually able to institute the leash protocol they had learned at the shelter and take her outside on foot. After all, Kaitlin points out to me, "Freckles is a dog who likes her routine, at least until she decides to change it."

There came a time when Freckles decided she would also like to change her crate routine. Unfortunately, this was at a time when Kaitlin and Chris needed to leave home. The typical routine, whenever they left home, was to make sure that Freckles as well as their own two dogs were

## I Know Your Dog Is a Good Dog

crated. But on this particular day, Freckles hesitated, and balked when it was time to go into her crate. Chris and Kaitlin had to leave, they knew the time had come to take a leap of faith and left Freckles free to roam in the house. When they came back everything was fine. That was the day, as Kaitlin told me, "Freckles decided she is no longer a box dog."

It was also about this time that they started letting Freckles outside into the yard instead of confining her to the exercise pen. She still had to be carried out in her crate, but then they would open the door to give her some free time. They would watch as she would cling to the fence and run from hiding behind a bush to the next bush that would give her cover. It was sad to watch but at least she was getting exercise and some freedom she had not had before.

Initially, this worked fine, because as soon as a person went outside the house into the yard, Freckles would dash into her crate. Then Freckles decided she wanted to change her routine again! They thought this plan would work but alas, one autumn evening they discovered things would not go smoothly.

Freckles was in the yard, and she would not go into her crate or come inside. What could they do? Their options were limited, they could not go get her, she would run away. She would not come to their calls, and they could not tempt her with food.

They had learned that Freckles had an aversion to being lured with food. If offered food to "do something" she would withdraw. Kaitlin suspects that Freckles related food lures to unpleasant things happening. So, while this would work with many dogs, it would not work with Freckles. They were stuck.

As the night grew long, Chris and Kaitlin stayed up watching Freckles wander the yard, then approach the door and then dart away. They waited until the wee hours of the morning to see if she would come in but then just became too tired. They decided to go to bed. They woke in the morning fearing that Freckles would be hurt or worse, gone. But they found that Freckles, ever the survivor, had burrowed into the pillows of the outdoor sectional to stay warm and sleep.

Still, they could not get her to come into the house. Freckles tried hard to be brave, she continued to come to the door and then run away, her fear overcoming her. It was into the second night when they heard Freckles whining at the door, Kaitlin would hop up and open the door, only to have Freckles look at her, then run.

Finally, at about 3:00 a.m. on that second night, Kaitlin opened the door once more and Freckles ran into the house and into her crate.

## 8. Freckles

Thus, was life with Freckles. Thereafter, she always wore a leash when she went outside so she could be retrieved without being touched.

Eighteen months have gone by. Freckles is still with Kaitlin and Chris, so far, a forever home that fits her needs has not been found. She is still a foster dog. I talk with Chris and Kaitlin about the progress Freckles has made. If we look at the last 18 months in view of the first two years of her life, we must admit she has made great progress. Actually, unbelievable progress. As a trainer and behavior consultant, I find Freckles' story fascinating. It is a rare story because most dogs like Freckles are not given this amount of time to recover. Most dogs like Freckles would have been euthanized before this much time had gone by.

What does progress look like for Freckles? What should our expectations be for a dog like her? Kaitlin tells me that Freckles spends less and less time in her crate. For the first six months she was with Kaitlin and Chris she would spend most of her time in her crate, this was by her choice. The door to the crate was left open. If Freckles became nervous or felt under pressure she would retreat to her crate. Then one day Kaitlin and Chris needed to leave home for a short time. Chris asked Freckles to go into her crate and she howled at him! This was a huge success. Freckles was engaging with Chris and expressing her opinion. Something she had never done before.

Freckles has also expressed her opinion by growling. Kaitlin believes that a growl is a dog's expression of what they are feeling at that moment, a need for space and for the people or other dogs to back off. Once Freckles began to understand her growl would be respected, she began to develop trust in Chris and Kaitlin. A circle of communication developed, Freckles would growl, Kaitlin and Chris would listen, Freckles began to trust, and the growling decreased. Kaitlin points out that fearful dogs usually need to grow to the point where they feel secure enough to growl, so, growling, for Freckles, was progress. This was a big deal.

Freckles' big move out of the crate was onto a dog bed. She had the ideal spot, a soft bed in front of the fireplace. Then one day Freckles jumped on the couch. Freckles had officially grown from being a "box dog," to being a bed dog, now she was a couch dog. Freckles began spending more time on the couch with Kaitlin's calm, squishy, American Staffordshire Terrier. Freckles seems to draw comfort from his calm presence and was often found lying bum to bum with her canine friend.

Recently Freckles has begun venturing onto the couch when Kaitlin is sitting there. She keeps her distance from Kaitlin and keeps her

## I Know Your Dog Is a Good Dog

hind end towards her, but what a milestone for this girl to voluntarily share space with a human. Freckles has also begun to accept having her leash placed on while she is sitting on the couch instead of in her crate. The protocol of attaching the leash only below her chin without touching her collar remains, but she no longer needs the safety of her crate to tolerate this process.

Freckles will freely go outside by herself. She no longer wears a leash, and she readily crosses the threshold to go out. Coming back inside is still hard and Freckles will stop at the door and scan the room, once she feels all is well, she will scurry across the threshold and run to the safety of her bed. But remembering the dog who had to be carried outside in her crate, this is huge progress!

Kaitlin tells me that when Freckles is outside, her motion is less frenetic, her movement is more purposeful, and she looks around at her environment. She stands taller and stretches, she sniffs the grass and does less darting from hiding place to hiding place. Kaitlin has seen her sit down on the grass, which was a new behavior, and recently for the very first time, Freckles rolled in the grass. It is now the norm for Freckles to spend a little time playing before coming back in. Amazing!

In her progress with people, Freckles has begun to take treats from the hands of familiar visitors to the house. And the dog who went from a crate to a dog bed then to the couch? Now sleeps in the bedroom with Kaitlin and Chris and their other two dogs.

Kaitlin has observed that Freckles' progress has been speeding up. Where before she would only be able to tolerate one new thing about every three weeks before becoming overwhelmed, she is now trying new things daily. Kaitlin believes most dogs will reach a tipping point in their rehabilitative process. Initially, progress is slow, then along the journey, they reach that tipping point, where their progress begins to speed up. It took a year, but Freckles has reached that point.

Kaitlin and Chris continue to face challenges with Freckles. They still cannot touch her, although she does sometimes choose to touch them. While sitting on the couch Freckles will gently touch her hind end to Kaitlin's hip and Kaitlin has gently moved her elbow along Freckles' side. Freckles will occasionally bump Kaitlin's hand, asking for a treat.

And those flashbacks? Kaitlin is convinced that Freckles is replacing some of her scary past with new happier memories. Occasionally she will see Freckles wag her tail while she is sleeping and has heard her make soft chirping sounds in her dreams.

## 8. Freckles

I ask Kaitlin how they went about their approach to rehabilitating Freckles. I asked her to share some of her dos and don'ts. Kaitlin laughs as she tells me that she has taken a lazy approach to working with Freckles. She does very little active training. She does keep food with her and has always tossed treats to Freckles when she goes near her or when Freckles draws nearer to Kaitlin. Kaitlin points out it does not matter what the food is or how much food she has. It is important that the presence of a human always predicts that food is following. Kaitlin also campaigned for medication for Freckles and Freckles is now on a low dose of medication to assist in reducing her stress level.

In addition, Kaitlin and Chris created a physically safe place for Freckles both indoors and out so that she has the freedom to explore without them intervening. Unless there is a safety issue, they let her do what she wants in her exploration. If she wants to jump on the couch and is not jumping on top of another dog, they let her jump.

They also remain willing to experiment. At one time they thought Freckles would like to be in one of the bedrooms on her own with the opportunity to explore. Freckles did not like being closed in a bedroom by herself so that idea was shelved. On to the next idea.

Kaitlin and Chris embrace creativity. They believe Freckles is at the point where she really wants to affiliate with people but is scared. Kaitlin and Chris must figure out how that can be done and work to set up those safe experiences for her.

As for don'ts, they do not focus on training skills. That may happen in the future, but Freckles is not ready for that. They also make sure that their own dogs and no human visitor is ever allowed to push Freckles past what she can tolerate.

Kaitlin tells me the hardest part of living with Freckles is not celebrating loudly when she does something wonderful. These days, those opportunities happen frequently, like jumping up on the bed to be with the humans. Overall, they are pretty proud of Freckles. I tell Kaitlin they should be proud of themselves too. This is the story of a dog who spent years being abused and then years physically safe but without much opportunity to grow.

Freckles will be a permanent foster until the right home is found and they still hope that is the future that awaits. For now, she is a lesson in what post-traumatic stress in dogs can look like and the amount of time and effort it can take for them to get better. Freckles' story is amazing!

# 9

# The Behavior Modification Plan—Part 3

Finally we arrive at the heart of the matter. The part of the plan you were waiting for. It is time to actively work on your dog's concerning behaviors.

## *Changing the Emotional Response—Conditioning Exercises*

While what we think of as traditional training is used to teach specific skills that are placed on cue, such as sit and stay, what I am going to call "conditioning exercises" focus on changing behavior by addressing the underlying emotion that drives the behavior. This is the bulk of the behavior modification plan. The parts that came before are important and lay a foundation for the conditioning exercises. This behavior change is created by using classical conditioning, counter conditioning, and operant conditioning.

Dr. Karen Overall, a Veterinary Behavior Specialist, describes requirements for behavior modification as involving:

- Shaping behaviors in a non-threatening context.
- Possible implementation of classic desensitization (DS) (e.g., the patient learns not to react to stimuli that increase in intensity) and counterconditioning (CC) (e.g., the patient is rewarded for exhibiting a preferred behavior that is incompatible with the undesirable one).
- Replacing a set of rules that encourage reaction, regardless of context with a new set of rules that allows the animal to relax and take his or her cues from the contextual environment.[1]

Using conditioning to modify behavior is a method that grew out of the fields of human psychology and learning theory. There are fancy

## 9. The Behavior Modification Plan—Part 3

scientific definitions of these methods but don't worry about getting too bogged down in that. If you have a scientific, curious mind there are whole, big books written on the topic. Here is my brief, and I mean brief, explanation of conditioning.

When thinking of classical conditioning, think Pavlov. You probably remember learning about this Russian scientist in a high school science class. Although Pavlov's research was much more complicated, what we remember is that he would ring a bell before feeding the dogs in his laboratory. The dogs began to associate the sound of the bell with mealtime. Eventually, even if the food was not present the sound of the bell would cause the dogs to salivate as if the food was there. The dogs had been conditioned to associate the sound of the bell with their food, the bell predicted the food was arriving and created the same physiological response. Classical conditioning happens a lot without us even knowing about it or trying to produce it.

When I was young, we had a little dog named Ginger. Ginger loved cheese. Our large family ate a lot of Velveeta cheese. If you do not know what this is, think of a yellow-orange, brick size, soft cheese food. Velveeta cheese was sliced with a small metal wire slicer. When you would pick up the slicer there would be a small metallic "clink!" Ginger learned this clink sound predicted the cheese was out and she would likely get a bite. We did not set out to teach her the clink meant to come running. Just like Pavlov's dogs, Ginger was conditioned to the sound of the slicer predicting cheese.

Classical conditioning can produce very strong connections. Have you ever had a dog that knows a walk is ahead when you are putting on your walking shoes? They were conditioned to that predictor. Classical conditioning can also work to create a negative response. I have known dogs with separation anxiety that will become anxious when the owner gets out a suitcase or picks up the car keys.

Counter conditioning is similar to classical conditioning but allows us to pull a switcheroo. It allows us to replace an unwanted response to a stimulus or trigger with a new, desired response. The sound of the mail truck predicts that dangerous mail carrier is invading my property. What if the sound of the mail truck predicted something fun would happen, like getting a treat or playing a game of tug?

In counter conditioning, we are typically trying to change your dog's response to something that frightens them. After all, that is why you called a trainer in the first place, because of your dog's reaction to a specific trigger.

# I Know Your Dog Is a Good Dog

Counter conditioning is typically used along with something called desensitization, more properly called systematic desensitization. Desensitization involves very, very gradually exposing your dog to the thing they are afraid of while using counter conditioning to change their response. It is "systematic" because desensitization is done in very small, pre-determined steps. Plans for counter conditioning and desensitization need to be thought out carefully. So it's best to have a trainer help you through this process.

This brings me to another term used in behavior modification called flooding. Where desensitization exposes an animal to something that is adverse in very small increments, flooding overwhelms the animal with an exposure of what they are afraid of.

Think of someone who is afraid of spiders. When they see a spider nearby, they may jump and scream. They may flail their arms to remove an imaginary spider from their body. They may run away, they may hide.

Let's assume this person finds this fear unpleasant and it impacts their quality of life. They would like to overcome this fear. Let's say further that they proceed through a systematic desensitization program and are exposed to spiders only in pictures, they learn more about spiders and when they are ready, they are exposed to a live spider at a far distance. They work on this fear through a behavior modification plan and improve.

Now, let's imagine instead of a desensitization program they report to their mental health provider who promptly locks them in a small room filled with spiders for one hour. When the door is unlocked the person is no longer screaming or flailing. They are quiet and calm, they may even have a crooked smile on their face. You may even talk them into turning around and going back into the room. Are they cured? I think you know the answer. That is a somewhat silly, unlikely scenario. But let's think of it this way.

Your dog is afraid of having their nails trimmed. When they see the nail trimmer they jump and scream (I mean howl). They may flail their arms (I mean legs) around and run away. They may hide. Sounds similar to the spider situation above, doesn't it? Maybe their owner pins them down, even lying on top of them. Maybe they wrap their head in a blanket or place a muzzle on them. Maybe, the dog grows still, stops barking, and stops struggling. He may remain lying down after he is unrestrained. Has he learned to like having his nails trimmed? No. He has been flooded, overwhelmed.

It is more likely the dog has given up, is exhibiting learned

## 9. The Behavior Modification Plan—Part 3

helplessness, is in shock, or is repressing behavior because it no longer feels safe to express. Flooding has a valid place in human psychology when used in the hands of experts. It is not a method that should be used by dog trainers or behavior consultants. But, back to conditioning used in positive reinforcement training.

Changing behavior also uses a type of conditioning we call operant conditioning. Operant conditioning differs from classical and counter conditioning in that the dog participates in the process with some type of action.

In force-free or reward-based training, positive reinforcement is used. Positive reinforcement is when something the dog likes follows the desired behavior. If that "something" is reinforcing to the dog the target behavior will increase. In fact, you may hear some trainers refer to themselves as positive reinforcement trainers.

To return to the sciency stuff, there are different types of operant conditioning. You may have heard of the four quadrants. They are positive reinforcement, negative reinforcement, positive punishment, and negative punishment.

In this case positive and negative are used in a more mathematical sense. Positive means add, and negative means to take away. Reinforcement increases a behavior. Punishment decreases a behavior. So, positive reinforcement adds something the dog likes to increase behavior. Negative reinforcement removes something the dog does not like to increase a behavior. Positive punishment adds something the dog does not like to decrease behavior and negative punishment removes something the dog likes to decrease behavior.

A dog trainer or behavior consultant should focus on positive reinforcement. On occasion, I find, we all use negative punishment without realizing it. Think of walking away from the dog that jumps on you. You removed (negative, remember minus), yourself (something the dog wants) to decrease (punish) the jumping.

In my opinion, dog trainers and behavior consultants should not use positive punishment or negative reinforcement. Remember the humane hierarchy. If all the steps that come before positive punishment and negative reinforcement fail, the dog should be referred to a higher-level professional. The reason for this is that these methods can easily backfire, causing problem behaviors, and sometimes dangerous behaviors to worsen. But let's leave the science stuff and talk about the great change we can accomplish with conditioning.

If my dog is nervous when approached by other dogs and has a

## I Know Your Dog Is a Good Dog

history of pulling and barking at other dogs, I may decide to teach my dog a new response. Perhaps instead of pulling and barking, I would like my dog to look away from the other dog and look at me for instructions.

To accomplish this, I use operant conditioning. It is operant because my dog will participate with an action, looking at me. To set up an operant conditioning exercise for this behavior I need to think about the steps I will take to work towards my goal.

First, I will decide what action I would like from my dog. In this case I would like my dog to look away from the trigger and look at me. Then I decide what reinforcement I will use. The reinforcement must be something important enough to the dog to work for. I decide to use high value treats. Then I will decide on the trigger to use while practicing. For practice I will use a dog that is calm, and I know will not react to my dog. When I start the exercise, I will keep the trigger dog far enough away so my dog notices it but does not react. My next step is to plan what I will do when my dog engages with the trigger dog. I decide I will make a kissy noise; this causes my dog to look at me and when he does I give him a treat. I have used operant conditioning to teach my dog a new response to a trigger.

As part of operant conditioning, it is important to understand the difference between a reward and a reinforcement. A reward is something given for a job well done. It may have different levels of meaningfulness. I always appreciate a nice certificate, but a plate of brownies is the way to my heart. A reinforcement, by definition, is something that increases the likelihood of a behavior being repeated. The dog must tell us what works for them as a reinforcement. We cannot decide that for a dog.

If my son mows my lawn and I reward him with a piece of candy it may not be very motivating, especially if he doesn't like candy. But if I reward him with cash, he is likely to mow the lawn again. I can choose what the reward is, but I cannot choose how reinforcing it will be. And if I am asking my dog to do something really hard, I will make sure the reinforcement is very strong. My dog may do some sits and downs for pieces of kibble, but if I am asking him to spin in a circle, sit and shake hands, I better get out the smelly treats. And if I am asking him to look at me instead of looking at that very scary person or dog, I should just get out the pork chops.

This can all sound very scientific and complicated. The way I explain behavior modification to my clients is that we are going to try to develop a plan that attempts to change the dog's emotional response. Instead of, "oh my gosh, I see a stranger, they're going to kill me." I want

## 9. The Behavior Modification Plan—Part 3

them to think, "Hey! Maybe it's not going to kill me, maybe I need to stop and think about this," or even, "hey it's not going to kill me, it's going to give me a cookie, yay!"

### A Word About the Emotional Response

When we talk about the process of changing that emotional response to "Yay!" it is science based. I tell you this to reassure that a qualified trainer or behavior consultant will have a method to their madness. In fact, the term used in learning theory is conditioned emotional response or CER. This response is the result of conditioning. A conditioned response can be negative. When I get that reminder about an upcoming dental appointment, I have a conditioned emotional response. I have a great dentist, but I have a long childhood history of not so pleasant dental experiences that has created that strong response. When I was a student, and the time came to take an important test I would have a strong negative emotional response.

Emotional responses can be positive as well. As soon as I hear the first Christmas carol of the year or smell the first pumpkin pie baking, I get all warm and fuzzy inside. These emotional responses have been conditioned over time.

Most of the time the reactions in our dogs that we find problematic are conditioned emotional responses. In one of my early reactive dog classes I had a student, a very petite woman, who owned a Great Dane. When the Great Dane would see another dog, he would "go ballistic." In talking with the owner she explained that when she got him as a puppy, many people told her she needed to get right on top of training and to make sure she had control of the dog. This worried her to the point that she bought a prong collar for her dog when still a puppy. If out walking and another dog came into view her puppy would pull, this sounded like normal puppy curiosity and an effort to meet another dog. Because she was so worried about controlling her dog she would pull hard on the prong collar. It wasn't long before her dog became reactive at the sight of other dogs. The puppy curiosity turned into adolescent reactivity.

It is possible that her dog had learned that the sight of another dog equaled painful pulling on his neck. This pain had created a negative emotional response to the sight of another dog. You may say that I am guessing at this. I would say I am extrapolating. I say this because of the many, many dogs I have seen develop reactivity because of punishment using force and electricity. This is almost always done with good intentions by owners who have no desire to hurt their dog or create new problems. The magic of conditioning is that we can create a positive conditioned emotional response.

Emotions can be changed using conditioning, but it is the behavior that is being reinforced or punished, not the emotion. That can be confusing, but I point it out because of the many times I have seen owners told not to comfort an upset or frightened dog. I hate to hear this advice. I hate to see an upset dog seeking comfort or reassurance ignored. You will not make your dog worse by comforting them. So if your dog has just had an upsetting reactive experience, or was frightened, please by all means comfort your dog. Remember Pink at the beginning of this book. Her owner comforting her at times of stress and panic was an important part of her healing process.

As I said it is not necessary for you to be able to recite the definition of counter or operant conditioning, but if your trainer cannot explain the techniques, it is probably not the right trainer to be working with a dog with behavior concerns.

## *Engage/Disengage*

Which conditioning exercises are developed and how they are utilized depends very much on the individual dog. But with reactive dogs, I will almost certainly work on teaching the engage/disengage game.

There are several exercises that teach this process. I will say that most of them have their roots in an exercise called "Look at That" developed by trainer, Leslie McDevitt and described in her book, *Control Unleashed*.[2]

There is also a wonderful training philosophy developed by trainer Grisha Stewart called Behavior Adjustment Training (BAT) that is built on, among other things, the process of using distance, pacing, and leash skills to work with reactive dogs. It is a wonderful method and I highly recommend any of Stewart's books and videos.[3] Check out her website, if you are ever lucky enough to be close to one of her workshops, it is very worth getting there.

With all these methods, the process is to take a dog's defensive response and replace it with a desired response. A dog who is reactive is engaging with a trigger and displaying a response we as the dog's guardian do not want. I want to help the dog learn to disengage from the trigger and pay attention to me. Then I can tell the dog what we will do next.

The engage/disengage game can be used for many triggers, not only

## 9. The Behavior Modification Plan—Part 3

triggers a dog sees but can also be used for triggers they hear. I commonly use this for dogs that live in apartment complexes and bark at every sound.

As an example, let's take a dog who is reactive to people. When I set about to develop a conditioning exercise, I need to thoughtfully plan out the steps. I would start by determining the dog's threshold to other people, let's call them strangers. The threshold depends on the distance between the dog and the stranger. The threshold is the point at which a dog reacts to the stranger. For most dogs, if a stranger is far enough away, the dog is able to hear, see, or smell the stranger but will still be able to pay attention to the owner and take treats from the owner. They are able to keep themselves under control despite the presence of the stranger. The dog is under threshold.

If the stranger moves closer to the dog, there will be a point at which the dog reacts, cannot be distracted, and will not eat. It will only react to the stranger, typically by pulling, barking, or growling. The dog has gone over its distance threshold.

When your dog is over threshold the brain is in the flight, fight, or freeze mode, and learning cannot take place. All conditioning exercises must be done when your dog is under threshold. If you are in the process of a conditioning exercise and your dog goes over the threshold, then increase the distance away from the stranger, and give your dog a chance to catch their breath.

Here is the thing about thresholds though: they move. Surprise! On a good day, your dog's threshold may be 50 feet from intruding dogs or people. But if it's a bad day, suddenly your dog is reacting to other dogs or people at 20 feet. What the heck?! You've been working so hard. You are likely to feel discouraged. But do not worry, this is not unusual. Many things can cause this shift. Maybe your dog (or you) is stressed that day. Maybe your dog (or you) is overly tired that day. Maybe your dog doesn't feel well.

Often what happens is something we call trigger stacking. You know the day. You leave your home to take your dog for a pleasant walk. Suddenly a cat runs across your path, and your dog's prey drive kicks in. Then the trash truck that is running late comes lumbering down the street. Just as you turn in the other direction, here comes the kid on a skateboard. One trigger stacked on top of another too quickly. When this happens, I tell folks to "get the hell out of Dodge!" and go back home. These days will happen. There will be a new day.

When I do start teaching the engage/disengage game, I typically

## I Know Your Dog Is a Good Dog

start working far under threshold. If your dog can tolerate the sight of another dog at 50 yards away, I may start working with a distance of 100 yards.

Another part of the plan is to be well-prepared with a lot of reinforcements. I want to make sure they are high value and I have enough. If using food for reinforcement for conditioning exercises do not worry about using too much. Make any treats tiny. And hand them out generously. I have been in a situation where I ran out of treats before I realized my bag was empty. When I discovered there was no food, I went about making a fool of myself by praising and patting, and running in circles with my dog. It worked at that moment but not really something I want to repeat often.

Next, I decide if I need helpers. With my clients, I often ask another trainer that is in my network to volunteer to be the stranger. Whomever I use I need to make sure the human understands the task at hand and will take direction. The middle of the conditioning exercise is not the time for the helper to come up with suggestions or new ideas.

I also plan how I will communicate with my helper. I typically have my phone in my pocket and use a hands-free device to talk with my helper. Remember we may be 100 yards apart. This way I can ask my helper to move farther away, or closer, to stand still, or walk in a specific direction. Being able to communicate at a distance will make the exercise go more smoothly.

If I am using a helper dog, I want to make sure the dog is calm, and stable and will not react to the dog I am working with. It helps nothing if I am working with a dog who fears other dogs and the helper dog starts barking.

When using helpers I also must consider their safety and comfort. If there is inclement weather, I make sure there is shelter for the human or dog helper. I make sure there is water available and a place to rest.

I consider the area I am using. Are there hills someone may stumble down or traffic nearby? I make sure the harness and leash on the helper dog are secure. I do not want any escapes happening on my watch.

I have the same consideration for my client dog and human. If the dog has a bite history or will possibly aggress toward my helper, I will ask that the dog wear a muzzle. I will use barriers if necessary or tether the dog securely. I also make sure the dog's owner understands how to safely handle the leash.

After planning out all these steps it is time to actually do the work. I pick a spot such as a park or a schoolyard on a weekend. Maybe we are

## 9. The Behavior Modification Plan—Part 3

working in a business park on the day the business is closed. I have my treats and helpers in place. Then a group of small children on bicycles ride right in the middle of the exercise and it all falls apart. Happens every time. I say that a bit tongue in cheek, but it is a reminder that even with the best planning you and your dog are living beings and there will be good days and bad days, and flexibility will be the name of the game.

But when I am actually ready to start this is what the exercise looks like. I have the stranger at a distance well under the dog's threshold. I wait for the dog to notice the stranger, this may be by looking at the stranger, sniffing the air, or turning an ear towards the stranger.

As soon as I see that happen, I will click my tongue to get the dog's attention. As soon as I see the dog disengage from the stranger by look at me, turning their ears toward me or disconnecting their gaze from the other dog, I give the dog a treat. In the beginning, I do not require the dog to look straight at me or make eye contact with me. I just need the dog I am working with to disengage from the stranger. The second I see that happen I give the dog a great treat.

It can be hard to get your dog's attention if it is nervous. Saying its name hardly ever works. Our dogs hear their name so many times a day and in so many different contexts it may not be attention getting. I find clicking my tongue or whistling works well, even patting my leg or making a silly noise. Sometimes I move my hand or myself into the dog's peripheral vision.

After I give the treat, I wait for the dog to look at the stranger again. As soon he does, again, I get the dog's attention and give a treat. I continue to repeat this engage/disengage game several times and then... I quit. That's right, in the beginning, my goal was not to get close to the stranger. My goal is to teach the dog this new game. Look at the stranger, look at me, get a treat! This may be as small as ten repetitions. This process requires a lot from your dog mentally and emotionally and it can be exhausting.

In future sessions, the next step I am looking for is when your dog sees the stranger and then looks at me expecting the treat. Aha! We call that an automatic look back. Remember conditioning? An event or thing begins to predict a new event or thing. The sight of the stranger predicts food. That is what we are working towards.

Once my dog gets pretty good at this game, I start to close the distance between the dog and the stranger. This can take a long time and we can help the dog, but not force the dog. Mistakes happen, all the time. If I get too close and the dog goes over threshold we just start over at a bigger distance. And I never set a goal of a reactive dog meeting and hanging out with the thing they are afraid of.

There is absolutely no reason anyone must come and pet your dog when you are out and about. That should never be a goal. Your dog has been telling you and telling you they are afraid. You are spending all this time helping them learn to deal with that fear. Nothing is accomplished by making your dog available to the whims of others.

A good goal for a reactive dog is to be able to walk past another dog or person at a reasonable distance, such as across the street, without having a reaction, and having a relaxing walk. The progress achieved and the goals that are set will be different for every dog.

And that noise or motion I made to get my dog's attention? That becomes a cue for my dog to look at me. I have had such wonderful, creative owners make this game their own. Some will use silly words as a cue, like Popcorn! Some click their tongues or whistle. Owners have also created wonderful reinforcers for their dogs. See a dog, look at me, we are tossing a toy in the other direction and running to get it. See a dog, look at me and I toss a handful of food on the ground for you to find. See a dog, look at me, and we play a game of tug.

This is just an example of a conditioning exercise and will be different for every dog and will be developed with your trainer. Some common tips I give for operant conditioning exercises are:

Work under threshold, move the threshold slowly.
Make training sessions short, a lot of learning can happen in five minutes.
Make sure you are using a great reinforcer.

Remember your management plan so you are not inadvertently exposing your dog to triggers when you are not working with them.

Look for opportunities to practice. I have stealthily followed people and dogs at parks without them knowing they were helping to train a dog.

You can practice this game with anything that gets your dog's attention. It does not have to be a trigger. Sit on the front porch and practice with every passing car for example.

## *Relax on Mat*

While the engage/disengage game is directed towards dogs with reactivity there is one exercise that I will include in the plan for every single dog. That is, relax on mat.

## 9. The Behavior Modification Plan—Part 3

The relax on mat exercise serves multiple purposes. This exercise helps a dog learn to be calm and can lower arousal levels. It gives the dog a mobile, secure space. Relax on mat can also be grown into a cued behavior of having a dog move to a safe space. These goals are helpful for all dogs (and people!) but are especially helpful for dogs that are anxious or fearful.

If I was forced to choose only one thing that would help families living with dogs that have behavior issues, it would be "relax on mat." I would toss out everything else before I left out this exercise. But it is one of the things I have the most difficult time convincing people is beneficial. Maybe because it seems too easy, or maybe because I do not bother explaining the scientific reasoning behind the process, lest eyes glaze over. But I am a firm believer in the benefit of relax on mat, so much so that I teach all dogs this process regardless of age or temperament.

There are multiple protocols for relax on mat. In dog training circles, two of the most well-known are one developed by the trainer Nan Keene Arthur and one developed by Veterinary Behavior Specialist Dr. Karen Overall. Keene Arthur describes her protocol in her book, *Chill Out, Fido! How to Calm Your Dog.*[4] Keene Arthur outlines an easy-to-follow process and I have used her method quite often. Dr. Overall's protocol is described at length in her text, *Manual of Clinical Behavioral Medicine for Dogs and Cats*. Dr. Overall describes the science behind her method, "This protocol contains the essential, basic behavior modification program on which all more complex programs using DS and CC will be built."[5] DS stands for desensitization; CC stands for counter conditioning. Dr. Overall's protocol is detailed and provides a thorough step-by-step method.

After using multiple protocols and their derivatives throughout the years, I have settled on a process that I find is manageable for families but still effective. Families living with dogs with behavior concerns are already overwhelmed and busy. I believe in simplifying anything I can for my clients. I encourage families to go through the process twice a day, five days a week, if possible. Here is the protocol I teach my clients.

Get a mat. This can be a rug, a flat bed, a towel, or anything you would like to use. It does need to be small and light enough that you can roll it up and put it away when not working on this exercise, so you do not want to use a bulky bed. I usually recommend an inexpensive bathroom rug. Besides being cheap, the rubber backing prevents slipping.

Each day measure out half of your dog's daily food allotment into a container. With your dog in a room with you, sit in a comfortable chair and place the mat on the floor near you. Then, disengage from your dog. This means that you will not be looking at, talking to, or interacting with your dog. You are simply there to deliver the food. This is a good time to watch television or read a book. The goal is to establish a relationship between the dog and the mat. If you have more than one dog, you will need to work with only one dog at a time. So, you will need to remove the dogs you are not working with from the room.

Next, drop a piece of kibble on the mat about every five seconds. Make sure to count the five seconds, you might be surprised how long this really is. Your dog will discover the food and eat it. When the food you have measured out is gone, you are done! Pick up the mat and put it away. That's it. Repeat, repeat, repeat. Your dog will learn that the mat predicts food, that predictability is important, which is why you put the mat away when you are not working on this exercise.

At some point, on some day, while you are dropping kibble your dog will sit down on or near the mat awaiting the next piece of food to be dropped. When this happens, you are going to quickly drop several pieces of kibble, one after another onto the mat for about ten pieces or so. Then slow back down to one every five seconds. Each time your dog sits or lies down the treats will bombard the mat from your hand. The message to your dog is, the more relaxed you are, the more food will fall. Soon you will find that it takes less time for your dog to sit or lie down on the mat.

After continued practice, you will notice your dog increases the amount of time they are sitting or lying on the mat while you drop one piece of food at a time. Your dog has learned that the mat predicts food, food is pleasurable and makes your dog feel happy. The mat is now the stimulus that creates calm. The mat becomes your dog's happy place.

Once your dog has built a relationship with the mat, you are going to "take the mat on the road." You will build one new location at a time. Start with locations where it is easier for your dog to relax and build up to the more challenging locations. Try it in other rooms of the house, then outside at home, then start at locations away from home.

To move this behavior forward, after several weeks of practice, you will extend the amount of time in between dropping the pieces of food. Five seconds will become 15, 20, or even 30. You may also see your dog remaining on the mat even after the food is gone. Typically, I see this process grow organically. There is no step-by-step rule to follow. Once a dog knows this is your place to hang out and rest you can begin to leave the mat out. You can even have your trainer help you teach your dog to go to the mat on cue.

## 9. The Behavior Modification Plan—Part 3

Once the relationship is established with the mat you can use the mat as a cue for calm in several scenarios. The mat can help your dog feel calmer on car rides and I ALWAYS take the mat to the veterinarian's office. Not only is this security for my dog, but it also gives us something to do while we are waiting for the vet to enter the exam room. I make sure to have my dog's mat ready when I have visitors in my home. My dog knows if he hangs out on the mat instead of pestering people, he will get treats.

Seems simple right? Remember to be patient. My Great Dane spent three weeks standing and eating the food then walking away. There was a moment when I thought she would be the ONE dog who did not catch on. Finally, almost a month later she lay down on the mat. I had almost given up! I am glad I didn't. That mat went with us everywhere for the rest of her life and provided much security for my anxious dog.

The purpose of using half of your dog's daily food is simply to avoid adding extra calories. If you are doing this exercise only once a day, then use half of one meal. If you are doing the exercise twice a day, then use half of each meal. If plain kibble does not interest your dog, use treats, the calories are worth it for this exercise. Again, if I was going to recommend one thing for a dog with behavior concerns, it would be this exercise. I have seen relax on mat change dogs' lives.

## *The Big Picture*

That was a lot of information. Most dog owners seeking help do not know what to expect and can become a little overwhelmed when they find out about the behavior modification plan and everything that is involved. I think it is helpful to review and review again. Remember that there are foundation steps and future work will build on that foundation. You will not need to tackle everything at once. So, let's review the behavior modification plan. The specific steps of a plan will differ between professionals, but typically all plans will contain the same process. Once you find the professional you will work with, the plan will likely contain a mix of the following parts.

The trainer or behavior consultant will send you a lengthy form to fill out and return. Don't be afraid to include any small details. The more we know about your dog the more prepared we will be. The consultant will obtain a history either over the phone or in person. This is an opportunity for the trainer to fill in gaps or flesh out information from the form. When I review a questionnaire returned by an owner, I will review and jot down the questions I have in response to the information I received before I contact the owner to review.

An in-person observation will be conducted for the trainer to see the concerns firsthand. This observation, the initial questionnaire, and the history will make up the evaluation. Your professional will discuss with you if they are the best fit and if they are, you will proceed with scheduling. If they decide they are not, expect they will provide you a referral to the appropriate resources.

Expect to set goals with your trainer and discuss expectations. You will set up a management plan to prevent your dog from practicing unwanted behavior and to keep everyone safe. You will learn more about canine body language than you ever wanted to know and how your dog communicates with you. You will decide what skills are important and learn how to teach your dog with positive reinforcement training.

The bulk of the behavior modification plan will be using conditioning to help your dog change their emotional response to the things that scare them. This will be when you focus specifically on the concerns that led you to seek help. Don't worry if this does not happen right away. The management and training skills are the needed base for the conditioning exercises.

Remember when embarking on a behavior modification plan to go slow. You will undoubtedly have a long list of goals and things you would like to improve. It will go much more smoothly if you tackle one or two goals at a time. When you do, you will see progress in many areas, I promise.

Take small steps in advancing any behavior. It is better to be repetitive at the level where you are than to jump ahead. For example, when training new skills, I use the rule of five. Let's say you are teaching your dog a targeting exercise and when you hold out your hand and say the word "touch" your dog will move towards you and touch your hand with his nose. Your dog has been successful with this skill when you hold your hand four feet from him. He is doing so well that you decide to increase the distance to ten feet. Think about the rule of five.

Stand four feet from your dog and repeat the behavior five times in a row. You will only make the task more challenging for him and increase the distance if he can complete the behavior on cue successfully four or five times out of five. If your dog is only successful three times, then you need to stick to where you are and keep practicing. If your dog is successful only one to two times out of five something has

## 9. The Behavior Modification Plan—Part 3

gone wrong in the communication. Back up the exercise—for example, go from four feet to two feet. Review if you are clear with your cues and if your dog really understands what is wanted. If your dog is successful and completes the cued behavior four or five times out of five, consider moving from four to six feet instead of ten. Slow, steady progress is always better.

When I am training my dog to do something new, I set my dog up for success because by being successful we learn! If I am teaching my teenager how to drive, I am not going to take them to the four-lane high-speed highway for the first lesson. Think about what might happen. They would be overwhelmed. I will be scared. There will be tears and they may refuse to learn how to drive at all.

But if we start the lesson in a quiet parking lot on a Sunday morning, they are going to feel successful. This will build their confidence and they will be willing and ready to try something a little more challenging the next time.

We can apply this same metaphor to our dogs. If I know they are not going to be able to do what I ask, I will not ask. If I have just begun teaching my dog to drop something from his mouth when I say the word "drop" I am going to begin practicing with something that is low value. I am not going to begin "drop" when he is eating the chicken he stole off the counter. I am pretty sure when I say "drop" his reaction will be to run and swallow as fast as he can. That is not the time I am going to work on that cue. But if I have practiced and really reinforced the drop with great treats and he knows that by dropping the chicken he will get something better then I will give it a try. I want to set up my dog for success! Thereby, learning will take place.

Lastly remember that when you are overwhelmed, as will happen at times, you are not alone. Reach out to your trainer during those times.

# 10

# Even More Help

As you are working through your behavior modification plan, at some point you will wonder, how long will all of this take? When will my dog be okay? When can I take my dog for a walk without returning home in tears? When can I leave my dog home alone while I go to work? I don't know. I cannot tell you, no one can.

That can be hard to hear, especially when you've just seen the ad for the boarding and training program that promises to fix your dog in six weeks. Dogs are living beings; any given behavior has a multitude of factors. The success of a behavior modification plan is impacted by many things. Often changing behavior is truly a matter of two steps forward, and one step back. Continue to work with your behavior consultant and your veterinarian to make progress. While you are working on your plan there are several tools that can help you on this journey.

## *Medication*

Just as humans with mental illness can benefit from medication, so can our dogs. It would be unethical, if not inhumane, to not consider an evaluation for medication for our dogs. A behavior diagnosis for a dog is a medical diagnosis and should be treated as thus.

Discussing medications can be a touchy subject. I have had many clients express discomfort with giving their dog medication. The top reason I hear for this discomfort is that owners do not want to have a dog that is continually sedated. They are afraid of altering their dog's personality, of losing the dog they know. Other reasons may be a personal view that medications can be harmful to the physical nature of the dog. Some feel that giving medication is admitting defeat.

Discussions of medication can be touchy for the trainer as well. All considerations for medications should be conducted with a veterinarian. A trainer should never suggest or recommend a particular

## 10. Even More Help

medication or even indicate that your dog should be on medication. A trainer does not possess the knowledge base or the license to make these decisions. A trainer certainly can make a referral to the veterinarian for this discussion. I am sharing my personal experience with dogs that have benefited from being prescribed medication. I hope that by learning a little bit about medications used to treat dogs with behavior issues, some concerns can be alleviated.

Medications are an important component of treatment for dogs with behavior issues. Medications must of course be prescribed by a doctor. Medications are important because dogs with behavior issues, or problems, or concerns, or whatever label we choose, are really dogs dealing with a mental health diagnosis.

Though not all dogs with behavior concerns need medication, I have seen the use of therapeutic drugs make the difference in the success of the behavior modification plan. So much so that for some dogs, I will delay any training or conditioning exercises, and focus only on management, until the veterinarian has the time to stabilize the medication protocol. Some medications that are used in dogs can take up to 12 weeks to have a full effect. With dogs who have very complicated behavior issues, it can be beneficial to give the medication time to start working before beginning a training program.

One of the goals of using medication is to lower the threshold for triggered behavior. For example, in working with reactive dogs, distance is important. A reactive dog may be able to tolerate the sight of another dog at 50 yards. We call this the threshold. If a dog is over that threshold and in a reactive state, she cannot learn.

A goal of the behavior modification plan may be to help the dog tolerate other dogs at a distance of ten yards. Medication plays an important part in lowering arousal which allows the trainer and owner to work with the dog in the presence of a trigger. This allows the dog to learn and change to take place.

One of my own dogs, Bayou, was severely frightened by fireworks. Luckily, this was a trigger that was periodic and somewhat predictable. At the first sound of a pop or the smell of gunpowder, Bayou would panic and attempt to climb on my lap. Did I mention she was a Great Dane? When she heard fireworks, Bayou would pant and salivate, refuse to eat, and search for an escape route. She was in fight or flight mode. After the fireworks ended, she would remain in a high state of stress for the next 12–24 hours. Our veterinarian prescribed medication to be used during times when fireworks were expected.

## I Know Your Dog Is a Good Dog

After we started using the medication Bayou still did not like fireworks, but what I noticed is that she began having less of a reaction to fireworks that were very far away. I also noticed her stressful period after the fireworks ended, was shortened from 12–24 hours to about six to eight hours.

The medication was not a magic wand, but because with the medication on board she could tolerate some fireworks that were further away, I was able to get her attention when she heard those far away pops and bangs. She would look at me and she would eat a treat. I was able to begin a counter conditioning program to help her better tolerate fireworks. The combination of the medication and the behavior modification created further improvement. Even though my dog remained fearful of fireworks, I was able to comfort her instead of having her panic.

Along with the medication and behavior modification I also used management. I would play white noise, close curtains, and go to the basement to help lessen the sight and sound of the fireworks. In Bayou's case, the use of medication helped to improve the quality of her life and mine.

From a scientific standpoint, Dr. Karen Overall gives an example of how one of the medications used for anxiety in dogs works: "Clonidine is a member of the class of medications known as centrally acting, alpha-2-agonists. These medications decrease cardiac output and lower blood pressure, and so should beneficially affect the increased heart rate, tone and arousal that are reactions to stress, threats, or excitement. Medications like clonidine are thought to act by preventing the physiological effects of arousal in upsetting situations (e.g., storms, loud noises, novel situations that cause panic)."[1]

There are factors that owners should be aware of when considering medication for their dogs. Most of the medications prescribed for pets for behavioral issues are being used "off label."[2] In the United States, this means these medications have not been approved by the Food and Drug Administration (FDA) for the specific conditions for which they are used to treat pet animals.

Many medications are used in this way for humans too. An example is the drug Gabapentin. This medication was developed to help control certain types of seizures for patients that have epilepsy. With the broadened use of the drug, it was discovered that a side effect of Gabapentin was a reduction in nerve pain. Gabapentin is now a common treatment for nerve pain but was "off label" for its original purpose.

There are other examples. Many drugs that are approved in formulation for adults are used "off label" for children. Drugs that are prescribed in this way by licensed practitioners are legal and it does not mean the medication is not safe.

There are side effects to medications, some common and temporary and some rare. Your veterinarian should explain these to you. There may also be specific medical conditions or health history that preclude your dog from a specific medication.

It is important for your veterinarian to know all of your dog's history. This includes any nutritional supplements that are given as well as flea, tick or heartworm medication that is used. It is important to remember that many of these medications cannot be stopped abruptly and must be weaned to prevent unwanted physical or psychological effects.

If your dog has medication prescribed by a specialist and is seeing the general practice veterinarian for routine care, please make sure the specialist is communicating with the general practice veterinarian. The Veterinary Behavior Specialist is the expert on these types of medications and the best to advise on protocols for how these medications may need to be altered in the course of routine care, such as when anesthesia is needed or when medications are prescribed for other medical conditions.

## Mental Enrichment

I recently saw a dog food commercial for a company touting that their product is made for the wolf inside my dog. The ad showed something like a wild wolf running over hill and dale and morphing into the neighborhood poodle running across the manicured yards of the suburbs.

I've seen several memes lamenting the thousands of years it took the wolf to evolve into the domesticated dog next to a picture of a pit bull in a bubble bath. Those always make me chuckle. But it does make me reflect on the way the lives of pet dogs have changed. A century ago, dogs were kept mainly for the purpose of working. It was the privileged that were able to keep dogs as pets.

I was having a conversation with a veterinarian about the issue of knee injuries in dogs and he pointed out that often the dogs he sees are "weekend warriors." Dogs that are home alone 40+ hours a week and then taken out for a run on the weekends. These dogs are typically de-conditioned and overweight. He noted that dogs he sees that live in

## I Know Your Dog Is a Good Dog

the country or on farms who are allowed to exercise at will are not as prone to these injuries.

It made me reflect on how humans have impacted the life that pet dogs lead. I thought about my dog. When I am at home for what would be an eight-hour workday my dog sleeps about six of those hours. He is an adult and is past the stage of the puppy and adolescent energy. But it makes me realize that my dog's social and physical life is completely dependent on me.

Dog owners focus a lot on physical activity for their dogs. Sometimes too much and sometimes not enough. But they may have never focused on mental exercise, beyond a few toys. Lucky for my dog, I am aware of the importance of mental enrichment.

I knew that it was important to prevent boredom with dogs, especially young active dogs. Boredom can lead to frustration. Frustration can lead to unwanted behavior. Not only destructive behavior to the environment, whether that be outdoors, in a crate, or in the house but also self-injury. Dogs that are bored may develop physically harmful behaviors such as hair pulling or licking different body parts. But I never thought of mental enrichment as an essential part of caring for a dog and as a responsibility of being a dog owner.

Then several years ago, I learned of a dog toy that was becoming popular called a Jolly Ball™. This is essentially a large rubber ball with a large rubber handle. They are great toys. They do not collapse or deflate, even when the dog chews the handle off, which mine always do, the ball remains an object of entertainment. What surprised me is that the original Jolly Ball was not a dog toy at all, it was a toy made for horses. Knowing nothing about horses it came as new information to me that horses were given toys!

I knew that captive animals were given novel objects to explore. I would see the birthday cakes made for the elephants at the zoo comprised of hay and ice with special treats tucked inside. The videos of the elephant, or gorilla, or even bird finding the treasures were always charming. But before I became a dog trainer it did not occur to me that paying attention to the mental environment of our dogs was so important.

Focusing on mental enrichment is one of the most important things we can do for any dog, but for a dog with behavior issues, it is an important part of the overall behavior modification plan. What is mental enrichment? Simply, mental enrichment is altering or adding to the dog's environment to provide opportunities for the dog to express

## 10. Even More Help

natural dog behaviors. The opportunity to express these behaviors can lower stress, improve cognition, and expend energy. The result of this is a dog who is more relaxed, can think more clearly, and obtain more restorative rest and sleep.

It is fairly simple to create a mentally enriched environment for your dog and to provide mentally enriching activities. Think of this process in a few categories:

- **Food:** Use different feeding methods, different food items, or varying feeding schedules to prolong feeding time or stimulate natural feeding methods.
- **Sensory:** Use novel items, scents, etc., to engage the five senses (touch, taste, sight, sound, and smell).
- **Cognitive:** Enhance mental stimulation and occupy an animal's time through the use of puzzles or novel feeders.
- **Social:** Interact with other animals of the same or different species.
- **Physical Habitat:** Utilize the space in the enclosure by hiding food, rearranging the exhibit furniture, adding natural objects or toys.[3]

Here are some ideas that I and some of my clients have used with success. If you have a dog, I bet you have a dog bowl and a water bowl in the kitchen, or pantry, or laundry room? I'm right, aren't I? Why do we feed our dogs from bowls? I know I do because that is the way I have always known it to be. That is the way I grew up. When you get a dog, what are the first things you get? A leash, a collar, a tag, and food and water bowls. But here is a tip, stop feeding your dog from a bowl. And ... try different ways of feeding them on different days. Here are some ways I've fed my dog.

Commercially made dog puzzles. You can find these in pet supply stores and online. They are typically plastic trays with raised areas that make it a little harder to get the food out of the tray. You can also make your own. Use a muffin pan, put toys or your dog's balls in the pan on top of the kibble. Use multiple small bowls spread around the kitchen. Help your dog find the bowls and she will soon learn she has to hunt for her food.

One of the times I've seen my dog have the most fun and become the most excited is when I took her cup of kibble outside, tossed it into the yard, and said, "go find!" She loved it and I loved watching my dog be a dog, using her nose to hunt down her meal.

## I Know Your Dog Is a Good Dog

A word of caution here. If you have a dog that is a resource guarder, that guards its food and may snap or bite if he thinks another animal or person is going to take his food use caution. Have your dog trainer help you think of creative ways to feed your dog.

For sensory enrichment think of your dog's strongest sense, her sense of smell. My friend Kate and I taught a great class called Fun Scent Games™. The class involved hiding pieces of hot dogs in boxes placed in a large room. The dogs would take turns searching for the hot dog. One thing that surprised us was the number of dogs that had no idea how to use their nose to find anything! We talked in orientation about how powerful the dog's nose was. How dogs are used to find people and truffles and even endangered plants and animals. Then come class time we would have dogs blankly looking at their owner as if to ask, now what am I supposed to be doing?

In talking with other trainers that worked in the area of scenting we realized that our typical pet dog rarely has to use their nose. Certainly not for survival or to find food. They may search out the missed piece of popcorn that was left under the couch and may follow the trail of an interesting animal in the yard, but our "students" were not required to use their nose and were not sure how to go about the game. Once this was demonstrated a few times though, the dogs caught on. And they loved it! It was one of our most popular classes and we often heard from owners how tired their dog was after "hot dog" class.

I almost always recommend to owners to think of a way to create their own scent games at home. Start by saving all those boxes that are left at your front door with deliveries. Save tissue boxes and the tubes from paper towels or toilet tissue. These can all be used as containers. Save plastic food containers with lids, you can poke holes in those lids.

Start slow. Use maybe two or three boxes hiding a special treat in only one. Once your dog catches on, expand the search area, and add boxes. Then you can change the vertical level of the boxes. The dog that has learned to easily find the box on the floor that hides the treat really has to think when the box is put on a chair. Start out with a small circle of boxes then put a box or two in the hallway or another room.

If you are in the midst of a behavior modification plan you have been training your dog and that is one of the best ways to exercise your dog's brain. Especially by teaching a simple trick. I taught my dog Rocket to do a down on cue. I also taught him to go from a down to lying on his side. For no other reason than to just have fun teaching him something. Then in a moment of human boredom I decided

## 10. Even More Help

to make these tricks fancier. I changed the cue for lying down from "down" to "tired" I did this by adding the new cue right before the old cue. Think N for new, which comes before O for old in the alphabet. I would repeat tired, down, tired, down. My dog soon learned that when I said tired the word down would follow and he understood the word tired meant to lie down.

Then for rolling over I added the cue, bed. So now tired meant to lie down and bed meant to roll over. I had to demonstrate his new trick to everyone I met and they were always impressed when I asked my dog, "are you tired?" (dog lies down). "Then go to bed!" (dog rolls onto side). It was fun for me, and my dog and I know the time we spent together was meeting the need for his cognitive enrichment.

Social interaction can or might be important for your dog. But always have a caveat, for dogs with behavior issues this may or may not be true. Yes, social interaction with people and other animals can be important, but for a dog that is people reactive or dog reactive, or a dog with a high prey drive we must exercise common sense about having them around other dogs, people, or critters.

And now comes the time for my lecture on dog parks and day cares. I've already stated how day care may be an important tool for dogs that have separation anxiety and cannot be left alone but not all day cares are equal. I have been allowed to observe dogs I am working with at their day cares and always appreciate that opportunity. But most of the time I leave feeling stressed and sad. I have seen many worse-case scenarios and very few good examples of well-run dog day cares.

This is going to ruffle feathers but there is no reason any dog should ever be put into a group of 20 to 30 to 50 dogs. I am an expert on dog body language and when I have observed dogs in this type of environment, I see the rare dog that is relaxed and having fun. I have seen dogs expressing stress in all manners, shadowing day care staff, looking for an escape, sleeping, and snapping at any dog that comes near.

If you have a dog with behavior issues that is going to a dog day care for anything other than separation anxiety, consider taking them out until your trainer can give the facility their stamp of approval.

I am not anti–day care; in fact, I had a day care that two of my dogs would attend regularly. This was also where I would board my dogs when necessary. My Great Dane was not a people person and I would often park her at her day care when I had gatherings at my house. Here are the things I like about the day care I used.

The day care was Fear Free™ certified. The staff were trained using techniques from a nationally known trainer with whom I was familiar. Staff were required to be familiar with Nicole Wilde's books and videos on dog play.[4]

Playgroups were small, with three to five dogs at a time. Playgroups were observed for play style. If there were mismatches, the dogs were re-shuffled. Staff would make suggestions for owners of dogs that were good matches to come on the same day.

Staff kept notes on each visit of who played together, their reactions, and any noted issues. The facility did not hesitate to tell some owners that the day care environment was not right for their dogs. It is possible to find a good day care if you really search. If you want to know how your dog's experience is going, ask if someone your dog does not know, so they will not attract your dog's attention, could come and video for a nice long period of time, not just a few minutes. If the day care does not allow this, then do not go back. There should be no reason they should not be open and transparent.

And now my lecture on dog parks. That is a tough one. It can be wonderful for dogs to have a chance to run and stretch their legs. It can be an important source of physical exercise and play. But again, not all dog parks are equal. And again, should be avoided if your dog is reactive to other dogs and people.

Almost anyone can tell you of an experience they had or someone they know has had when a visit to a dog park went sideways. A better option may be to create a meet-up group with people you know, with dogs that are known to be friendly. Keep the group small and beg or borrow a space where your dog can run. One of my favorites is when I find an old, out-of-use, not maintained tennis court that still has a secure fence.

Remember puppies and adolescent dogs should never be taken to a dog park. Puppies may be susceptible to disease in an area where you cannot control or know the health status of other dogs. Older puppies and early adolescent dogs go through something we call secondary fear periods. It is a developmental stage during which, if something frightens a dog, they may keep that fear for the rest of their life.

An adult dog may be able to overcome a scuffle or fright from another dog or person, but if a dog fight breaks out with or near a dog that is in the midst of one of these fear periods the result may be a life-long fear of dogs.

How can you make a physical environment enriching for a dog? Does this mean having lots of toys or beds? Think of the physical

## 10. Even More Help

environment as an opportunity for a dog to express those natural dog behaviors. Behaviors like digging, urinating on things, sniffing through the grass, rolling in the grass, and hunting! Good news! This does not have to be in your living room or even your backyard! It doesn't even have to be every day. Think of these as general principles to provide opportunities. My dogs get these opportunities every time we take a walk.

For example, digging. If you have a dog that digs, I bet someone has recommended you build them a digging pit. A digging pit is an idea of providing your dog a designated digging area on your property. I've tried this. I have. I've tried sectioning off an area filled with topsoil. I've hidden treats and toys in the area to encourage digging in only that area. I've tried filling a wading pool with sand and toys. Do you know how well this worked? It didn't. It didn't work at all. I think it is a great idea and worth a try, but my dogs wanted to dig where they wanted to dig. So that was a no go for me.

My current dog is not much of a digger, but he loves to dig after moles. Fortunately, or not for my ankles, the woods we walk in has a lot of mole holes. It is an area that is not maintained as a lawn, so my dog is allowed to dig to his heart's content and to this day has never found a mole. Even when he has dug holes big enough for his head to fit into.

At home, if I have a dog that likes to dig where it should not, I have found a solution that works for me. I bury plastic-covered chicken wire in that area. This has worked great for me and eventually, grass has grown up through the chicken wire making it invisible, but close enough to the surface to make digging unenjoyable.

My dogs are also able to roll in the grass when we walk. It is their walk. I have learned to carry wipes in my car in case there are smelly things to be rolled on. I also had an interesting experience on a walk when my dog was happily rolling on her back and the latch from the harness that was between her, and the ground became unhooked by her rolling. So now I have a double latch. We also wade through water, climb hills, and take different paths when we walk.

Creating mental enrichment can sound like a lot of work but you do not have to tackle everything at once. Pick one thing, maybe stop feeding your dog from a bowl. I know you will see a result. Your dog will become more engaged, more relaxed, more interested in their environment, and more willing to listen. Mental enrichment will help your dog to be happy.

## *Holistic Treatments*

There are a variety of treatments that I group under the "holistic" umbrella. Technically the term holistic means treating the whole animal. These are treatments that may or may not be supported by scientific research, but they do tend to have strong anecdotal support. I will be honest; I have seen few of these treatments have a strong impact and I've never seen any of them solve a problem on their own. However, there are some that I recommend based on feedback I receive from owners and believe are worth a try. All these treatments work best when integrated as part of an overall behavior modification plan.

### *DAP*

DAP is one of the treatments I recommend early and often; it stands for Dog Appeasing Pheromone. The brand of DAP that I am most familiar with is Adaptil™. According to the website for Adaptil, a dog appeasing pheromone is a hormone released by dogs who are nursing puppies. These hormones send "comforting messages" and provide a "strong signal of security and comfort to dogs of all ages."[5] I have used Adaptil collars for my own dogs and I have seen small improvements. I have seen a reduction in nuisance barking and lowered stress when in unfamiliar environments.

Adaptil™ comes in a collar form, a spray, and a plug-in diffuser. I have not seen success with the diffuser other than in small spaces, such as an exam room at the veterinarian's office. The cost of the spray may be prohibitive to some. But I do recommend a trial of an Adaptil collar. The collar, which looks similar to a flea collar, must be worn snugly against the fur. Never attach a leash to the collar and follow the manufacturer's instructions on replacing the collar.

I see many products promoted as "calming collars" and I suspect there are some subpar knockoffs on the market. I recommend the Adaptil brand only because it is the brand with which I am familiar. I would like to make it clear that I have no relationship with the Adaptil company. The worst-case scenario in using DAP is that it will do nothing, but in some dogs, it may be beneficial.

### *Wraps and Shirts*

Dr. Temple Grandin, a noted animal scientist, author, and professor, writes about her experience of growing up as a person with autism in her book *Animals in Translation.* Dr. Grandin writes that at a young age, she discovered that the application of gentle pressure was calming to her.

This brilliant scientist set about designing a squeeze machine, this was an apparatus that she would lie in while it applied gentle pressure to her body.[6] Later in life, Dr. Grandin applied these principles to her research in the livestock industry. Her study and understanding of the animal mind have had a great impact on the way holding pens are developed for livestock animals. Dr. Grandin writes, "I think the explanation may have to do with oxytocin. Oxytocin also goes up with physical contact."[7]

Oxytocin is a neurotransmitter whose main function is to facilitate childbirth. Oxytocin is also produced when we fall in love. It is active in attachment and social behaviors.[8] A true "feel good" hormone.

This principle of reducing anxiety in animals by applying pressure triggered an influx of products directed to dog owners. One of the better-known products is Thundershirt™, a vest that wraps around the dog and is secured with Velcro straps that go under the dog's belly. The snug fit of the vest is meant to apply that gentle pressure.

I have also seen the use of small-size human t-shirts or even Ace bandages used to wrap dogs to accomplish the same purpose. A commercial product may offer the advantage of a better fit. Caution should be used if creating your own garment, if not done correctly wrapping things around a dog may cut off circulation or pose a risk of entanglement or strangulation.

I have received reports from owners that these products seem to help in some cases. My experience is that a more noticeable improvement is seen when these vests or wraps are used in conjunction with a dog appeasing pheromone, DAP, or with medication. And for some dogs, I've seen them make no difference at all. If worn appropriately these products should not cause any harm, although I have seen shy dogs frightened by the sound of the Velcro straps. As with any new accessory, wraps or shirts should be introduced appropriately in a non-threatening way.

## *Nutritional Supplements*

There are a variety of nutritional supplements on the market that are promoted as helping to reduce anxiety and to help keep dogs calm. I always recommend proceeding with caution with these products.

## I Know Your Dog Is a Good Dog

Because nutritional supplements can impact your dog's overall health, and because there may be medical conditions specific to your dog that would prohibit their use, I always recommend these be discussed with your veterinarian.

Purina Calming Care™ is a product directed specifically at treating anxiety in dogs. On their website, Purina claims that "the beneficial probiotic strain, BL999 is believed to positively impact anxious behavior via the microbiota-gut-brain axis, a bidirectional communiat system between the gastrointestinal tract and the brain."[9] The product is a food supplement in the form of a powder sold under the brand name Calming Care™.

The gut-brain connection has been supported by several scientific papers including Kirchoff, Udell, & Sharpton's, "The Gut Microbiome Correlates with Conspecific Aggression in a Small Population of Rescued Dogs (Canis familiaris)."[10] Mondo, Barone, and Soverini's, "Gut Microbiome Structure and Adrenocortical Activity in Dogs with Aggressive and Phobic Behavioral Disorders,"[11] and McGowen et al.'s, "Tapping Into Those 'Gut Feelings': Impact of BL99 (Bifidobacterium longum) on Anxiety in Dogs."[12]

Common sense should tell us that if a dog does not feel well, if it is sluggish or has stomach aches, it is likely not going to be on its best behavior. But there may be more scientific reasons that addressing nutrition can address a dog's behavior. Nutrition should always be considered when working with dogs with behavior issues.

# 11

# Arlo

"Life happens in between medication doses; we live our lives in those intervals."

I have a soft spot for Rotties, they are one of my favorite breeds. I have affection for all my clients, but I have to remain objective in my job as a behavior consultant. Objectivity helps me provide the best care. However, I must confess, a picture of this 80 pound, mostly Rottweiler mix, hangs on my fridge.

Arlo was adopted as a young puppy by Kelly and Richard. They had owned other dogs in the past, including a Rottweiler. They were experienced and knowledgeable about the breed. They were well aware of the energy level and the need for training and work for Rottweilers. But Arlo was different. He was wild. He was beyond destructive; he would rip furniture apart and he would steal and tear clothing. He also seemed to scare easily. He barked, and paced, and cried, a lot.

This behavior was noticed by Arlo's owners almost immediately. In an attempt to address their concerns they got him into a puppy class right away. The trainer in this early class described Arlo as hyperactive

**Arlo**

and stubborn. The trainer was constantly using the leash to give Arlo hard corrections, jerking his head and neck with the leash. He explained to the owners that Arlo needed these corrections frequently. He also told them they were not giving their puppy enough exercise.

Kelly tried to explain to the trainer that exercise was difficult because at times Arlo was too frightened to leave the sidewalk in front of their house. The trainer responded that Arlo was not afraid, just stubborn. Deep down his owners felt this was wrong. They began to feel it wasn't right to subject a young puppy to this type of treatment, but the trainer was the expert, wasn't he? Arlo did learn new skills in the class, but his overall behavior did not change. After a while, Richard and Kelly began to wonder if Arlo was a normal dog.

Kelly became more and more uncomfortable with the advice she was being given by the trainer. Yes, she knew Arlo could be stubborn, but this was different. When Arlo was about a year old, Richard was walking him at the school that borders their backyard. A groundskeeper was running a large commercial mower at the school. Arlo took one look at the mower as it zipped past them and pulled to go back to his house. He was petrified.

From that time forward if they went out for a walk and Arlo saw mowers or even heard them, he would try to flee home. As he got older his fearful behavior grew into reactive behavior and he would bark and pull and jump toward not only mowers but now any vehicle with large tires; trash trucks, pickup trucks, and even school buses. Trash days became unbearable. If inside the house, Arlo would hide and shake when he heard the large trucks. His fear was so apparent that Kelly would be in tears watching his distress.

Arlo began showing other concerning behaviors. He started reacting toward other dogs. The puppy they used to take to outdoor events and to the farmer's market was gone. Arlo started showing signs of separation anxiety too, especially when Richard was away from home. Even with Kelly there, Arlo would spend his time pacing and whining and hiding.

He developed some odd behaviors such as hitting and biting on a door stopper repeatedly or repeatedly running to the bed and grabbing and throwing pillows that he would then destroy. He started scratching at the floor and floor registers over and over. This was not just the behavior of a fun, high energy dog, these behaviors could not be interrupted, and Arlo could not be distracted from them.

Arlo was friendly when meeting new people, but he was more than rambunctious. When I first met Arlo he jumped onto the back of

## 11. Arlo

a couch and then onto me, all 80 pounds of him. For those not in love with him, this could be a lot to handle. Kelly and Richard began to recognize this was not just high energy or high-drive behavior, remember they were experienced with high-drive breeds. This was something different.

They recognized they needed help and sought treatment with a veterinarian who was board certified in behavior. The Veterinary Behavior Specialist diagnosed Arlo with global fear, generalized anxiety, fear related aggression, pain, and irritability. Arlo was started on medication for his behavior, and that did help, but it took months to arrive at the right combination of medications at the right dosages. It took quite a bit of trial and error to find the most therapeutic combination of medications that would help Arlo. Thankfully, his family has reached a regimen that seems to help, but it requires dedication. Arlo was being given medication four times a day and the times each day must remain consistent. This makes it difficult for Richard and Kelly to be away from home for any length of time.

Somewhere in the process of finding help for Arlo, Kelly came upon a book called *Decoding Your Dog: Explaining Common Dog Behaviors and How to Prevent or Change Unwanted Ones*, by the American College of Veterinary Behaviorists.[1]

This book changed the way Kelly thought about dogs and their fears and how she thought about Arlo. It validated her gut feeling that "traditional" obedience training was not helping him and likely making many of his problem behaviors worse.

*Decoding Your Dog* became instrumental in giving Kelly insight into how dogs think and experience the world. This was a turning point, and it was about this time that Kelly and Richard reached out to me to help with training and behavior modification.

Together we worked on many things with Arlo, his reactivity, his separation anxiety, his obsessive behaviors, and his leash walking skills. The behavior plan for Arlo was complex and encompassed many goals. The plan included working on exercises to reinforce calm behavior, both indoors and out. It included basic training to build skills and confidence. We taught Arlo games and used nose work to provide mental enrichment and distraction. And the plan required practice, practice, practice.

Kelly would often joke that Arlo could play and run hard outside and then come back into the house and still act like you had given him a pot of coffee. The mental enrichment tools we implemented as part of

## I Know Your Dog Is a Good Dog

his plan were a game changer. Kelly tells me, "You may not be able to out-exercise a Rottweiler, but if you can provide enough mental enrichment activities you might just stand a chance." Again, proof that Arlo's energy level was not just a matter of not having enough exercise.

As Arlo was working through his behavior modification plan Kelly and Richard were also working with a veterinary nutritionist to address a chronic digestive condition. This condition had likely been causing him pain which was contributing to his behavior. Having this condition treated made an additional positive impact on Arlo's behavior and is a good reminder of the necessity to address any health issues for dogs with behavior concerns.

The time came when Arlo and his family completed their in-person visits with me. A year had passed since I had seen Arlo when I met with Kelly and Richard to talk about their journey. Kelly tells me that many of Arlo's behaviors have improved in the past year. She feels a change in vets and focusing on his stomach problems has helped. He has even been able to wean some medication. Arlo is now a dream to walk and something she looks forward to every day if they remain aware of the presence of any triggers.

At my visit, the dog that happily jumped from the couch to my shoulders was now excited to see me but kept all feet on the floor. He calmed quickly after my arrival and was soon snoozing on the couch. He seems wonderfully improved, but his owners warn me that it sometimes seems he exchanges one problem behavior for another.

Arlo still reacts to cars and recently got out of the house when a guest opened the front door without noticing he was nearby. Kelly stretched to grab Arlo as a car turned onto their street, but just missed reaching his collar. Arlo ran towards the car and the driver stopped suddenly. Arlo ran smack into the car. The poor young driver was shocked and sobbing thinking she had hit a dog. They had to explain that no, Arlo had hit her. Luckily neither car nor dog was injured.

Arlo also continues to develop some perseverating behaviors. He will still get anxious if Richard is not home. He has developed the belief that standing outside in the yard makes Dad come home. So now if Richard is not home, Arlo has difficulty relaxing inside and cries to be outside in the yard. Even though his problem behaviors are not as severe as they used to be, life with Arlo remains a challenge. He is a wonderful example of a dog that has complex and intricate behavior issues that will be lifelong. And Richard and Kelly are a wonderful example of human perseverance and love.

## 11. Arlo

The exhaustion of living with Arlo is made more complicated by his need to have one of his owners with him most of the time. As a result, Kelly and Richard very rarely, almost never really, get to be away from home together. They did have one friend that was able to care for Arlo, but they lost that service due to the friend's life changes. Because Arlo has so much nervous behavior and odd behavior, they fear he would be difficult to tolerate by anyone.

At times the stress of caring for and worrying about Arlo is overwhelming. They admit they sometimes feel stuck. This is not helped by the comments they get from other people. They have been told, "that dog runs your life," or "I guess we'll just have to schedule around your dog." Kelly describes these comments as hurtful on another level. She and Richard are trying to do their best.

Kelly and Richard speak fondly of the dog they had before Arlo. That dog died with cancer. When that dog was entering into her end of life, they thought about the quality of her days, not the quantity. Kelly points out that if we looked at behavior diagnoses in dogs as illnesses, we would see that quality of life is not always measured. I asked Kelly and Richard what has been helpful in their journey with Arlo, and I am told that a good vet and good dog sitter are worth more than gold, "they are worth any amount of money." A good dog sitter gave us some normalcy.

Resources that pointed away from punitive training were helpful. The book, *Decoding Your Dog*, was most helpful. It was the beginning of learning things about Arlo that were specific to him and helped move them down the path to the right treatment. Kelly feels that understanding your dog and what they are trying to communicate with their behavior is key. Arlo's behaviors are complicated, and the book allowed her to make sense of them. She recommends it to all dog owners, behavior problems or not.

One of the most important things they have learned is to give Arlo choices. This was critical to his improvement. Kelly describes taking Arlo for walks and if he spooks and tries to return home, then they return home. Kelly advises that in the past her knee-jerk reaction would be to positively encourage Arlo, to give him treats, and to help him work through his fear. A, "come on buddy, you can do it" attitude.

While that may be an effective approach for some pups, Arlo wasn't having it. He didn't care if you packed a peanut butter coated filet mignon to-go. He wasn't interested. Kelly tells me so many people would tell her, "You're teaching him that behavior is ok." Like that was a bad thing. She felt that advice basically translated to; "No wonder your dog is a brat, you need to show him you're the boss and that's not ok." She would think, "Wait, what, not ok for him to communicate with me?"

But, after reading *Decoding Your Dog*, Kelly had a lightbulb moment. It was a heartbreaking moment, but a critical one. Granted, encouraging Arlo to continue walking by using praise and treats wasn't necessarily a correction or negative reinforcement, but she realized she was teaching her pup that he couldn't trust her. Imagine a friend "bribing you into an uncomfortable situation after you've tried to tell them, repeatedly, that you're uncomfortable."

Again, that book and realizing the importance of giving Arlo choices changed everything. Kelly tells me, instead of "talking" I started "listening." When Arlo would balk while out on a walk, Kelly would tell him, "Ok Arlo, you're clearly uncomfortable. I 'hear' you and respect that." Kelly would do her best to make sure there was no tension on the leash and started saying to Arlo, "show me where you want to go." Not that I thought he understood the words, but by taking any and all tension out of the leash, I was attempting to communicate: "your call, buddy!"

Kelly continues, "Once Arlo learned that the second he put the brakes on, that I respected his declining comfort level and would give him a choice, that I would no longer encourage him to 'just stop being afraid,' (I mean, how ridiculous does that sound?), both his trust in me and his confidence grew, slowly, but surely. This took lots, and lots, and lots of repetition, consistency, and patience. But, goodness, was it worth it. He started wanting to go further and further on each walk. And really, he's a dream to walk if we can avoid roads and other pups."

And Richard wasn't exempt from the trust and confidence building either. Arlo had a sudden fright while on a hike with Richard. Richard was frustrated that he had driven out to the site and Arlo put the brakes on not even a minute into the hike. Kelly and Richard discussed how to apply the methods she used on walks when Arlo displayed that same behavior.

Kelly encouraged Richard to keep taking him for hikes. Even if they were driving 20 minutes to walk two minutes. Once Arlo knew that he could trust Richard to give him an option and that he will neither be "in trouble" nor "bribed" out of the choice, he started going farther and farther on each hike. Arlo began to understand that he had control. Once he understood this, he was able to walk further. And eventually, instead of bolting from some triggers he would stop and observe them. "Dogs thrive with choice."

## 11. Arlo

Kelly tells me that what has not helped them is unsolicited advice. Unless you have lived with a dog with behavior issues you cannot know what it is like. Kelly recommends to other owners of dogs like Arlo, "forget what you think you know, you will have to relearn everything. This is not a matter of they need more exercise."

I ask Kelly and Richard if there will be future dogs in their household? They tell me that is a hard question to answer. Kelly states that on one hand she doesn't want to waste what she has learned in life with Arlo, but on the other hand the thought of another special needs dog is daunting. Kelly advocates for "adopt don't shop" but absolutely understands and respects the reluctance there for people who have lived with a behaviorally challenged dog.

They have had great experiences adopting in the past, but an "Arlo dog" can definitely make you more apprehensive and they are not sure they have it in them to take on another dog as challenging; physically, mentally, emotionally, and financially. However, she would like to say that "I don't think you're guaranteed or immune to any behavior issues purchasing from a breeder either."

But a home without a dog? They are not sure that's a home they want to be in. They are confident that this experience of life with Arlo will be incredibly beneficial for any future pups whether it be with their own dogs, volunteering at the shelter, or even just being an advocate for dogs overall.

Kelly believes that most dog owners know they are taking on a massive responsibility, one that they're aware of and up for. But a pup like Arlo? He has exceeded all expectations of responsibility that you could potentially find yourself with. Some you didn't even think were possible until you have one. Having said that, Kelly can't imagine a home without a dog, but they will certainly need to proceed with extra caution and carefully consider that when the time comes.

Kelly goes on to say that "As difficult as Arlo has been, I always think about how glad and grateful I am that he ended up with us. Because I don't think there are many people who could or would be able to take on a pup like him. There have been plenty of tear-filled days that we question his quality of life and our own. There are many sacrifices we've made. I once read a quote saying: 'we've done everything versus we've done everything we could.' We feel we've done everything we could a hundred times over."

Kelly continues to say, "And if nothing else, we have gained a lot more compassion for those that have had to make an incredibly difficult decision. Resources are limited to all of us, and they aren't just limited to time and money. Because even if you have unlimited amounts of both, those aren't the only resources that start to run low, including your own personal wellness and quality of life."

In the meantime, Kelly and Richard continue to enjoy the best of Arlo. There is so much he does that they love. They love his doggy parkour when he gets the zoomies. They love when he decides to carefully remove their socks from their feet and carry them around, sometimes burying them and sometimes regifting them back to his owners. They love his sweetness. And I love having Arlo's picture on my fridge. Arlo brings with him an incredible amount of joy. His snuggles are the best.

# 12

# Becoming an Advocate

In my lifetime, I have had two dogs that were reactive to people. They either did not like anyone outside the immediate family or, even worse, would only tolerate a few specific people. Their stranger danger reaction to people entering the home or seen on walks or from the car was to growl, lunge and bark.

One of those dogs was my beautiful blue Great Dane. It was difficult to take her anywhere without someone asking to pet her. She was a striking dog and most people do not see Great Danes every day. I understood the attraction. When asked, "Can I pet your dog?" I would always have to answer no with an apologetic smile. To friends, I would joke that my dog already had three friends and has told me she doesn't think she needs more.

But in truth, it can be challenging, even difficult to live with a dog like this. Any owner of an "unfriendly" dog has experienced the frowns, the shaking heads, and scoffs from friends, family, and even strangers. Some of us have been turned down by groomers, declined to be seen by veterinarians, and asked to leave the day care. Sadly, some people just do not like our dogs, and that can be hard to hear. My dog may be living in a world where it is not wanted. That leaves me, as my dog's guardian, to be its advocate. And advocate we must!

When my friendly Golden Retriever was a puppy, I took him to puppy class. My puppy was behaviorally sound, and I had no concerns about any developing behavior issues. I knew a good-quality puppy class would help him learn some beginning skills and give him a chance to socialize with new experiences, dogs, and people.

I was a dog trainer so knew what to expect and had a clear idea of my objectives. I am sure I received stares when I arrived at class with my equipment bag over my shoulder. While other students arrived with their dogs and one bag of treats, I arrived with enough supplies to weather a three-day siege. I had three varieties of treats, a treat bag to attach to my belt, four toys, two teething chews, paper towels in

## I Know Your Dog Is a Good Dog

case there was a potty accident, and a rug for my dog to lie on. I was prepared.

It was a great class with an experienced teacher. My puppy and I had fun and I was proud of what he was learning. But there were some exercises that I chose to opt-out of. That is correct, we declined to participate in some activities. The first time I did this the assistant teacher asked, "Oh! Are you sure?" I noticed the side eye of the students on either side of me, but I didn't care. My priority was for my puppy to have a positive experience and there were some activities that for him would not be ideal.

One class exercise was to have all the humans sit in a circle and one at a time the owners would lead their dog around the circle to say hi to each person and receive pats and treats. When I stood up to take our turn, I felt my puppy's weight lean back against my legs, I felt his front feet suddenly glue to the floor. He was nervous. "No thanks! We'll pass this time," I cheerfully said. My puppy happily sat in front of me saying hi to each owner and puppy that came around the circle but being the center of attention and making his round, was too much for him that day. I knew it would not be a good experience and if forced may ruin his attitude towards coming to class. I watched other puppies make the rounds, most of them loved it, but a couple clearly did not.

One of the fun things about the puppy class was that the dogs were exposed to a lot of novel objects. Noisy toys and moving skateboards were on the floor during playtime. Agility equipment was placed around for the puppies to explore, ramps to climb, and tunnels to crawl into. There was a hoop just a few inches from the floor that the puppies could jump through.

During free play time, I approached the hoop with my puppy and held treats on the other side to tempt him through. He thought the better method was to go around the hoop to get the treats. Smart dog. I tried several times, and he had no interest in going through the large circle. An assistant in the class came over, picked up my puppy, and said, "here let's put him through a few times." I saw my puppy's eyes go wide and feet stretch out in protest. "No!" I said in a not-so-cheerful voice this time. I grabbed my puppy back. "But, if you…," the assistant started to say. "No, thank you," I said. I was not about to have someone force my puppy to do something that might frighten him. I had to speak up.

You may be thinking, but you are a professional. You know these things and can make an educated decision about what is right and

## 12. Becoming an Advocate

wrong. I also have a belief in following your gut and asking questions. Questions such as, what is the purpose of the exercise, what will it accomplish? Is there a risk of unwanted fallout from doing this? Is this absolutely necessary? If your gut is telling you this is not the right thing, don't be afraid to hit the pause button.

I have a dear friend and fellow dog trainer that often shares an experience she had when she was first exploring the world of dog training. At the time my friend had no formal knowledge of training. She loved animals and volunteered with a rescue group. She thought it would be interesting to learn more about how dogs learn and are trained. She thought a great starting point would be to visit and observe some dog training classes.

She was observing a class taught by an old-fashioned, coercive trainer. The class was held in a small room. There was a circle of chairs for the humans, and each student sat in a chair with their dog sitting on the floor next to them. As an observer, my friend was sitting behind the circle. She was near a young woman who had a beautiful pit bull. In chatting with the student before class she learned this handsome, meaty dog had been recently adopted and was this young woman's first dog.

The trainer had instructed the students to have their dogs sit and stay. As the trainer was walking in the middle of the room the pit bull stood up and walked over to him. My friend told me the dog's body language was soft and he did not jump on the trainer, he seemed to want to say hi. The dog was wearing a prong collar, the trainer walked over to the dog's owner, took the leash from her hand, and jerked the leash hard to give the dog a correction for breaking his sit.

The dog then walked around to stand behind his owner's chair. The next time the trainer came by my friend heard the dog give a small growl. The dog had learned. He learned that guy hurts me.

My friend came back to observe the second class, but the young woman was not there. After the second class, my friend did not return either. She was just learning about dog training, she was not yet an expert, but she knew she was not comfortable with this type of training. She listened to her gut.

My friend kept doing her research and found a local training club that used force free training. She knew this was the program for her and eventually became a force free dog trainer. She has helped hundreds of dogs since that time. She never knew what became of that young lady and her pit bull. We can only hope that the young lady also followed her gut feeling and found the right training for her dog.

One of the first steps in becoming your dog's advocate is to examine your own relationship with your dog. Living with a dog with behavior issues is so challenging. I have had times with my own dogs, when I may have had enough and lost my cool and shouted at my dog. Yep, it happens. There were times when I had to heal a relationship to get things back on track. There are a few techniques I suggest that will help strengthen your relationship with your dog and grow the role of advocate.

## *The Power of Choice*

Some of the saddest dogs I have seen are those who have lost all control over their lives. This is often seen in dogs that have lived their life on a chain. Or puppy mill dogs that live every single moment of their life in a small cage.

Learned helplessness is a psychological term that means an individual, after facing continuous negative and uncontrollable situations, stops trying to change their circumstances, even when they can. Interestingly, the term was coined by psychologists Martin Seligman and Steven Maier after conducting experiments in which they would deliver electric shocks to dogs. In the long-ago experiments, an electric shock was delivered to the dogs that were contained in pens. The dogs were given no way to escape the shock. Then later, after many repetitions, the dogs were given a route to escape the electric shock but did not seek escape. They had developed learned helplessness, a severe psychological condition.[1] How sad that today we still use shock to control our dogs.

We already control much of our dog's life. We control when, where and how much they eat. We control which room of the house they spend time in. We control when they go outside and how often they are allowed to relieve themselves. It is important to search for opportunities to provide our dogs a choice.

When I started incorporating choice as part of my behavior modification plans for dogs with behavior issues, I saw many positive changes. I would see dogs grow in confidence and react with less fear and anxiety. I cannot say why this happened; I think it would take someone with a lot more knowledge about animal behavior than I to explain. But I think part of it is that for any animal, learning that they have some control over their destiny and that they are not merely the recipient of the whims of humans, must make them more comfortable in their world.

## 12. Becoming an Advocate

Here are a few ways you can provide opportunities for your dog to make a choice:

- Keep all toys in a drawer or bin. When it is time to play, present several of the toys to the dog and let him choose which one to play with.
- Feed meals in multiple bowls, instead of putting dinner in just one bowl on the floor divide it into 3 bowls. Your dog gets to choose which portion to eat first.
- If your dog likes to sleep on a blanket or in a dog bed provide multiple blankets or beds, another way to provide choice.

There are many creative ways, every day, we can provide choices for our dogs.

## *Consent for Contact*

Another way of providing choice for our dog is the idea of asking for consent before interacting in ways that may be stressful or aversive. This is a fairly new idea in the world of animal behavior. It is a concept that is under study, especially by experts who work in zoos and sanctuaries. The idea of consent is based on the principle that the animal is an active participant in how and when it is touched, handled, and treated.

You will typically see consent discussed when providing medical, grooming, or other physical care for an animal. For dogs, especially those with behavior concerns, consent is a way to improve a dog's confidence, sense of self, and comfort, and is a show of respect for your dog.

I have used the concept of consent with brushing my very furry Golden Retriever. He loves to be brushed and groomed, except for his tail, which is mostly what needs to be brushed and groomed. Typically, when it is time to brush his tail, he will try to escape or he will turn and put his mouth on my hand to signal he is not comfortable. At that point continuing to brush becomes a power struggle. I usually lose.

I first learned about the idea of consent and allowing a dog to say wait or no, from a method developed by trainer Chirag Patel, called the Bucket Game. Patel has wonderful workshops and videos to teach the Bucket Game and I highly recommend his process.[2]

The technique I use for my dog is to put a smear of peanut butter on a rubber mat that has suction cups on the back. These mats can be found for purchase online. I adhere the tray to the floor or even a vertical surface. I've used the dishwasher or a tile wall.

While my dog is licking the peanut butter, I start to brush his tail. If he stops licking, I take that as a signal that I should stop brushing. When he starts licking the peanut butter, I resume brushing. By using this method my dog has learned that he has some control over what is happening to him, that he is not going to be forced, and that he gets peanut butter. He has become much more tolerant of having his tail brushed. In fact, I really don't have to use the tray with peanut butter any longer, I just keep a handful of treats handy and give those throughout the brushing.

If there are occasions when a dog must have care, for example, a dog with overly long nails that is afraid of having her feet touched, I recommend a visit to the vet for sedation for the procedure. This will allow you to continue to work on consent without breaking trust.

Another way we can use consent for our dogs is to think about how we allow interaction with other people. The Family Dog organization focuses on improving the lives of dogs and kids. The Family Dog teaches the Pat, Pet, Pause technique.[3] PAT, your leg or lap to call the dog to you, if the dog comes to you, PET the dog once or twice, then PAUSE. If the dog wants to continue the interaction, they will let you know. Most dogs will lean on you or put their muzzle under your arm or paw at you. If they do not signal that they would like to continue the interaction, no further petting is allowed. This is a great way to allow your dog to offer consent. This is also an awesome way to keep kids safe from dogs that may show their distaste for being touched in more forward ways.

Providing the opportunity for choice or consent may sound like a small thing, you may even think it is a silly thing in a conversation about animals. But offering consent can provide a healing process to a dog that is hurting. "The power to control one's own outcomes is essential to behavioral health. When a lack of control becomes a lifestyle, it may result in aberrant behaviors"[4]

## *Advocating for Your Dog in Your Home*

Just say no. If your dog is uncomfortable with visitors in your home it is your job to help your dog, to set her up for success, and to protect her. It does not mean you cannot have visitors, but you must have a plan. The best plan is to just give your dog their own space, so they do not

## 12. Becoming an Advocate

have to deal with the visitors. This can be in a room, behind a door, or behind a gate. But what do you do with the people who insist on seeing your dog? "Dogs love me!" "Oh, I can always make friends with a dog." "I'm not afraid of dogs." "But I want to see them." Just say no.

You can try to explain your dog is not comfortable around people. If that doesn't work, tell them your dog doesn't feel well today. If that doesn't work, tell them your dog has ringworm, which is contagious to people. Your dog's welfare is more important than your guest's desire to interact with your dog.

With the right training plan, a dog may learn to tolerate and even enjoy visitors. My dog Thelma was not crazy about company. She greeted visitors at the door with growls and barks. Even though I was pretty sure Thelma would choose to flee over biting, each guest that came into my home was given the same cheerful instructions. Do not reach for her, do not make eye contact, and do not talk to her. Thelma had the choice to stay around visitors or go away. She always chose to stay but would remain at the periphery. She was scared but also curious. She was interested in visitors.

I worked hard with a behavior modification plan to help Thelma with her fear. Over the years Thelma grew much calmer with visitors entering the home. She would gradually move closer, and she would remain calm if she was ignored. Towards the end of her life, Thelma even enjoyed sitting next to me on the couch and listening to and watching our guests. She was social but afraid. I continued with my special Thelma instructions. I knew my dog and knew she wanted to be part of the action but wanted to be an observer only. I never allowed visitors to move close to her or try to pet her.

Another of my dogs with stranger danger, my Great Dane, Bayou, however, had no interest in meeting new people. Bayou did have friends outside of the family, she loved the staff that worked at her day care, and she enjoyed my visitors that were dog-savvy females, as long as they did not wear hats or carry purses. She was a funny dog. But if anyone outside of her circle of friends visited, she preferred to be alone in her room away from visitors.

I taught Bayou that when there was action at the door this was her cue to retreat. I would say, "time for your room" and Bayou would trot down the hall. She knew that in her room awaited her bed, treats, and her favorite toys. She would happily hang out away from the scary visitors. And for those that asked, "Can't she come out, I would love to see her." My answer was, "nope."

# I Know Your Dog Is a Good Dog

## *Advocating for Your Dog Away from Home*

I love to walk and hike with my dogs at parks. But... People. I was walking my dog, Thelma when we encountered one of her worst nightmares. We came over the crest of a hill to find a children's birthday party. Several children came running to pet the pretty dog. I stepped in front of Thelma, held out my hand, palm forward, fingers pointed up, and said, Stop! I have learned that people don't really listen to what we say but they do respond to that body language, the universal sign for stop! The kids stopped in their tracks and Thelma and I did a U-turn and went on our way. Stopping an interaction before it starts is always the best, first step.

I was walking my overly friendly Golden Retriever, Rocket, and my people-shy, reactive Great Dane, Bayou, at our local park. As we were returning to the parking lot. I could see we would have to pass several people to get to my car. I shortened both dogs' leashes to keep them close to my side. As we got closer, one of the adults, with child in tow, began walking towards me while saying, "Oooh, is that a Great Dane, can we pet her?" "No, sorry," I said, "she is not friendly. But you can pet this one," as I unwound my Golden's 30-foot leash. My friendly dog was happy to get some attention and my shy Great Dane was spared. It can be embarrassing to admit to people that our dog is not "friendly." But I didn't care. I did not know those people and was likely never going to see them again. One look at my dog's grateful eyes was all I needed.

I often train dogs in public places. It is a common part of the behavior modification plan. For most people being able to take their dog into public is an important goal. So many times, we have been in the process of having a wonderful training session when here comes the off-leash dog, followed by the owner shouting, "don't worry, she's friendly."

It is my job as the trainer to take control of this situation. I will walk towards the owner, distract their dog to follow me, and explain that we are in the middle of a training session and to please leash their dog. I have been on the receiving end of dirty looks and under-the-breath comments. I have often had to point out to these people that the sign right at the entrance does say that all dogs need to be on a leash. I do my best to be polite and professional, but I must do this, not only to keep my client dog safe but to also model this behavior for owners. It is difficult to act in ways we are taught are not polite. It can be hard for more introverted people to speak up. But it is an important way to advocate for our dogs. I promise it is something that becomes easier with practice.

## 12. Becoming an Advocate

## *Advocating for Your Dog at the Veterinary Office*

All dogs must attend veterinary visits at some point in their life. It is unavoidable. I strongly recommend finding the closest Fear Free™ Certified veterinarian in your area or at least a veterinarian that is willing to accommodate your dog and is not afraid of your dog. But regardless of which veterinarian you use, visits to the clinic are a time to advocate for your dog. Here are some ways to do that.

Brief the clinic staff about your dog's concerns. Give them a chance to be prepared. Let them know what makes your dog more comfortable. Maybe it is a slow approach from staff or staff wearing street clothes instead of a lab coat or scrubs. Perhaps your dog needs plenty of time to sniff around the door before they enter. Confirm that you will be able to remain with your dog during the exam.

Ask for an appointment that is at a time of day that is the quietest, with the fewest patients. When you make the appointment let the clinic know you will be waiting in the car until they are ready for you. Ask them to call you when it is time to come to the exam room.

If you attend appointments at a large clinic, ask if you can use an alternate door. Most clinics have a back door. Your dog may be more comfortable avoiding the lobby altogether. If the scale is in the lobby and your dog must be weighed there, ask them to clear the lobby or have people step away. Bring your dog's stuff! Bring the treats, bring the toys, and bring the rug. Don't worry about getting odd looks; this is your dog!

Ask the veterinarian what the priorities are for the visit. Is it immunizations, a blood draw, or listening to the heart? Start with those because you may need to step in and say that is all my dog can do today. I have been so lucky to have understanding vets caring for my behaviorally challenged dogs. They regularly check in with me during the visit. They ask how I think my dog is doing and if they can continue the exam. There have been times when I've had to say that is all we are doing today; we will come back another day.

Ask for medication for your dog. If my dog needs to have a thorough exam, if they need nails trimmed, if they need something more invasive like anal glands expressed, I ask that my dog be medicated. Sometimes the medication may be something I give my dog at home before visits. At times the medication is given in the clinic. The veterinarian will help make that decision. Some medications can help your dog feel calmer and some medications may completely sedate your dog for more invasive procedures. If medication is not offered, then advocate for your dog and ask. A good rule of thumb; is if you have a dog that must wear a muzzle at the vet's office your dog should receive medication for the visit.

If you have a veterinarian that will not answer your questions or accommodate your dog's needs, then find a new one. I have had many, many people hesitate to do this because they are afraid of offending their veterinarian or hurting their feelings. It doesn't matter. Your dog's welfare comes first. And I will let you in on a little secret, it is a common thing in medicine, and they will likely not care that much. Some of them may be happy to see you go!

Clinic staff matters too. You may have the most wonderful doctor in the world but if the staff does not work with you or worse, tries to undermine your efforts you need to find a new provider and you need to let the veterinarian know why you are leaving the practice. First and foremost, I am my dog's advocate and need to speak up if she is in a situation that is not the best for her.

## *Muzzles*

When you see a dog wearing a muzzle, what kind of emotion does that create in you? Muzzles have a very negative connotation in our society. But I love muzzles! In fact, I think every single dog should have their own muzzle. Teaching your dog to wear a muzzle is another way you can advocate for your dog.

That's right. When I was a child my beloved Dalmatian Snoopy got hit by a car. He ran into the house and hid under the kitchen table. As a 10-year-old child, my instinct was to crawl under the table with him, to comfort him. "Don't!," my mom said, "he might bite you." She wasn't wrong. Any dog can bite; they have the equipment for it and sometimes it is the only way they can express themselves.

My gentle, sweet, Golden Retriever ate a cat toy when he was young and ended up having major surgery. I would not expect him to bite me in a million years but when I was changing his surgical dressing over the tender incision, I made sure to stay clear of the business end of my dog. Even the most gentle of dogs may bite given the right circumstances.

Dogs who are nervous or growly at the veterinary clinic should wear a muzzle for all visits. My veterinarian tells me that my growly dog wearing a muzzle is what keeps me on her Christmas card list! Here is why. I've been afraid of some dogs I work with. I have been afraid they

## 12. Becoming an Advocate

may bite me. It is no fun. I acknowledge that fear and I have practices in place to stay safe while providing good care for my clients. It doesn't matter how experienced you are or how many hundreds of dogs you have worked with, a large, growling, dog with big teeth makes you nervous. It is a perfectly normal, really good survival skill and our fear of growling animals was a great evolutionary tool! It is there for a purpose.

If I take my scared dog to the vet or groomer, my vet or groomer is going to be nervous. My dog will feel that nervousness and become more scared. But, if I take my scared dog to the vet and my dog is wearing their own comfortable muzzle, the vet is going to be more relaxed, which will help my dog (and me) feel calmer, which will make my vet calmer. A positive feedback loop! Muzzles are a good thing.

Not all muzzles are equal. There are two main types, sleeve and basket. There are also a variety of custom-made muzzles for dogs with hard-to-fit heads, such as bulldogs. Sleeve muzzles are narrow tubes, usually made of nylon, that fit over the closed mouth of the dog and make it impossible for the dog to open their mouth beyond the slightest degree. Most clinics and groomers keep them on hand. A basket muzzle, on the other hand, allows the dog to open their mouth somewhat. A dog with a basket muzzle can pant, can take a treat, and drink out of a water bottle.

I strongly prefer basket muzzles over sleeve muzzles. I think sleeve muzzles can make dogs more nervous. It is as if they know their method of defending themselves, biting, has been taken away. Imagine being in a fistfight and someone pins your arms behind your back. Probably not a good feeling.

But basket muzzles must be fitted to the correct size and worn correctly to remain secure. Therefore, it is not expedient for clinics to keep them on hand, which is why it is important for your dog to have their own muzzle.

My dogs have their own basket muzzles because this is a piece of their own familiar equipment, no different than a collar, harness, or leash. I put my dog's muzzle on them in the car before we enter the clinic. Every dog should have and be comfortable wearing their own muzzle.

It is not unusual for a dog with behavior issues to be afraid of new equipment. Neophobia, the fear of new or novel things is common. Many dogs will balk at wearing a muzzle. To help a dog learn to wear a muzzle comfortably, I use the process of conditioning.

The first dog of my own that I taught to wear a muzzle was my dog

# I Know Your Dog Is a Good Dog

Thelma. Thelma was a large Shepherd mix, a black and tan dog with a fluffy tail that curled over her back. Thelma was very shy and worried about people. She was a dog I thought might bite if she felt trapped. My main goal in teaching Thelma to wear a muzzle was so that she could safely receive the veterinary care she needed throughout her life.

I started the whole process by changing what I called her muzzle; it became her fancy hat. In my mind, that took away any negative connotations associated with saying the word muzzle, out of my voice. It is hard to say, "Thelma let's put on your fancy hat" without a smile in your voice. I wanted to communicate to my dog that this was not a punishment or a negative thing that was happening.

The next step was to begin exposing Thelma to the muzzle. Since I know that predictability is an important part of the conditioning process, I first began by holding the muzzle behind my back. Then, I would bring the muzzle in front of me and as soon as Thelma looked at the muzzle, I would mark that look by saying, "yes" in a happy voice, and then quickly give her a treat. Then I would hide the muzzle behind my back again. I repeated this process of showing her the muzzle about 5 to 7 times in a row, then we would stop. I did not want her to get bored with the game. We played this muzzle game once or twice a day at least 5 days a week.

Once I saw Thelma showing an understanding of the muzzle game, I began to ask a little more of her. Where before, I would hand her the treat as soon as she looked at the muzzle, now I would continue to hold the muzzle in front of me after she looked. When Thelma realized she was not immediately getting the treat, she would try something to let me know I owed her. One of those things was to touch the muzzle with her nose. As soon as she did that, I would say "YES!" and hand over the treat.

Now the game became, touch the muzzle with your nose and get a treat. This increased her comfort level of physical contact between her nose and the muzzle. This allowed me to turn the muzzle into a bowl. I would hold the muzzle in my hand and place treats or a little smear of peanut butter on the inside. Thelma was willing to place her whole snout into the muzzle. When she did this I would still say, "yes" and give her a treat. Double treats!

Next was the process to begin moving the straps around gently while she was eating food from the muzzle. I stayed at this step for a long time because the movement and the sound of the metal buckle were scary. After a few weeks, I would begin to hold the straps in place

## 12. Becoming an Advocate

over her head for a few seconds. Seconds grew into a couple of minutes at a time. It took about three months to reach the point where I could have Thelma place her nose into the muzzle and allow me to buckle it and she would get many, many treats through this process.

I was not in a hurry to complete this lesson. Thelma lived with me for another six years after her muzzle training. Taking three months to make her comfortable and not scare her by rushing the process was a blip in her life. When we pulled into the doctor's parking lot, I would say, "Let's put on your fancy hat"! We remained on our veterinarian's Christmas card list.

# 13

# Walt

"Sometimes it feels like we are living with a third roommate, it can be hard to feel close to him; he is a companion, but not always a great companion." This is how Matt and Katie describe life with Walt, their 75-pound, black and tan hound mix with long floppy ears. At the same time, they declare the many things they love about Walt. Katie tells me, "He knows when I am sad or grieving and in his own way he tries to help." "It is just heartwarming to see him get so excited about little things, like car rides. He loves a car ride." Matt adds, "He is also smart, maybe too smart. He knows how to manipulate you in the cutest way to get what he wants. He may not be the best roommate, but he is here, and he is someone to come home to and spend time with." But there were also the bites.

Matt and Katie were Walt's third home. He had been adopted from a rescue as a young puppy and in a short amount of time returned to the rescue. Walt was adopted a second time and that person, after a year or two, decided they no longer wanted him. But instead of returning Walt to the original rescue, this time Walt was taken to an open-intake shelter with a history of high euthanasia rates.

That shelter did take the time to scan Walt's microchip, which was still attached to the original rescue. His owner had never taken the time to register him as their pet. The original rescue scooped him back up and for the third time, Walt, now about two and a half years old, was once again placed up for adoption. That third adoption is when he came to live with Matt and Katie.

Matt and Katie do not know why he was returned. The rescue either did not have that information or did not share it. It never occurred to Matt and Katie that they should ask for more details. The thought that a rescue would adopt out a dog who was not safe was not in their mind.

Walt has always been a bit of a handful; he is a big dog, and upon adoption, did not have the best manners. When out on a walk, he would bark and pull at any passing dog. He was determined to chase cats and

## 13. Walt

other critters. If people passed by his home, he would vigorously bark and jump at the windows.

But Walt is also silly and fun-loving. He loves taking a car ride to visit Matt's parents, two of his favorite people. Walt gallops around his house and takes up most of the couch when he naps. The first few years of life with Walt had been busy but relatively peaceful.

His new owners did notice that Walt seemed to be a generally nervous dog. They recognized that his behavior towards other dogs and people appeared to be more a function of his anxiousness than wanting to hurt anyone. They also recognized that Walt had some issues around food. He would steal food from the counter or find bits and pieces of things when out on a walk. When he did have food, he made it clear that it was his to keep. He would stiffen and growl if anyone came close to take his prize away from him but never snapped or tried to bite.

Then one day, while out on a walk with Katie, Walt picked up a dead squirrel. Quite the trophy for a hound dog. Katie, rightfully worried about disease, tried to take the dead thing away from Walt. Walt snapped at her and came very close to biting her. That surprised Matt and Katie; he had never come that close to making contact.

The next event came during a time when Walt was lying on Matt and Katie's bed. He was not feeling well, and Katie was sitting with him to monitor him and to provide comfort. Walt seemed to be in pain and Katie became worried. She leaned close to listen to his heart and his breathing. Suddenly Walt jumped and bit Katie on the forehead. Immediately after he bit, he retreated and acted chagrined. The bite from this large dog was bad enough to require medical attention and stitches.

That was the first bite, Walt has bitten both Katie and Matt twice in the five years they have had him. The events they described to me, when we first met, seemed defined and circumstantial. Walt has bitten or attempted to bite when being hovered over, being handled for medical treatment, or grooming, and once when Matt reached into his crate. He did not appear to be a dog that was aggressive or unpredictable. On the occasions when he did bite, he seemed to be in defensive mode or resource guarding.

I have performed many evaluations of dogs that displayed clear distance-increasing body language. I respected what these dogs were saying. I always act carefully and appropriately. I am conscious of my own body language and never push boundaries. For some dogs I meet, I require the dog to be on a leash or behind a barrier to keep myself, the dog, and everyone involved safe. This was not the case with Walt.

## I Know Your Dog Is a Good Dog

When I met Walt, I had no fear of being bitten. He was not a dog who showed threatening behavior toward me. In fact, Walt soon figured out I was a source of treats and stuck to my side. I could see Walt was smart. He loved to play and figured out the puzzles and games I brought quickly. Still, I was cautious around Walt, I kept in mind his history of resource guarding and possible touch sensitivity. I did not challenge him for possessions and I remained alert to where he was and what toys or treats may be close by. Because when Walt did bite, the bites were significant, almost always requiring medical treatment.

As we combed through his history, I could see that typically, incidents with Walt would happen around the 4th of July. This makes sense because Walt is afraid of loud noises like fireworks and thunder. His family notices there is always an uptick in his anxiety around this summer holiday. He tends to try to hide and look for escape routes when he hears these loud noises. He is hypervigilant. Matt and Katie notice he drools and shakes if there are continuous loud noises. Matt and Katie usually try to leave town around the 4th of July and go to their place in the country where it is quieter. But they cannot stay there forever and back at home the celebration may go on for days or weeks.

During those times, when Walt's anxiety increases, and he exhibits his reactive behavior more quickly, when he is frightened, and hard to calm, when he cannot be touched or comforted, is when his owners worry about the quality of Walt's life. Is it fair for him to live in misery? Is it fair for him to be put into situations where he so strongly feels the need to protect himself from everything around him? This is the time they will debate with themselves if they have let this go on long enough.

Once noisy holidays are over, months can go by without incident. During those times Matt and Katie begin to question why they would think of taking more drastic steps, as Walt seems perfectly happy. They tell me it is like there is a hidden personality in Walt, waiting to pop out. A canine Jekyll and Hyde. In fact, when they adopted Walt, his name had been Roscoe. During Walt's somewhat unpredictable periods they will tell each other, "Roscoe is here."

Matt and Katie think of life divided into periods of life before Walt, life before Walt bit them, and now life after Walt has bitten. They have learned to live with this unpredictable roommate. They have worked hard with veterinarians and trainers and the focus of life with Walt is preventing another bite. Therefore, life with Walt is closely managed. This management includes plans for many different situations.

Walt has a plan for visitors. The overall plan is to not have visitors,

## 13. Walt

so they rarely entertain. When they do, Walt goes to stay with Matt's parents, who love him. For safety, Walt is never around children. If adult visitors do happen to be in the house with Walt home, they are given instructions on how to interact with Walt.

There is a plan for the possibility that Walt may decide to guard objects or spaces. Matt and Katie manage this by planning ahead. If Walt has something he is likely to eat, if it is not something harmful to him, they let him eat it. The pork chops on the kitchen counter are not more important than Walt's safety. A case of worms from a dead animal can be easily treated with medication. It is not worth the risk of trying to remove that object from Walt's possession.

Walt has been known to guard his sleeping spaces. Now that he is an older guy, he will more frequently take himself off to nap on Matt and Katie's bed. If this extends into bedtime, then instead of physically moving Walt, Matt and Katie keep a container of kibble stored in the nightstand drawer. The kibble can be tossed onto the floor to lure Walt off the bed and into his crate.

There is also a plan in place to manage Walt's fear of storms. Medication is part of the plan for Walt to manage his noise phobia and extra medication is prescribed to be used to reduce anxiety during thunderstorms. However, the medication must be timed to be given right before the storm arrives. This can be hard to do as not all storms are predictable, so at times the storm arrives without the benefit of medication being onboard.

Walt has established his storm "safe place" in the guest room. During these times, Katie, unable to ignore his trembling and fear, will sleep there with him. She explains her process of building a wall of pillows between herself and Walt to prevent touching him accidentally. I picture Walt and Katie starring in their own canine version of an old Lucille Ball and Clark Gable comedy.

There is also a plan in place for handling Walt to provide necessary physical care. Walt has learned to comfortably wear a basket muzzle. He can wear this for trips to the vet or the groomer when needed. This is also used after they visit the country. Everyone, including Walt, needs to be checked for ticks on those summer days. Matt and Katie are careful to use a tick preventive, but we all know a tick will occasionally be found hitching a ride. The process for tick removal is to have Walt wear his muzzle, while one person feeds him and the other removes the tick.

But even with the best of plans, things can go wrong. Trainers are fond of saying, "management is great until management fails." That is almost always due to the unknown quantity, people. Even the best-laid plan can be undone by other people.

Such as the bane of any reactive dog owner, the off-leash dog. Like so many other owners, Matt and Katie try to give instructions to those who interact with Walt. "Please leash your dog, please give us distance, please don't let your cat wander into our yard, please don't try to hug Walt." They can become tired of being the dog police. Other owners may not worry about their own dogs, but Matt and Katie, and Walt are the ones who would have to deal with the fallout if anyone got hurt.

Dealing with fallout comes up again when we discuss the relatives, friends, and co-workers that tell them Walt should be euthanized. They know this advice usually comes from a place of love and that their friends want them to be safe. But Matt points out that it is he and Katie who would have to make that phone call telling the vet that it is time. They are the ones that would have to hold Walt while he died. It is Katie and Matt that would come home to an empty house. It is just not that easy.

This has led to some heated discussions with friends and relatives. As a result, they share very little about Walt with others. I hear this from almost every one of my client families. Not talking about what is a major relationship in life frequently leads to feelings of isolation. It also saddens them that other people never get to learn about Walt's good qualities. Most of the time he is a sweet, loving, funny dog.

I ask Katie and Matt what they think the future holds? They are not sure. Life with Walt can be challenging, and they must remain on their toes. They realize they are always monitoring Walt, at all times, they always know where he is and what he is doing. Life with Walt is not carefree, it can be exhausting. Matt and Katie admit that they sometimes feel stuck with Walt. I assure them that I hear this comment from almost every person living with a dog that has serious behavior challenges.

Matt and Katie are not sure they will get another dog after Walt. If they do, they will want to know more about the dog and the dog's history. Sadly, they have learned that not every dog should be in a home. A decision that can be unpopular and not always respected by some rescues. It is frustrating that they were not told more about Walt before they adopted him. They will still sometimes wonder if they are the right home for Walt, but what would the right home be? For now, Walt has a safe space to live out his life.

Walt is 8 years old now and Matt and Katie know that the time will come when they must make the decision to say goodbye. In fact, over

## 13. Walt

the past couple of years, we have touched on that heart-wrenching conversation from time to time, wondering if the risk was too great and if it the time had come.

I think only people who live with dogs like Walt understand how the heart can be pulled in different directions almost every day. The dog that you love so much may not be safe to live with. The heart that desires to protect and defend your dog competes with the brain telling you your dog may harm you or someone else. As with all my clients, Matt and Katie know I am here to support their decision whatever that may be because I know they will make the best decision for Walt.

Why have they decided to keep living with Walt? This dog that has sent both for medical care. Because they love him. Because he is family.

There is a postscript to Walt's story. Many months after last meeting with Matt and Katie I learned that Walt had died. Walt lived a good long life, but his behavior did contribute to the end-of-life decisions for Walt. A topic often overlooked by those who work with animals is the impact that behavior can have on those decisions. The behavior may not be the sole reason for a dog being euthanized but it can certainly impact the decision to treat other physical illnesses. Dogs with behavior problems may be more likely to have a shortened life even if the primary reason for a euthanasia is a medical diagnosis.

# 14

# Help for the Human

I want owners to advocate for their dogs and I want to advocate for you. Living with a dog who has behavior problems can be hard. Families living with these special dogs face challenges that other owners do not. Sometimes, these challenges can feel relentless. Whether a dog suffers from anxiety, reactivity, fear, panic, or some other diagnosis, these are chronic conditions. It may get better, then worse, then better again. But the challenges will never completely go away. The humans living with these dogs need support.

Living with a dog with behavior issues can be physically exhausting. Many dogs with behavior problems have poor sleep patterns. They may not sleep or not sleep well at night. Many of them pace, they may have long periods of whining, and they may pant continually. And if you ever had a large dog on your bed that is panting you will know your sleep will be disturbed. Sleep disturbance in the dog can lead to sleep disturbance in humans. Poor sleep can impact emotional regulation and physical health.

Living with a dog with behavior issues is mentally and emotionally exhausting. Schedules must be planned, often to minutiae. If a dog is on a complicated medication schedule, then daily activities must be arranged around that drug regimen. If the dog's meal schedule impacts the medication, then mealtimes must be planned too. No more "I'll feed the dog when I get home."

Exercising a dog can become a challenge. Owners must consider when and where their dogs will be walked. Walks may suddenly get cut short if the dog becomes upset and needs to retreat home. No more, "I'll squeeze a walk in sometime today." When out with a reactive dog, the owner must be ever vigilant and aware of their surroundings. This can be exhausting.

There are practical worries that add more pressure. Many owners worry about what they will do if there is an emergency, and they are called away from home. Many dogs with behavior issues cannot be

## 14. Help for the Human

boarded or cannot be around people other than the owner or family members.

The larger consideration is the self-judging and doubt that owners live with. Owners that constantly ask themselves, "Am I doing the right thing? Should I try a different training method? Should I have put my dog on drugs? Should I get rid of my dog? What if my dog hurts someone?"

People living with dogs with behavior concerns need help, but they need the right kind of help. One hundred percent of the clients I work with have received well-meaning but unwanted advice on what to do with their dog. It is rarely helpful and often conflicting. A family will be told by one person that their dog is fine, and they are overreacting while being told by someone else their dog is dangerous and should be euthanized.

It is important that while families are getting help for their dog, they also seek help for themselves. Whether you are living with a dog who has behavior issues or grieving the dog you lost, do not hesitate to seek help. It is not unreasonable; it is totally understandable. Seek out a therapist or a support group. Many large shelters and university veterinary programs sponsor support groups for pet loss. There are groups that are in-person or online.

Lastly, create a way to defend yourself against unwanted opinions. For my clients, who are working with professionals and have a safety plan in place, I suggest the following. When confronted with judgment or input simply reply, "We are working with our veterinarian and trainer to decide the best plan for our dog and our family." That's it; you do not need to explain further.

## 15

# When You Can No Longer Live with Your Dog

Many families living with a dog who has behavior problems will arrive at the point when they wonder if they should place their dog in a new home. Often when we think of sending our dog to live elsewhere, we think of the separation difficulties we would have as humans. The sense of loss and grief, and guilt. Sometimes, we assume our dog will have the same emotional experience.

Dogs certainly do have emotions and can suffer loss as well. But the millions of dogs that are adopted from shelters every year testify to the ability of dogs to adapt to a new, happy home. In her book *The Other End of the Leash*, Patricia McConnell discusses the topic of rehoming dogs at length. Dr. McConnell, a well-respected animal behaviorist, states, "Rehoming your dog into a situation where he will be safe and happy is not a betrayal."[1]

I have adopted adult dogs myself and can unequivocally support my wholehearted love for those dogs and their love and attachment to me. It is okay to rehome a dog. And there are many factors that can create the need to rehome a dog. But there are several things to consider when making that decision for a dog.

## *Cost of Care*

Living with a dog that has behavior issues is expensive. I tell owners that if their dog were diagnosed with cancer and they decide to treat with a specialist, to undergo chemotherapy or surgery, and perhaps rehabilitation, they would not be surprised to be told that treatment will cost thousands of dollars. When one of my dogs started limping and I feared a ligament tear in the knee, I started budgeting the thousands of dollars I knew it would take for surgery. We need to

## 15. When You Can No Longer Live with Your Dog

look at a behavioral diagnosis in the same manner. A behavior diagnosis is a chronic condition that can require multiple providers and multiple treatments.

Cost of care can vary greatly in different parts of the world. In the Midwest United States, in 2022, the average prices for common treatments and supplies look like this:

- Veterinary exam to rule out underlying health issues. This can include laboratory tests and x-rays, $200–$400
- Trial medication from a general practice veterinarian, $30–$100 per month
- Evaluation by a certified trainer or behavior consultant, $150–$300
- Harness, $30–$35
- 6-foot leash, $10–$20
- Long line leash, $15–$20
- Treats, $50–10 per month
- Chew toys/treats, $15–$35
- Mental enrichment items such as food dispensing toys, $40–60
- Spray Shield Bite Deterrent, $15
- Training sessions with a trainer, $350–$600 for six sessions
- Evaluation with a Veterinary Behavior Specialist, $500–$600
- Follow Up appointment with Veterinary Behavior Specialist every three months, $150–$200
- Dog sitter or Day care, $30/day

Now imagine you are a college student and just adopted a dog that has started lunging and growling at other dogs or people. Or perhaps you are a single parent supporting a family. The cost of care is a real factor that must be considered. You should not be ashamed to say that you cannot afford this. The onus our society places on people who cannot keep their dogs because of cost is wholly unfair.

## *Time and Energy*

Do you have the time and energy to meet your dog's emotional and physical needs? For example, a dog with separation anxiety needs to have almost constant human company while working through a behavior modification plan. If an owner cannot be home much of the time, due to other commitments, that dog is likely to be happier in a home where a family member is almost always present. In that case, re-homing may be a wonderful solution, if the new owner knows and understands the needs of the dog.

Is your dog a working line dog showing frustration and destruction because it is not getting enough mental and physical exercise? If you really cannot meet the dog's needs, your dog may be happier in a new home.

## Safety from Your Dog

Is your dog a safety risk? That is a hard question to answer because we may all define that question differently. What does it mean to be safe from a dog? Typically, we define that as physical safety. Has your dog ever bitten you? If they have, how severe was the bite? Did it break the skin? Was there more than one bite? Did you need medical treatment? Those are some of the factors that we look at when considering a bite history. All dogs can bite; they have teeth! And most dogs, given a certain set of circumstances, will bite. But not all bites are the same.

I once had a client whose dog had bitten her more than once. Those bites had very much damaged her trust in her dog. She felt those bites were unpredictable. After a bite incident, there would be a period of peace. But she was never quite sure if her dog would bite her again. It was a burdensome cycle, and she was constantly nervous around her dog. She loved her dog, but it was difficult to ever feel safe in her own home. Should a dog with a bite history be rehomed? That can be a difficult decision.

Noted animal behaviorist, James O'Heare discusses this topic in his book, *Aggressive Behavior in Dogs: A Comprehensive Technical Manual for Professionals*. "If there is someone who is prepared to take on the problem and is in a better position to deal with it, rehoming is sometimes a viable option. This measure is more acceptable when owners are unable or unwilling to change the behavior and the potential new home allows for avoiding the provocative stimuli. For example, if the dog aggresses toward other dogs or children and the new home does not have these evoking stimuli, rehoming could be a good option. The owner must be very clear with the new owner about what the problems are and have them sign a waiver accepting all responsibility."[2]

This is not a decision to be made lightly and is a decision that has moral, ethical, and legal ramifications. But the decision to rehome a dog can be fraught with guilt, shame, and sadness. It is difficult and the loss

### 15. When You Can No Longer Live with Your Dog

of that dog needs to be grieved. Often it is the right thing to rehome a dog. And sometimes it is not.

A dog does not just live in a home, a dog lives in a neighborhood, in a community. Is your dog a danger to the community? If so, they should not be rehomed. It may be difficult to judge the level of risk. Consider this. What if you rehome a dog that is aggressive towards children to a home with only adults? Are there children in the new owners' lives? Do children visit? Do children live next door? Even if the new owner signs a waiver, if the dog injures a child do you bear any moral responsibility? These are very hard questions to answer.

Many municipalities have stated definitions for dangerous dogs. Where I live the official ordinance reads: "A dangerous animal is a dog or cat or other animal that, without provocation, has attacked a person or other animal and caused serious injury or death; or a dog, cat, or other animal for which three or more citations for violation of subsection 611.210.e.f. or g. has been issued within any twelve month period."[3]

Any family considering rehoming a dog with a bite history should have the dog evaluated by a Certified Applied Animal Behaviorist or a Veterinary Behavior Specialist. The question of rehoming a dog with a bite history should not be taken lightly and experts should be involved in that decision.

## Safety for Your Dog

Is your dog safe from you? That may sound like a funny question, but it should be considered. Is there anyone in your life, or in your family who might lose patience with your dog? Has your dog "almost" bitten anyone in the home? If he does bite, is there anyone that is likely to injure the dog as a reaction? Are there family members that will insist the dog is crated all of the time or banished to live outside? (This is cruel and no way for a dog to live.)

I recently saw a "lost dog" post on social media that was not the average case of a dog escaping a yard. In this case, one family member had been out of town for several weeks due to the demands of their job. While they were gone, another family member had taken the family dog to a shelter. The family member who had been out of town returned to find the dog gone and was desperately seeking its whereabouts. I spent years volunteering at a large open-intake animal shelter and can say this is not that uncommon. This is a scenario for a dog that may have been better off being rehomed. I should say, it is also a red flag for domestic abuse within a family. As a dog owner, you have the responsibility to keep your dog safe and the best way to keep them safe may be in another home.

I have been in many, many homes where owners or family members disagree on what should be done with a dog. It is a common situation for one partner to be invested in a behavior modification plan and one not. I have been told more than once "he/she said this is the last resort and then the dog goes to the shelter." It is very difficult for a dog living with adults who disagree on the plan to improve. I have seen these disagreements undermine any efforts and lead to the eventual failure of the plan. In fact, I do not accept clients unless every adult in the home agrees on treatment and understands the expectations.

A behavior modification plan is challenging, can be expensive, and takes time and a great deal of effort. Even if one partner is dedicated to the plan, not having the support of the other partner will almost always derail the plan. It is hard, but you may have to admit that there is a better home for your dog. If your dog has a great possibility of improvement with a behavior modification plan but your circumstances prevent carrying out the plan, re-homing may be a good option.

## *Only Dogs*

"We got a new puppy!" Everyone in the family is so excited, except the resident dog. No one asked her if she wanted a new canine friend. A common call that I and my colleagues receive is the situation where a new dog was added to a home with a resident dog and now the dogs are not getting along. In the best-case scenario, the dogs are grumbly at each other, but with time will get to know each other and peace will prevail.

The worst-case scenario is that the dogs are fighting, and one may be injured or killed. A training colleague describes these situations as arranged marriages. Someone else went out and picked a mate for the resident dog without asking if or what kind of mate was wanted.

I probably know more multiple-dog-families than single-dog families. There are many reasons for this. We love dogs! The more the merrier. I have lived with as many as four dogs at a time and they all got along splendidly. Having a dog friend can provide companionship, a playmate, and company for a dog when the humans are gone.

## 15. When You Can No Longer Live with Your Dog

There are a lot of dogs that need homes and people want to help. Out of the goodness of our hearts, we want to give a dog a home, so why not add one more. Most good shelters and rescue groups question potential owners about current animals as part of the adoption process. But sadly, some do not. Compounding the trend of multiple dogs is the belief that dogs are pack animals and living together in a group is "normal." This is not true. It is a mistake to assume any individual dog will like other dogs and a mistake to think that because a dog was attached to a dog that is now gone, it will attach to any other dog.

In the training community, we generally describe a dog's tolerance for other dogs as being on a continuum. At one end of the scale is the dog that does not like any dog it sees. It is likely reactive to other dogs, has no interest in dog friends, and very happily lives as an only dog. To bring another dog into that dog's home would be a mistake.

At the opposite end is the dog that likes every dog, little, big, young, old, it does not matter. Every dog is a potential friend. The problem with this dog is that not every dog will want to be that friend. Between these two extremes are a great potential for dog tolerance. Some dogs may like the dogs it sees frequently, but not new dogs. Some dogs may like fluffy dogs but not short-haired dogs. Combining dogs into a home takes thought and planning. Do not hesitate to seek help in adding a new dog to your home. If a dog is in a multiple-dog home and cannot adapt, that dog may be happier being re-homed to be an only dog. However, in my heart, I always feel that the dog that was already there has priority.

## The Right Dog in the Right Home

Are you your dog's dream home? There are good dogs and good homes but not every dog belongs in every home. Sometimes we don't know a dog's personality or their needs until we have lived with them for a while. Often what is interpreted as a behavior issue turns out to be a mismatch between the dog and owner. It is not unusual that I am called to evaluate a dog with behavior issues only to find a wonderful dog in the wrong home.

This is usually due to a particular home not being able to meet the dog's needs. This can be a question of exercise, perhaps a person who prefers quiet activities adopts a dog that needs to run miles a day. Or vice versa. An active person ends up with a dog that would rather be a couch potato. Maybe a family with five children adopts an elderly dog

## I Know Your Dog Is a Good Dog

that really just wants peace and quiet. There is a multitude of reasons a dog does not fit into a particular home. When working with a family who I feel has a dog that is safe to re-home I ask them, "if your dog was to describe her dream home, what would it look like"? Are you your dog's dream home?

It is not an easy decision to rehome a dog. I have made that decision twice. I once had two little, middle-aged, Shih Tzus whom I loved, but at heart, I am a big dog person. I decided to adopt a large, yellow, mixed-breed dog. The new dog thought the little dogs would be great playmates and loved to chase and stomp them. The little dogs were not so excited about this new lifestyle; they were stressed to the point of illness. They would hide and shake. After a period of trying to create peace, I knew this wonderful big dog was not in the right home. I returned him to the rescue, who happily took the dog back with this additional information about his needs and found him the best home, his dream home.

Another time, I adopted a hound dog who was described as "cat safe," which was important in my three-cat home. The new dog was sitting on the couch next to me. My cats are very used to dogs and assume it is okay to share space with them. One of my cats walked past on her way to her favorite resting spot. The hound dog leaped towards the cat; I heard the clacking of teeth. Luckily the dog was on a leash and was not able to reach my cat. If he had not been restrained, I really believe my cat would not be alive.

The attempt to catch my cat was not playful. It was done with intent. The hound dog was returned to the rescue and found a home with no cats. In both instances, the rescues were happy to have more information to add to the dogs' profiles to find the best possible home. A rescue should NEVER make an adopter feel guilty for returning a dog, or even worse, refuse to take back a dog.

# 16

# Grady

Grady was a foster failure. That is a term that those who volunteer in animal shelters and with rescues use with a dog that begins as a foster but is adopted by the foster family. It may seem like a negative term but is usually said with a knowing smile by those in the business of rescue. Most of us have fallen in love with at least one of the animals that have come into our home in what was supposed to be a temporary situation.

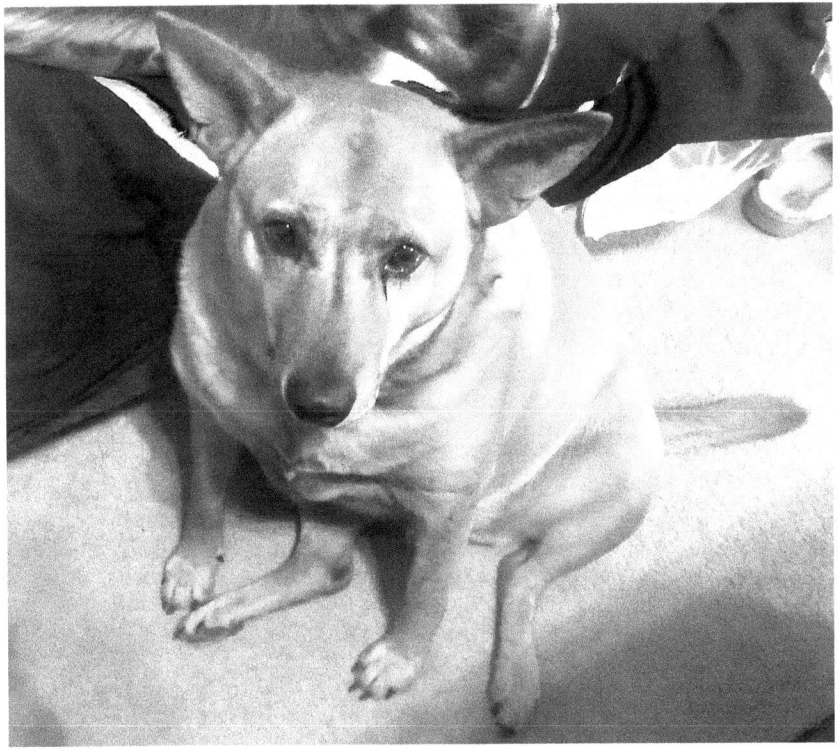

Grady

# I Know Your Dog Is a Good Dog

Grady was part of a large rescue. A group of dozens of dogs had been taken from a hoarding situation and had arrived at the local shelter where Lori was a volunteer. Grady was found to be infected with heartworm and needed to go into a foster home to complete the lengthy treatment. Once treatment was completed, he would be returned to the shelter to be placed for adoption. Lori got the call to foster and that is how she met Grady.

The hoarding situation Grady came from was dire. When the rescuers arrived at the location where Grady and the many other dogs were being kept, they found dogs living two to a cage, with cages stacked one on top of the other. All the dogs were filthy and smelly. When they were fed it was with food that was tossed into the small cages with each dog fighting for what they could get. The food not grabbed quickly would fall to the cage below. The shelter's intake papers on Grady noted his bowed hind legs due to malnutrition and lack of exercise.

Grady was about 4 or 5 years old when he came to live with Lori, which means he had been trapped in hell for 4 or 5 years. He was a skinny 35-pound mixed breed. Lori always felt he looked like a mix of Basenji and Chow.

Understandably, Grady was a fearful dog and Lori admits she really did not know what she was getting into. This was years ago, early in her volunteer career, and she had never cared for a fearful dog before. Even the dog training community was, at that time, just beginning to understand how damaging deprivation can be to the mental and emotional development of dogs and how that damage is expressed. Grady expressed his fear by staying at the back of the crate. He would hunch his shoulders trying to make himself smaller. If anyone came close to Grady, especially men, Grady would growl, bark, and lunge towards them with teeth bared.

Grady completed his heartworm treatment over the next five weeks and soon it was time for him to return to the shelter for adoption. Lori knew Grady had made progress in his physical health, he was now a normal weight, and his fur was fluffy and shiny. But progress in his behavior had been slow and she knew he wasn't where he needed to be to find a home.

Grady had adapted to Lori and had integrated well with the dogs in her home, but he remained fearful of people and would flinch if anyone around him made a sudden move. Lori couldn't stand the thought of bringing Grady back to the noisy, busy, shelter which would be a very stressful environment for him.

## 16. Grady

Grady was beginning to learn what it meant to be a house pet. His confidence was slowly growing. He had grown attached to Lori and she worried that staying at the shelter while waiting to be adopted would undo the progress that he had made. And how would shy, fearful Grady ever be able to meet any potential adopters? A dog that cowers at the back of a run and has little interest in new people does not get much attention from potential families.

Lori had become devoted to this growly fluff ball and began to think it would be better for Grady to remain where he was, safe with her. Besides, Lori had three other dogs, two of whom were bonded to each other. That left an odd one out, Hooch, her lumbering Mastiff. Lori thought maybe Grady could be a playmate for Hooch. So, Grady was adopted and became a permanent member of Lori's family. He never had to return to the shelter and the "foster fail" had been concluded.

Unfortunately, Grady never did bond with his intended dog friend, Hooch. Although they had a mostly peaceful co-existence, Grady would occasionally need his distance and would remind Hooch of this with growls and snaps. But easy-going Hooch was not a provokable dog and always remained calm in the face of these reactions. And though their relationship improved over time Hooch and Grady never did become the fast friends that Lori had hoped. But that was okay, Grady had a safe, comfortable home.

His behavior did improve but on occasion Grady's past would resurface. Every now and then he would have a sudden outburst and react to the people or dogs around him. On one occasion Lori had a coworker and her two young children visiting. The children were playing, they were not doing anything out of the ordinary for kids their age, and they were not being especially noisy or even running. Suddenly Grady rushed across the room and nipped at the children. Luckily, no one was injured, only frightened. But this incident made Lori more cautious, and she started putting Grady in another area of the house when she had visitors.

To keep all dogs safe, it became the norm in Lori's household to rotate dogs in and out of separate rooms or crates. This made sure that each dog was getting attention and play at different times. This prevented the dogs from becoming overly aroused and having active play flip over to any aggressive acts.

If Grady and Lori had been one of my clients today, these are exactly the kind of management techniques I would have recommended putting into place. A plan to alter the environment to reduce the unwanted

## I Know Your Dog Is a Good Dog

behavior and keep all dogs and people safe. But at the time Lori had Grady not as much was known about behavior modification for dogs. Looking back, Lori realizes she was managing life with Grady without thinking about it. And she was doing a great job. Lori says now, "I was just used to living with crazy dogs."

Regrettably and perhaps inevitably, a point came when the management failed. Grady had been with Lori for about four years, and she had resumed her volunteer duties as a foster home for the shelter. She was fostering a single puppy who needed to complete medical treatment before adoption.

It was Lori's practice to keep foster puppies away from her own dogs. On this day, a young family member who had recently moved in with Lori was holding the puppy in a room next to the kitchen. There was a gate in place and Grady was lying under the kitchen table. As they will do, the wiggly puppy got away from the person holding him, squeezed past the gate, into the kitchen, and ran up to Grady. Lori could see Grady did not like this and recognized this could be a dangerous situation. Lori instructed her relative to leave the kitchen and then Lori scooped up the puppy. The puppy started squealing in protest as only puppies can do, and Grady reacted.

Grady jumped up and bit Lori severely in several spots on her legs and arms. She was bleeding from the wounds where her skin had been torn away. She was glad at the moment that neither her family member nor the puppy had been harmed but she was seriously injured.

Lori was taken to the emergency room. Her injuries were treated, and she was sent home. The injuries to her legs were debilitating. She was unable to walk for several days. She had to have help completing simple household chores and she missed work. To this day she carries scars both physical and emotional.

Lori had adopted Grady because she knew she could give him a good life that would be difficult for him to find anywhere else. And she did give him a happy life. But Lori was no longer the only one living in her home. She had to think of her family. Lori had to make one of the most difficult decisions a dog owner can face. Lori knew that she, her family, and the other dogs in the house were not safe and she decided to have Grady euthanized. Lori took Grady to the vet for the last time. All Lori will say about this day is that "it was awful."

Now many years later and looking back in hindsight, I asked Lori how life changed after Grady. She tells me she grieved for Grady, but the grief was mixed with moments of relief. Lori had adopted another dog,

## 16. Grady

a sweet three-legged beagle named Roy. Life with Roy was a breath of fresh air. She was able to take him out in public and take him along to visit friends. She didn't have to put him away when visitors came to the house. It was such a change.

With Grady, she had to be always in control of the situation. She was not able to leave him with anyone else, some of the veterinarians and veterinary technicians that treated him were obviously afraid of him. She was often in a position of having to advocate for Grady when he needed care. She didn't think much about this while it was happening, it was just her way of life. But looking back she does realize that Grady was never able to relax, causing Lori to be as constantly vigilant as was her dog.

She looks back and tells me about the things she loved about Grady. The fat rolls around his neck which earned him the nickname Pikachu. His rolling walk, reminiscent of a retreating rhinoceros. She knows she made Grady feel safe and loved and she is happy about that. But was it enough?

Was it enough for this dog who had survived a tortured existence the first few years of his life? Who had only known cruelty at the hands of humans? I tell her I think it was. She had gifted him love and kindness, food, and warmth. And when it was time for Grady to leave this world, he went gently, surrounded by her love.

## 17

# Behavioral Euthanasia

Behavior Euthanasia or BE is the term used when dogs are euthanized not because of physical illness or injury but because of their behavior. Most of the time this is done because the behavior presents a safety risk to people or other animals. But it may also be a choice for dogs who have unremitting anxiety, fear, or depression and because of these illnesses have a very poor quality of life.

I anticipate there will be people reading this chapter who will be shocked, or even become angry at this topic. I suspect that it will be those who have never lived with a dog with severe behavior issues. They have likely never lived with a dog that has killed another dog or caused injuries to a human that required hospitalization.

This is not a topic for families who are tired of their dog or just don't have time to walk the dog or refuse to rehome their dog. This is a discussion for those families that I know have tried many things to help their dogs. Families who are crushed by the decision they must make. Families who want to be responsible citizens and who want to do the best, kindest, thing for their dog. This is a decision that is made when the quality of life for the dog, the people who live with the dog, or other animals in the home is severely compromised.

Behavior modification programs are focused on improving quality of life. Often the quality of life is improved by diminishing problem behaviors and reaching the goals set in the plan. Quality of life may also be improved by reducing the frequency or severity of the problematic behaviors. It may be that problems are stabilized and prevented from becoming worse. Unfortunately, there are times that despite great effort and the involvement of many experts, good quality of life is not achieved. And at those times the discussion of euthanasia may arise.

But how do we measure the quality of life? It is challenging because it is somewhat subjective. I know what makes my life worth living, but can I judge your life? Dogs are certainly sentient beings, but we really cannot sit down with them and discuss their hopes and dreams.

## 17. Behavioral Euthanasia

Weighing the value of a life and holding the responsibility of ending that life is one of the most complicated, burdensome, and important duties we have as pet owners. I once heard a veterinarian say that no matter the cause for the decision of euthanasia, we never feel like we chose the right time. We will always feel like we were too early or too late. If I am asked to discuss this topic with a family, I ask them to consider the quality of life for all involved.

# 18

# Tex

"That's not an Australian Cattle Dog." Those were the first words out of my mouth when I saw a picture of Tex. Tex, a small to medium white dog with a large black patch over one eye and ear, was now living with my friend Maureen. As she was a friend, my words were a bit more blunt than the usual diplomatic approach I take with clients. Maureen and her husband had always wanted an Australian Cattle Dog, and when a friend of Maureen's told her about a cattle dog in trouble, she stepped up to help. Since she already had two dogs of her own, her intention was to act as a foster home for Tex and help him find a new family.

Very little was known about this little dog. Maureen's friend, who had alerted her to this dog in need, knew that Tex had originally been purchased as a puppy from a cattle ranch in Texas. We came to think of this as clue #1. That first family re-homed him while he was still a puppy because he was "too active," clue #2. Now Tex's second owner wanted to re-home him because they lived in an apartment and did not have the room or the time for him. Maureen volunteered to help and found herself with an underweight, undernourished, six-month-old, "not an Australian Cattle" dog that was nothing but bones and ears, clue #3 that things with Tex were not going to be simple.

Australian Cattle Dogs are typically stocky and muscular and compact, with broad skulls. Their coats are typically blue or red speckled with black patches. Tex was skinny, pointy, and mostly white. He definitely had herding dog traits. He had a piercing stare, a tendency to stalk, and did not hesitate to chase and nip.

Knowing he had come from a working ranch, we researched other types of cattle dogs and the closest we could come is that Tex was an Australian Koolie. Not a common dog in the United States. Koolies are typically bred for work, not looks, so they come in a variety of colors. Tex sure looked like the pictures of Koolies we found online.

From the beginning, Maureen discovered that Tex could not be crated. If placed in a crate, he would bark and scratch and tear at the

## 18. Tex

Tex

sides of the crate to the point of injuring himself. But if home alone and not crated, Tex would soil the house, bite at the door frames, and chew the windowsills. And Tex would cry, oh how he would cry. This only happened if he was home alone. If family members were present, Tex seemed just fine. Maureen wondered if this working dog had spent too many long periods alone and confined as a young puppy, living in an apartment with the family that decided he was too much. He never was able to let go of his aversion to being crated.

Keeping her intention of being a foster home, Maureen did find a family for Tex nearby. He lived there for about four months, but unfortunately, the dog that lived there first never adapted and decided this was not going to work. He asked Tex to pack his bag and get out.

Another neighbor offered to take Tex but during the one and only

## I Know Your Dog Is a Good Dog

day Tex lived with her, he sat by the door and cried. "That's it," Maureen told me, "Tex is not going anywhere." They were not going to put him through re-homing again. Tex was there to stay. All those clues? They were coming together. Tex was in his fifth home.

Tex settled in. He loved his new family and home, but there were always challenges. He was very active, as a working dog should be, and his family had to be creative in keeping Tex's body and mind busy.

Tex would steal food. Since moving in with Maureen, Tex had regained his health and was now well-nourished. His new family gave him plenty of food and treats. That included his daily cuppa, each morning sitting in a chair at the table with Maureen while she had her morning coffee. But when home alone Tex would sneak into the pantry he had learned to open, remove packages of food, and carefully distribute them throughout the house. The family was surprised one day to arrive home and find an unopened pack of Pop Tarts™ on each family member's bed.

They wondered if he was naturally good at sharing or was he hoarding food. Sadly, they considered if in addition to spending all of his time in a crate in his earlier homes if he had also been given enough food. He had been underweight on arrival, was this causing him to store away for the future? Then again, maybe this working dog had just created his own job, making sure each member of his family had a ready snack. Tex was that smart, just ask the UPS driver. Tex learned to open the front door and any delivery driver was given an ear- (and mouth-) full for entering his property.

As time went on, life with Tex remained challenging but manageable. However, when the youngest son of the family went off to college, life changed for Tex. The amount of time he was home alone grew. There was not as much activity or the same number of people at home to interact with him. There was a further loss when the two older dogs Tex lived with eventually passed away.

Tex had become more secure in his new life and the destruction when left alone had become infrequent. But now, without his canine companions, Tex expressed his increasing anxiety by returning to urinating and defecating in the house. He would rip up the carpet and tear curtains and blinds from the windows. He chewed the steps to the basement and the trim from around the front door.

Maureen asked for help. Since she was a longtime friend, I wasn't sure I would be able to be objective when it came to Tex, so I called on a colleague who was a certified professional dog trainer and had worked with many dogs with behavior concerns. Tex was started on a

## 18. Tex

behavior modification plan. He was referred to a new veterinarian, who pronounced a diagnosis of separation anxiety and started Tex on medication to help reduce his stress. He also got a new dog friend, a sweet little hound mix named Winnie, so he would never have to be completely alone. Things began to improve.

Tex's life changed again when Maureen and her husband bought several acres of rural land. Tex loved country life. He played with visiting farm dogs, he had streams to gambol through and he would run for miles along the four-wheeler that Maureen's husband used to inspect the land. This way of life made Tex happy, but this was a weekend activity, and once he returned to the suburbs, Tex's anxiety would increase again. At times Maureen would ruminate that she should have tried harder to find Tex a working or country home. But the reality is those "farms where dogs can run" can rarely be found.

With the combination of behavior modification, medication, the opportunity for physical and mental exercise, Tex had a wonderful life, much of the time. But as the years went by and Tex grew older, his illness would have occasional exacerbations. When that happened, his medications would be adjusted, and he would improve for a while but then eventually would decline.

As Tex became a senior dog the exacerbations became more frequent and would last longer. His treatment plan grew less effective. Even at his home in the country, if left alone, Tex would pace and drool, never being able to relax. If Maureen and her husband had to drive into their small town, they would take Tex with them whenever possible.

If the weather was mild enough to leave Tex in the truck, he would ride along for visits to the hardware store or to get gas. Maureen and her family could even grab a bite to eat at the local diner, as long as they sat by a window where Tex could see them from the truck's driver's seat he would occupy. But it soon reached the point that Tex was only happy if everyone was home and in the same room together with him.

Tex's family tried many things. They thought maybe he would be happier if he had access to the garage while home alone, but he was not. Maybe he would feel better if he could go outside and they built all manner of secure pens and enclosures. Tex was not happy with this. Tex could jump over, go under, through, or around any barrier they built. They tried a dog day care, hoping this would be an alternative to being home alone, but were told Tex would panic until they returned to pick him up.

A turning point came during a weekend Tex and Maureen were at the country house. Maureen had to make a trip to the store, it was too hot to take Tex along. She did a perimeter check of the house, making sure there was nothing on which Tex could injure himself. This included unplugging all electrical cords he had been known to chew through, securing doors and windows, and picking up any items that may be a choking hazard.

When Maureen returned to the house after her quick errands, she was alarmed to discover that in his panic, Tex had climbed up and pushed a window air conditioning unit out of the window, tearing the electrical cord in the process. Thirty-five-pound Tex had hurled himself out of the window and had been wandering in the woods looking for his family. Luckily Tex had not electrocuted himself, been physically injured, or even killed.

Maureen called me to have a heart-to-heart. It is not the money and that had been plenty, vet visits, medications, equipment, training, and it wasn't the destruction, although there had been plenty of that too. It was about the quality of life for Tex and for his family. His anxiety and panic had been getting worse. We talked about how that must feel for him.

It didn't happen that month, but the time did come when Tex's family made the decision to let him go, to free him from his turmoil. They lovingly said goodbye and Tex was euthanized. Now, almost a year after Tex died, I talk with his family about life with Tex. I asked how life was with, and after Tex.

They talk about the changes in their own lifestyle. One thing they noticed is that they can travel as a family again. They were able to attend college graduations for their children. When Tex was alive, someone had to be home with him at all times, having a neighbor pop in was not an option, and boarding was not an option, so they were never able to all travel at the same time. For seven years, unless Tex was able to go along, trips were made with only parts of the family at a time. Which means during their children's middle and high school years a family trip was a rare thing.

Yet Maureen points out, even though they feel they had made the right decision, they also feel they failed Tex. Maureen's daughter tells me that for seven years it was all Tex, all the time, and then suddenly he was not there. It is such a significant change that you don't know what to do with yourself.

It was not just the humans in the house that had to adjust, Tex's companion dog, Winnie, did miss him, she was lethargic in the days

## 18. Tex

after he was gone and would search for him. But they also noticed Winnie was able to completely relax and sleep. A full night's sleep was not something that happened when Tex was alive. His hypervigilance would keep his canine friend awake.

Even now, a year later, the loss of Tex overshadows their life. Maureen says that it would have been easier to lose Tex to a physical illness instead of losing him to a mental illness. They do not talk much about why Tex died. Maureen and her family tell me that people do not understand. It is still taboo to talk about mental illness in people, let alone dogs. They feel they will be judged, indeed they were judged and received plenty of unhelpful advice throughout his life.

I ask about this advice, and Maureen explained they were told he "Just needed more exercise, that he needed a job, or that they needed to send him away for training." In the area where we live, board and train programs are almost exclusively punishment based. "What was I supposed to do," she asked, "he was already crazy, send him away and let someone punish him for being crazy?"

But she adds that people they knew well, like neighbors who saw Tex daily assured them they had done the right thing. Those people did not judge because they had witnessed life with Tex. Maureen felt that Tex had really not been happy for the last year and a half of his life. She just wishes you could explain to a dog that you are doing this to ease their pain. Now they remember Tex with smiles. He is remembered for the great hugs he would give and how smart he was. He is remembered for his sweetness and how much he loved his family. And of course, they remember that he took his morning coffee with plenty of cream.

# 19

# Quality of Life

There is physical pain and there is mental and emotional pain. Many dogs diagnosed with a behavior disorder are given the broad diagnosis of generalized anxiety disorder. Anxiety can be one of the most insidious, debilitating conditions to afflict a dog. "Anxiety is broadly defined as the apprehensive anticipation of future danger or misfortune accompanied by a feeling of dysphoria (in humans) and/or somatic symptoms of tension (vigilance and scanning), or autonomic hyperactivity, increased motor activity and tension."[1]

Autonomic hyperactivity is related to the autonomic nervous system, specifically the sympathetic branch of the autonomic nervous system. This is the part of the nervous system associated with the classic flight/fight/freeze response. Activation of this part of the nervous system causes symptoms such as an accelerated heart rate, a slowing down of digestion, dilated pupils, sweating, and increased blood pressure.

This response is a wonderful evolutionary survival mechanism. To use a somewhat tired metaphor, when an early human was surprised by a tiger, the flight/fright/ (and now freeze) response prepared the body to escape, to defend, or to hide. Blood is shifted from the extremities to the core of the body to provide more energy for the heart and lungs. The mouth goes dry, the stomach flutters and the intestines may react as digestion is shut down to divert more energy to the muscles. You may experience tunnel vision or vision becoming sharper to take in surrounding threats. All are very useful reactions unless the system goes haywire, as it may with anxiety.

In dogs, anxiety can be exhibited in many ways. Anxiety can erupt in reactivity, aggression, self-harm, destruction, or depression, and sometimes a mix of all of these. Medication and behavior modification can help these symptoms in some cases—but may not offer enough improvement to move the quality of life to a desirable level.

Think about a time when your sympathetic nervous system has kicked in. Think about those instances when you have had a close call

## 19. Quality of Life

while driving. A near accident, imagine how your heart pounds, you flush and feel hot, and your stomach may be upset. Now think about feeling this way most of the time without that close call ever happening. Living in constant fear and panic severely damages the quality of life.

My dog Bayou was fearful of people. During the time in my life that I had Bayou, there were not a lot of people in and out of my house. During those times that we had visitors, I had a structured plan for Bayou. When there were no strangers in our house, Bayou was a happy, silly, relaxed dog. Because the trigger of her anxiety was external and infrequent, she had a very good quality of life. She enjoyed her days.

My dog Tom had an internal trigger for his anxiety. His brain just didn't quite work right. He was miserable most of the time. Each day was a challenge. His quality of life was not so great.

## Quality of Life for the Family

It is not just the quality of life of the dog that matters. It is the quality of life of the humans living with the dog as well. This may be surprising as there are those who champion "giving all" for our pets and "would never imagine giving up on a dog." My guess is those people have never had to make the day-to-day sacrifices those of us who live with these special dogs have made.

I once worked with a couple who lived with a large, aggressive, Malamute. No one other than these two people could safely handle the dog. Because of this, the owners only left home to go to work and run errands. They could never be away together overnight because they could not leave their dog in the care of anyone else; it would not have been safe. These owners had not been to visit family or on a vacation as a couple for five years. Five years! There are very few people who would be able or willing to make that sacrifice.

A few years ago, I saw a "feel good" story on Facebook about a young woman that sold her car to pay for her dog's veterinary bills. That is a wonderful sacrifice to make if you can, but most people could not and a sacrifice like that may lead to financial ruin for some families.

I have had owners whose dog's behavior problems have caused so much stress in their life that it damages relationships with partners, children, and relatives. I have known more than one couple who have ended their own personal relationship because of the demands of living with a dog with behavior issues. These are very real, very difficult life challenges, faced by real people.

Early in my training career, I worked with a wonderful veterinarian who told me he always asked two questions of families living with behaviorally challenged dogs. The first question was: When you were thinking of getting a dog, what did you imagine life with that dog would look like, and how close is your reality to that picture? The second question was, What is your line in the sand? The answer to this question is different for everyone. I have had many people tell me that biting or harming someone else could not be tolerated. I have had others tell me there is no line.

I like these questions because they provide a reality check. The answers to those questions are helpful in considering how much of a problem the dog's behavior issues are causing for an owner or family. They can show how much alignment there is among family members. These questions can open a discussion around the emotional weight the family is bearing. It can be a starting point for developing a plan to move forward or a starting point for a frank discussion on re-homing or euthanasia.

Often when we live with a dog that has behavior issues, especially over a long period of time, we forget what life is like for other human-dog relationships. Sometimes we are surprised at how altered the reality we are living is. I have had more than one family tell me that they did not realize what a difficult life they had been living or how restricted their life had become until that dog was no longer with them. It is okay to look at your quality of life and consider if this is something you can maintain without damage to your own financial, mental, and physical health.

## *Quality of Life for Other Pets*

My first experience with losing a dog specifically to a behavior diagnosis was with a young, yellow Labrador. My dog had been diagnosed with severe generalized anxiety disorder. His was one of the worst cases I had ever seen. You can read about this experience in my book *Mental Illness in Dogs: A Guide for Trainers*. His disability was relentless and greatly impacted his quality of life. At the same time, I also had an adolescent Great Dane. The two dogs would snuggle with each other and nap together. I thought the Great Dane was a good anchor for the

## 19. Quality of Life

anxious dog and her presence prevented him from being alone when I was gone.

As part of the management plan for my anxious dog, I set up cameras in my home. I was able to monitor my dog's stress level and activity throughout the day. Because I had the cameras, I was also able to see that the Great Dane was causing the destruction that would greet me when I arrived home each day. My Dane loved to shred toys and had taken to shredding the couch. I would come home to find lumps of stuffing and foam strewn about the floor. I was not sure how concerned I should be. After all, she was an adolescent and a giant breed. Her dog bed was a twin-size mattress. Would it follow that her chew toy was a couch? The day I was able to see the wood frame of the couch I really began to worry.

Sadly, the time came when my anxious dog lost his battle with mental illness. Along with his veterinarians, I made the difficult decision to end his suffering and had him euthanized. I grieved hard for this dog and still do. To my surprise, after this dog was gone, my Great Dane's destructive behavior stopped almost at once. She never chewed the couch again. With time and study and thought, I now believe that living with an anxious dog was too much for her. I am sure I was not able to meet her needs because of the extra time my anxious dog took from our schedule. But I also think the other dog's barking, the panting, the constant motion, and stress created her own anxiety. I think the destruction was her way of expressing her stress. Living with a dog with a mental illness was damaging her quality of life.

It is important to consider the other animals that live in our home when considering quality of life. Dogs and especially cats are very good at hiding stress. Because of that, it may be difficult for us to notice if other pets in our home are showing signs of discomfort.

The needs of the behaviorally ill dog may divert attention and time away from other animals. That can impact the other animals' quality of life. They may not be getting the attention, the exercise, the play time, or the companionship they need.

Anxiety in one animal may increase that in all others. For homes where a dog's reactivity or aggression is aimed at another resident pet, that animal may live in constant fear for their safety. They may feel the constant need to escape. Chronic stress on companion animals can eventually lead to physical illness. We must consider the quality of life for all the animals that are in our care.

# 20

# Champ

Act first, ask questions later. I spotted this as Champ's modus operandi at our first meeting. I was hired by Champ's owners, Beth and Dan, to help develop a behavior modification plan recommended by the Veterinary Behavior Specialist treating Champ. At that first visit, the second and I am sure the third, Champ, would be crated or tethered to a bolt in the wall when I arrived. I would enter the house, quietly sit at the kitchen table, and observe this beautiful, 100-pound, barking, charging, German Shepherd Dog from the corner of my eye. Champ was practiced at reacting before he had all the information in any given situation.

At those early visits, Champ would be released after he calmed down. It would take several minutes, but once freed he would approach and take treats from my hand. He would then lie at my feet to keep a close eye on my movements. If I did stand up from my seat the barking would start again.

My interactions with Champ were slow but steady. As the months went by, Champ eventually accepted me into his circle of friends. I was able to move about freely, pet him and ask him for the behaviors we were teaching. I was able to walk next to him while we worked on conditioning exercises. But Champ persisted in his "act first" way of approaching the world.

Since Champ and I had gotten to know each other, I no longer feared his ferocious barks would turn into bites. He no longer needed to be contained for my arrival. But still each time I entered his house, I would steel myself for the bark that only a very large German Shepherd can generate. Champ would charge toward me with his loud protests. He would sniff my feet and look me up and down. Then his tail would begin to wag, and he would grin his, "oh it's you!" grin. There he was, my "Champers," the loving nickname I bestowed upon this dog. Act first, ask questions later.

Champ had earned the right to be suspicious and cautious. He was about three years old when he was adopted by Beth and Dan. Originally,

## 20. Champ

**Champ**

Champ had belonged to a man and woman in another state. Sadly, the woman passed away, resulting in the man and Champ moving in with a relative. The relative did not want Champ in the house, so he began life as an outside dog, living on a five-foot chain year-round, including through all the harsh Midwest winters and summers. He received little attention and minimal care.

Thankfully, a good Samaritan learned of Champ's situation. She worked with the family who realized they did not have the resources or interest to care for Champ. They eventually agreed to surrender Champ to a national GSD rescue.

The first goal for that rescue was to return Champ to good physical health. At the time he was rescued, he was carrying only 60 pounds on his large frame and missing all the hair on his back end. With good nutrition and veterinary care, Champ regained his physical health.

Once he was fit and his constitution returned, a local rescue group took over and Champ went into foster care with a plan for him to find a family of his own. Unfortunately, Champ did not adapt well to the children that lived in his foster home, so he was transferred to a boarding facility. It was while in that boarding facility he came to the attention of Dan and Beth. They were looking for a German Shepherd to add to their family and brought Champ home on a foster-to-adopt basis. The purpose of foster-to-adopt programs is to make sure a dog is a good fit for the interested family. Although from the time they met Champ, Beth tells me, she knew he was theirs.

Beth and Dan had lived with German Shepherds in the past and were well-experienced with the breed. The rescue had passed on that children made Champ nervous, but no other issues were mentioned. He had been living at a boarding facility and no problems had been reported between Champ and the other dogs or staff. What his new family was about to learn is that Champ was very good at repressing his feelings.

Within the first week of being in his new home, Champ began reacting to things he would see through the windows. He would rush the window, and hit it hard with his giant, fluffy paws while barking and growling. He reacted to people with dogs, people without dogs, cats, bikes, motorcycles, and pretty much anything that moved outside of his house.

With his large size and the level of his reaction, Beth was truly afraid that one day he might go straight through the window. In an attempt to reduce his reaction, she lined up a row of kitchen chairs along the window to create a barrier. Since Champ was so large this idea only partially worked, so next, she covered the windows with an opaque cling film to block his view. It blocked Beth's view as well, she no longer had a view of her front yard.

For his first walk, Beth chose a short path around the block. Champ pulled and barked at everything; he was difficult to hold on to for petite Beth. This barking and pulling included any neighbors, so introductions were out of the question. They were pretty sure the neighbors were thinking "What have they done?" Beth and Dan could see walking Champ was going to be another challenge. They started taking the first jaunt of the day in the early morning hours when it was still dark, and the streets were empty. They were beginning to see life with Champ would not be easy, but they were committed to him.

Beth and Dan knew they needed help and signed Champ up for a class with a local training club, which advertised using positive reinforcement training methods only and offered classes specifically for reactive dogs. They completed the evaluation and Champ was accepted into the class. But then they were told the class would not be starting for months.

## 20. Champ

Beth knew they could not wait, Champ was only getting worse, so they sent Champ to a board and train program. Once that program ended and Champ was back home, any progress he had made in his reactivity soon fell apart. Beth points out that he did learn many skills, but the program did not address his underlying behavior issues.

Beth and Dan had lived with dogs in the past whose behavior had deteriorated over time. This was usually due to illness or those health problems that come with old age. Champ was different. His behavior was severe and constant, it was all-consuming. It exhausted their time, their energy, and their emotions. Champ's general practice veterinarian referred them to a veterinarian who specialized in behavior problems. They were hopeful, but again, had to wait three months for an available appointment.

Eventually, Champ was seen by the Veterinary Behavior Specialist. He was diagnosed with generalized anxiety, global fear, fear-related aggression, possession aggression as well as separation anxiety, and confinement distress. A treatment plan was put into place for Champ.

Part of his treatment was medication. It took months to establish the right combination and dosages of drugs that would help Champ. By the time I met Champ, he was on a medication regimen that seemed to be helping. This plan required medication five times a day. Beth found that the plan worked best when the medication was given at the same time each day.

One can only imagine how the medication schedule and Champ's general needs impacted Beth and Dan's daily life. They adjusted their schedule around Champ's needs. They altered their work hours. They were not able to socialize, except on rare occasions and when they did, they had to be nearby and leave any event early. This is not a trivial factor. Socialization is an important part of human life and serves to decompress and reduce stress as well as add to the quality of life. And Beth and Dan's family did want to see them now and then.

Having someone else come to the house to care for Champ was not an option. Everyone was terrified of Champ. When visitors did come into the house, Champ would charge at them and bark very loudly. He was scary. In fact, Beth recalls that whenever her father stopped by, he would stand behind a chair during the entire visit. Crating Champ did not help. In his desperation, he had broken out of every crate invented, and every containment device they had tried.

Champ's reactivity was not his only issue, in fact, his fearful behavior, his need to be always close to Beth, and his continuous anxious

## I Know Your Dog Is a Good Dog

vocalizations could be exhausting. When I first met Beth, one of her goals was to be able to sit and watch a 30-minute TV show with Champ relaxed next to her. The simpleness of that goal was a reflection of how severe Champ's issues were.

Champ did improve over time. His quality of life and that of his owners got better. Beth was able to relax and enjoy some quiet time of her own. But even with the improvements that were accomplished, living with Champ required constant care and vigilance. Champ may no longer explode at the sight of a dog or person when out on a walk. But he would still pull and bark until distracted. He might not threaten visitors to his home in such an outward way. I saw for myself that with repetition and appropriate behavior from the human that he could learn to enjoy a visit. But that human had to be dedicated and tireless.

Beth and Dan channeled everything they had into Champ. Beth tells me, "It was really hard, really hard." But they never gave up because they loved Champ. Beth tells me one of her favorite things about him was his welcome-home routine. Each day when Beth came home from work, she would lie on the floor with Champ, and he would wrap his giant paws around her. It was their own special hug.

I can tell you that once I got to know him, Champ was funny, smart, and a loveable goof. I will not forget the mistake I made when we were doing an outdoor training session. I saw Beth and Champ walking towards me and while still 30 yards or so away, I yelled, "Champers!" in greeting. Here came giant Champ running towards me pulling Beth, running behind, barely hanging on. "Oops." Champ changed everything in Beth and Dan's life. In good ways, and in bad ways.

The time for my in-person visits with Champ came to an end, but Beth continued to update me on his progress with emails and phone calls. When Champ was almost ten years old, I received a call from Beth. I could hear the weariness and sadness in her voice as she told me that even with adjustments to his medication and their management routine, the plan was not working as well as it had in the past few years. Stress and anxiety were permeating this senior dog's life.

We talked about what a wonderful dog Champ was, and that Beth's goal had always been to give him a wonderful life, giving him the safety and love he had so little of in his past. We talked about the possibility that at this point in Champ's life the best way to keep that promise was to let him go.

It was many months later when Beth made the final decision. She didn't want Champ to suffer any longer. Beth did not share this decision

## 20. Champ

with many people. Only a few close friends knew how challenging it was to live with Champ. She felt most people would not understand and she did not want to be questioned. Making this decision was hard enough.

The day after Champ died Beth was sitting in the house by herself, she suddenly thought, "I can take the film off the windows. This is the first time I've been able to look out those windows in six years." But the nose prints on the windows, those stayed for the next six months. She couldn't stand to clean them off. What a perfect example of grief mixed with a glimpse of a new day.

Later, after Champ had been gone a while, I asked Beth to look back and tell me some of the things that were helpful in the journey with this special dog. She told me that an understanding vet is wonderful. Champ was treated at a multi-vet practice; a couple of the veterinarians were actually terrified of Champ. But the vet that cared for Champ throughout his life was amazing and they could not have made it without her. I asked more about what this veterinarian did that made things easier.

Beth told me how helpful it is when the veterinarian allows the owner to stay with their dog during exams. Giving the owner the power to advocate for their dog and being allowed to explain their dog's needs is important. Owners who work so tirelessly with these special dogs will always have information that will help a clinic visit go more smoothly and keep everyone safe. Champ did better with a doctor that would approach him slowly. He would calm down more quickly if the clinic staff would take just a few minutes to do some hand targeting with him.

Hand targeting is when a person holds their hand at a distance from their body and the dog touches the hand with their nose. Champ was, well, a champ at hand targeting. This skill gave him a chance to gain information about a new person without getting too close. To have a veterinarian that participates in greetings the dog is comfortable with is a true asset.

Working with a Veterinary Behavior Specialist was a necessity for a dog with Champ's diagnoses. The Veterinary Behavior Specialist is the highest level of a medical provider for behavior concerns. This is the doctor that has the knowledge and skill to manage medications. The medication regimen for Champ was intricate, finding the right balance of medications and dosages took time and an expert to prescribe them. Working with a force free trainer was also beneficial in helping Beth and Dan with the practical application of Champ's behavior modification plan. And working with the trainer in their home provided the opportunity to practice skills in a safe manner.

## I Know Your Dog Is a Good Dog

What did not help was unsolicited advice from family and friends and even strangers. In fact, Beth did not talk about Champ a lot because other people "just don't get it." People would ask, "Have you tried this or that? Have you tried CBD oil, agility, or sports or more exercise?" "Have you tried getting him out more, having him around people more." People with these suggestions would mean well, but they "just didn't understand what we were dealing with. Unless you have lived this you just don't know." Living with Champ required around the clock management and always staying two steps ahead. Beth tells me, "The last thing I needed was judgment, I did everything I possibly could."

I asked Beth how life with Champ impacted her decision to get another dog. She tells me that Champ broke her heart, and she doesn't think she can ever have another German Shepherd. In fact, after Champ died, the thought of another dog was untenable, so Beth and Dan got a cat. Beautiful Mabel. Mabel was able to ease Beth back into the idea of loving a pet again without getting hurt. Mabel helped heal Beth's heart.

After some time, she decided she was ready for a new dog but the thought of that made her really nervous. They decided getting a Golden Retriever from a breeder would improve the chance that the dog would be more stable, even though they understood there are no guarantees. Beth wanted a dog that could participate in a variety of activities. They had been living in isolation for 6 years. She wanted to walk in the neighborhood and have visitors to the house. That does not seem like a lot to ask.

Beth and Dan and I reviewed the breeder they had chosen. I looked closely for any red flags and found none. We used our phones to enable me to virtually attend their first visit to the breeder. This allowed me to see the mother and the puppies, as well as the environment they were in, and to observe for any concerns. Everything seemed to be in good order.

Still, even with careful planning, there were many moments of worry. Beth was concerned she was going to do something to make the new puppy anxious. I assured her that behavior issues such as Champ had are caused by a myriad of contributing factors. There is almost always a genetic basis combined with environmental factors that lead to the problems diagnosed in Champ. We also knew that Champ had suffered mistreatment in his younger years. I reassured her that she was taking all of the right steps in finding her next dog.

At my last visit with Beth and Dan, their adolescent Golden Retriever lay at our feet. He is a wonderful dog. Everything they

## 20. Champ

had hoped for, friendly, stable, and even working on a hunting title. Now when we talk of Champ, it's hard to hold back tears. Beth loved Champ, and I loved him too. We remember how with his own people, he was such a lover; he was sweet and smart. He tried so hard to do everything that was asked of him. There were times when Champ was happy, but life was very hard for Champ, and I am happy he is no longer suffering.[1]

# 21

# Saying Goodbye

A dear friend called. She was calling me from the hospital. Her dog had attacked her, and she had multiple, severe bites along both of her arms. She would need surgery and would be in the hospital for several days. She was calling to ask me if I would take her dog to our mutual veterinarian to be euthanized.

She knew it was necessary. She did not want to leave her dog in the care of anyone else during the time it would take her to recover. She knew her dog was a safety risk, and she was also concerned for her dog's wellbeing. She did not want to hand her dog over to animal control to suffer among strangers for the required hold time only to face the inevitable alone. She wanted her dog to be with someone that was familiar to him and cared about him.

My friend had met this dog while working at an animal shelter. She had grown quite fond of him and spent a lot of time with him. The dog had been adopted and returned twice. The reason for his being returned was that he was "too wild" or "hard to control." There had been no reports of aggression or biting. My friend did not want to see this dog in another failed home, so she decided to adopt him herself.

After living with him for some time, she did find that he had some anxious behaviors. She especially noticed that if the dog was over-aroused while playing or by seeing a passing dog or person outside of the home he would begin to jump on one of the other dogs he lived with, grabbing legs or ears while growling. This is something we call redirected aggression. A condition when a dog becomes frustrated at not being able to reach the object of his interest and excitement so then turns his energy towards whatever person or animal is nearby.

When overly excited around people, this dog would become very mouthy. He would grab onto the arms and legs of his owner or even visitors. His mouthiness was enough to leave bruises but never broke the skin.

There came a time when there was a very unfortunate incident in

## 21. Saying Goodbye

my friend's home. A loud argument broke out among people who were nearby. This seemed to trigger the dog and he turned and attacked his owner, my friend. She was taken to the hospital with injuries that were severe enough to cause permanent scarring and nerve damage that she deals with to this day.

My friend knew that her dog was a safety risk and that he could no longer live in her home. She also knew the likelihood of finding another appropriate home was small, and placing him in another home was not the responsible thing to do. But not able to be with her dog while hospitalized, she called me. I told her of course I would do this for her because I knew if I ever asked her to do something this difficult for me, she would not hesitate. She still loved her dog and through our tears, I promised her dog's last day would be filled with only kindness.

I made the appointment with the veterinarian and then went to her house to collect her dog. I tried to hide my heavy heart. I took the dog through the drive-up window at the local burger joint and got him a hamburger. We went to the park for a walk, and we sat and looked at the trees. We finally arrived at the clinic. I cradled her dog as he died that day and told him how much he was loved. It was one of the hardest things I have ever had to do in my life, and now years later I still remember the details as if they happened yesterday. It was a hugely difficult decision to make, but it was the appropriate decision for my friend.

The decision to have a dog euthanized because of behavior problems is a decision that is made by many people each day. In 2019, a Facebook Group was created called Losing Lulu. The Facebook group was created to support those who have lost a pet due to behavior issues. As of early 2022, the group had over 17,000 members from around the world. Pets that had been lost include not only dogs but cats, horses, and even birds. Remember that you are not alone but part of a large circle.

If you find yourself facing the extremely difficult decision of euthanasia for your dog, here are some suggestions, that, in my experience, may help ease the way. Let someone else make the appointment. It does not have to be you. Delegate this task to a trusted friend or family member that understands and supports your decision. That phone call is hard to make.

Consider home euthanasia. This may be easier for you and your dog. It can avoid the trauma of a trip to the clinic. It can also give other animals in your home a chance to say goodbye and to know their companion is gone. If your dog is an appropriate choice for this, Lap of Love is one such service and has multiple locations throughout the country.

## I Know Your Dog Is a Good Dog

Ask for support from someone who understands, even if it is your trainer. I often prefer to be alone with my dog when they breathe their last. I feel it is an intimate moment, a privilege, and one I want to share with my dog without distractions. But I have found it to be helpful to have someone there when it is over. You can have someone waiting for you. Someone who can drive if necessary and someone who will know if you need a good cry, a walk, or a stiff drink.

Remember that your dog is ill. Taking a physically healthy young dog to be euthanized is one of the hardest things I have ever done and will be for you too. It is hard for our brains to make sense of this. If a dog had been hit by a car or is dying of cancer, we may think of euthanasia as a blessing or at least a relief. In our society, we do not view mental illness in the same manner as we do physical illness. Not for people and not for dogs. But a dog that has been diagnosed with a behavior disorder has a chronic illness, and just like the dog that has been treated for a terminal physical illness but fails to improve, our dogs with behavior issues may fail as well.

Remember that you do not owe anyone an explanation. Ask your veterinarian or trainer or friend to help you think of a reply that will work for any questions or challenges. Here is what I suggest for my clients when they are wondering what they will say. "We made the decision we thought was best for our dog and our family." That is it, you do not owe anyone anything else. And that statement can be repeated over and over.

Seek help. Do not hesitate to seek help with your grief. "In a May 2021 survey conducted by Veterinarians.org of 400 US adults, 68% of respondents reported that the loss of their companion animal was, in some cases, harder to deal with than the loss of a family member or friend, while an additional 17% claimed that the loss was equal to that of a family member or friend."[1] That loss, compounded with the emotional toll that has already taken place can be calamitous for our emotional and mental health.

I have had clients tell me that they have been diagnosed with depression or PTSD after the loss of their dog to a behavior diagnosis. If your feelings are unmanageable or if you would just like a safe place to discuss your loss, talk to a mental health care professional. If you are not sure where to find one, ask your family doctor or check with your employer. Many companies offer free, confidential mental health programs. Look online for a support group.

One of my clients who had lost their dog to behavioral illness

## 21. Saying Goodbye

contacted me a year after their dog had died. They were calling to tell me they had recently talked with a pet psychic and how the experience helped them to deal with some of their grief. Without judging this experience or their choice to seek this route, I listened to their story. What struck me was not the experience of communicating with the lost pet, but that even a year later they were still seeking answers to questions. Here are the questions they sent to the psychic:

- Does he forgive us for the choice we made?
- Is he better? Is his mind finally at rest?
- Does he still visit us?
- Does he know how special and how loved he was to our family?
- Will he ever come back to us?

I was touched and impressed by the profound, utterly deep, life-changing loss they had experienced. Moments like this paint a clear picture of the love and the depth of loss owners feel about their dogs. Never make the mistake that someone that chooses behavior euthanasia has made that decision quickly, easily, or callously. They have not.

## 22

# Should I Get Another Dog?

Almost universally those who have lived with a dog with behavior problems express a hesitancy, if not downright fear, at the thought of getting another dog. Regardless of how much we love our dogs, living with a dog who has behavior issues can be hard. Most of us would probably not voluntarily take on that challenge a second or third time. I know I would not.

It is not unusual for me to receive a phone call from a past client, asking if an action or conduct they see in their new dog is normal, or if it is a sign of an emerging behavior problem. The emotions that we are left with after living with a challenging dog can hover close to the surface. Even as a professional I have gone through this apprehension with my own new dogs. More than once, I have lost faith in my own judgment and called on training colleagues to talk me through the perfectly normal adolescent opposition or the senior dog grumpiness I am observing. I need reassurance that this behavior is normal and not a sign of a diagnosable mental illness. It is okay and expected that you will have these worries with any new dog of your own.

Not only clients, but I have also had training colleagues, some very experienced dog trainers, call me to talk through the fear of getting another dog. I believe this speaks to the level of emotional upheaval that living with a behaviorally challenged dog can create. It can be scary to step into a new relationship with a new dog. And this is something that is difficult to understand if you have not been in that position. But if and when you decide you are ready for another dog, there are action steps you can take to lessen the concern and anxiety around bringing a new dog home.

First, don't hesitate to get help in choosing a dog. Many trainers and behavior consultants offer services in helping to add a new dog to a family. In my career as a trainer, this is one of the most delightful

## 22. Should I Get Another Dog?

tasks for which I am hired. Who doesn't want to go visit and play with dogs! However, I do tell my clients, you have hired me to say no, so be prepared!

To help with the quest, my clients fill out the following questionnaire. These questions can help you really think about what you are looking for and can help breeders, rescue or shelter staff identify potential matches:

**Tell me about your family**
Who lives in the home?
Are there other pets in the home?
Are there other animals that visit regularly?
Are there visitors with mobility concerns due to age or physical status?
How often will the dog be walked, exercised, and have playtime?
Where will you keep the dog when you are not at home?

**Tell Me About Your Home**
What type of residence do you live in—house, apartment, attached condo, or villa?
Do you have a yard?
Do you have a fence? If so, what type and height?
Are you willing to install a physical fence if necessary?
Where do you plan to exercise your dog?
Do you share a boundary line with anyone that has a dog?

**Please rate the following items on a level of importance with 5 being very important and 1 being the least important.**

Friendly behavior toward children.
Friendly behavior toward visitors.
Friendly behavior toward other dogs.
Friendly behavior toward cats.
Low energy, likes to lounge around.
High energy likes to hike, run, and play sports.
Does not shed very much.
Sheds a lot.
Needs to see a groomer regularly.
Is already housetrained.
Okay if not housetrained, we will work on it.
A dog small enough to sit on my lap.
A dog able to keep up with my active lifestyle.

## I Know Your Dog Is a Good Dog

And I always add the following caveat. Remember that many factors go into behavior. Some behaviors are considered normal animal behaviors that any dog may have, including but not limited to: barking, chasing, running, digging, and chewing.

When I am assisting a family with their search for a new dog, I refer to this questionnaire often. When the family that rated minimal shedding as important sends me a picture of a lovely German Shepherd mix, or the family that is looking at Siberian Husky puppies marked as an exercise preference, a few small walks a week, it gives us the chance to discuss further.

If you do not have access to a professional to help you in your search for a new dog, take along a friend who will help you stick to the items on your list and to remind you when you stray. It can be difficult to look at all of those dogs needing homes and say no.

You must remember that you are looking for a match with a dog that can stay in your home for a long, long time, no matter what life changes come your way. If you do not have children, a dog that is not fond of kids may be a good choice. But are you planning on having kids? The dog who is not fond of kids now is not likely to grow fond of them over the next few years. Do you have children that visit your home often, or live next door? Then that dog may not be the best choice.

I also highly recommend the book *How to Find Your Dream Dog*, by Dixie Tenney. This is one of the better books I have seen that addresses all the things involved when searching for a new dog. Tenney walks through the various ways to obtain a dog, be it rescue, shelter or breeder. She offers items to think about and tips for your search.[1]

If you are adopting a dog from a shelter or rescue look for an organization that has a foster-to-adopt program. It can be difficult to get to know a dog in one meeting. Most people choose a dog based on a listed breed or on looks alone. Many times, potential adopters will meet the dog, sometimes in a small room, and must decide to take the dog home then and there. Sometimes this works out great! But it is not a way to really know about the dog you're taking home for life.

A dog may not present their true self in a situation like this for several reasons. The dog does not know you, and just like people, many dogs may not be comfortable showing all their personality to a stranger. The dog may be suppressing its behavior or shutting down due to the stress of being in a strange, scary environment. I have talked to many clients who met their dog once and decided to take the dog home. Suddenly, the

## 22. Should I Get Another Dog?

dog growls or protects their food. The client will tell me, "He seemed so quiet and sweet when we met him."

Foster-to-adopt programs allow potential owners to act as a foster home for a dog and over time decide if this is the dog for them. This gives the dog a chance to decompress in a home environment and gives the family the chance to really get to know the dog. If it is not a good fit, the dog will go back to the rescue. The rescue gets the benefit of learning more about the type of home the dog needs. I think these programs are very valuable and kudos to the rescues that willingly and understandingly take the dogs back into their care. If the dog wasn't a good fit for your home, you were probably not the right fit for the dog either.

Be cautious when looking at shelter or rescue descriptions. Be aware that through the years there have been a variety of assessments and tests used by shelters and rescues to determine a dog's personality or temperament. The results of these assessments are used to make adoption recommendations. You may see things like, needs a yard, prefers a home without cats, and no kids under 12. Unfortunately, these assessments are not perfect and are open to interpretation. These tests have a high error rate because dogs are living beings and these tests are testing a dog on a particular day, in a particular environment. These tests may not be enough information to really know what is in that canine package. In addition, staff performing the assessment may not have been trained to do the tests correctly.

Be aware of listed breeds for mixed-breed dogs. Unless the parents are known, or a DNA test has been done this is just someone's best guess. I remember in my years of volunteering at my local shelter in the early 2000s when pit bulls were not adopted out because it was thought they could not make good pets. If a dog came to the open intake shelter as a pit bull unfortunately it was euthanized. Because of this, volunteers would campaign for every blocky-headed dog arriving to be labeled a boxer mix. It was an effort to save the dog's life. Thankfully, now we know better about the wonderful family members pit bulls can become.

We also would randomly change our guess about a dog's breed. If a fluffy black and white dog listed as a border collie mix was not getting any interest, we would change the breed to something more exciting, such as a Landseer Newfoundland mix. Try passing that up!

Some shelters have taken the wise step of doing away with mixed-breed listings completely. Now dogs are listed as small, medium, or large, short-haired, long-haired, spotted, black, or yellow. I always

## I Know Your Dog Is a Good Dog

smile at a term coined by my friend, Susan to describe so many average shelter dogs, MBD, Missouri Brown Dog.

Even with a purebred dog, caution should be exercised when assuming specific personality traits based on breed. In May of 2022, a seminal report was published in the well-respected journal *Science*. This report involved a study of more than 2000 pet dogs, a combination of purebreds and mixed breeds. The study focused on eight areas: human sociability, arousal level, toy-directed motor patterns, biddability, agnostic threshold, dog sociability, environmental engagement and proximity seeking. The study found that "Breed explains just 9% of behavioral variation in individuals."[2]

Genetics do play a part in behavior, but most of the genes dogs carry existed long before specific breeds were even developed. Most breeds are only about 200 years old. That is considered very young in evolutionary development.

In addition to genetics, the environment makes a significant impact on behavior as well. This is not to say that breed does not matter, but for an owner searching for a dog, the breed is not the only quality to pursue. There can be a wide variety of behaviors in any given breed. If all Labradors or all Malinois had the same temperament, then any Lab could be a service dog and any Malinois a police dog. But the reality is to find a Labrador to be a service dog, or a Malinois to be a police dog, or any other breed/job match, one has to go through many litters, and even within a litter, there may be only one puppy that fits the bill. That is one of the reasons these dogs are so expensive.

A conference I attended a few years ago provided a great opportunity for networking during lunchtime. One day I sat with a group with an individual talking about how hard it is to find good toys for Golden Retrievers, that they will chew through anything. I had to smile being a Golden owner myself. Others at the table made suggestions but were met with, "oh no, those may be okay for other dogs, but will never work for a Golden."

The next day, at another table, with a new group, the exact topic came up again. But this time the dog in question was a Boxer. The owner could not find chew-proof toys. Again, when offered ideas, the response was "Oh no, not for Boxers, you just don't know." On one hand, I can see this is a result of lovers of specific breeds holding their favorite as special and unique. And they are! On the other hand, it reminded me that many of the traits we ascribe to a breed are there because a dog is a dog.

## 22. Should I Get Another Dog?

One added piece of advice I like to give is to remember a puppy is a puppy. So many times, I have been contacted by a family that tells me they got a specific breed because their last one was so wonderful and easy and calm. Now they have a puppy who is driving them crazy! But what they are really remembering is the senior Doberman, or Poodle, or Maltese they so recently had. They are forgetting what that dog was like ten or 12, or 13 years ago.

## *Bringing Home the New Dog*

When you do decide to bring home a new dog, expect a lot of mixed emotions. This is perfectly normal. Especially if you lost your last dog to behavioral euthanasia. I often have conversations with families who express the guilt they are carrying. The new dog is a reminder of the loss of the last dog. Bringing home a new dog can take quite a lot of adjustment, but there are things you can do to ease the transition.

Hire a trainer before the dog comes home. Yes, that's right. Hire a trainer for a home visit before the new dog arrives. The trainer can help you set up a space for the dog. They can give you management tips and discuss initial training ideas. They can review what equipment and toys will be appropriate. This will help put your mind at rest and allow you to discuss your fears with the trainer and ask questions.

Look for two of my all-time favorite books. If you are getting a new puppy, I highly recommend *Puppy Start Right: Foundation Training for the Companion Dog* by Kenneth Martin and Debbie Martin.[3] If you are bringing home an adult dog, *Love Has No Age Limit: Welcoming an Adopted Dog into Your Home* by Patricia McConnell and Karen London will guide you.[4] Dr. McConnell includes tips from how long it takes an adult dog to adjust to a new home, how to introduce visitors, all the way to house training an adult dog.

## *How I Ended Up with a Golden Retriever*

It may be time to think outside of the box in your search for a new dog. What I like to call muscle dogs, are my thing. Give me a good pit bull or Rottweiler and I'm a happy dog owner. Although I have had the odd Shih Tzu in my life, my dogs tend to be short-haired, large, and active. My dog Thelma certainly encompassed many working breeds in

## I Know Your Dog Is a Good Dog

her mix. My boxer Lola was the dog of my heart. My Great Dane Bayou was my best snuggler. Then came Rocket the Golden.

I was looking for a new dog. I had a spot in my home and in my heart. But I just did not have it in me to live with another dog that had to have high management or could not be around people or other dogs. I wanted a dog my whole family could live with and enjoy. I wanted a dog that I could integrate into many parts of my life and take with me on the road.

So, I made a list. I preferred to have some control over the dog's socialization so I knew a puppy would work better for that. I wanted to be able to visit the puppy before I would be bringing them home so kept my search within a day's drive from my house. I wanted to meet the puppy's parents so I could see what temperament my puppy was likely to inherit. This list pointed me towards working with a breeder.

I set out on my search. When I start I first talk to the folks I know who have wonderful dogs and ask where they acquired their dog. Sometimes the farmer down the road is the best resource. I will also look at akc.org and look for breeders that have earned the Breeder of Heart designation. This is limited to breeders who pay attention to temperament. But I don't stop there. I also ask veterinarians, other trainers and friends.

I found a breeder that would soon have a litter of puppies, *check*. The breeder owned both parents, *check*. They did thorough health screenings, *check*, and had a specific socialization plan for puppies from the time they were born, big *check*! The breeder was a four-hour drive away, *check*. And both of the expected litter's parents were certified therapy dogs: this was the personality I was looking for in my new dog. A sound, stable

**Rocket the Unexpected**

## 22. Should I Get Another Dog?

dog. The breeder allowed home visits at an early age, so I had the opportunity to meet the parents and puppies several times before the puppies were old enough to go to their new homes. I felt I had a good picture of the dog my puppy would grow to be.

And what was the breed? Golden Retriever. Never in a million years a breed I would have considered. So, home came Rocket. Rocket grew into a dog that was sweet and friendly. Not the smartest, there would be no obedience competitions, that was not his style. But he learned enough of the basics to be a good family pet. He enjoys his once-daily mile walk; he loves to eat, and he does not retrieve. In fact, a friend has labeled him a Golden Observer. And the shedding, oh the shedding. But Rocket fits perfectly into our family. He loves everyone and everyone loves him. By thinking outside of the box and focusing on what I wanted inside of the dog instead of on the outside, I now have a dog who is the right match for me.

This is not to say that there are not some wonderful rescue dogs, there are, and I know many. Some who have become service dogs and therapy dogs. By working with a professional and keeping an open mind you can find the best rescue dog for you.

And it is important to remember that not every dog that comes from a breeder is a great dog. There are many things that contribute to a dog's physical and mental health. I have worked with many well-bred dogs that have had serious behavior concerns. What it does mean is that with time, and research, and motivation you can find the right dog for you. You can safely give your heart away, again.

## 23

# Celebrate Your Dog

I hope this book has shown that you are not alone in your journey with your dog. I hope it shows you that there is help available for you and your dog. I hope you can see that there are many people who have shared your experience. Most of all I hope you can find a way to celebrate your dog!

Celebrate by having fun. Take a virtual class with your dog. If you are living with a dog with behavior issues and the dog is not comfortable being around other dogs or people, this may be the perfect activity. There are many trainers from all over the world that provide virtual classes. You can work on goals with your dog, then show off their talents via video! You can even pursue titles for your dog. The American Kennel Club offers virtual classes in home manners, tricks, and even scent work! Check it out at akc.org.

Brag about your dog. Write about your dog. Share all the wonderful things your dog can do and is. Join a forum. Check out dogsinneedofspace.com, a wonderful site and one of the original resources for dogs with behavior challenges. Make your dog an Instagram star. Share pictures of the fantastic dog you have. I know your dog is a good dog.

## *Remember Your Dog*

Beatrix Kiddo was a feral cat, a community cat. She was tough and smart and as with most cats, Beatrix chose her own path. She never would have been happy living indoors with humans but did decide to set up house on my friend's front porch. My friend provided her with a pretty good environment. A heated house, regular food, and fresh water were always available for Beatrix.

After a few years of living as my friend's porch kitty, Beatrix stopped showing up. After some time of not seeing or hearing

## 23. Celebrate Your Dog

anything of her, my friend began to search for Beatrix. As feared, for this wild-living cat, Beatrix was found deceased.

Throughout her life of unknown length, Beatrix had adorned my friend and her husband with hours of entertainment and fellowship, if not companionship. Although Beatrix belonged to only herself, she was mourned. This homeless, independent cat would be missed.

The loss of Beatrix makes me ponder the grief we feel for lost pets. As a society, I do not think we express the same level of sympathy for all animals. Almost any kind human understands the grief of the loss of a pet dog. But as a cat owner, I can tell you that the illness or loss of a pet cat does not seem to generate the same level of sympathy as the loss of a dog, except from those dedicated cat lovers.

If we take this train of thought further, how do we feel about those pets from childhood, the goldfish, and turtles? Some are almost thought of as disposable. The level of mourning for the lost life of an animal is not equitable.

When a pet dog is euthanized, or "put to sleep" due to illness, the infirmities of old age, or because of sudden traumatic injuries, their owners mourn freely. Many will post eulogies on social media. Pictures and memories of their beloved dog are shared widely, as they should be. The loss of a dog, even an elderly dog that has lived a good long life, is painful.

The owners of those dogs are comforted with sympathy, cards, and memorial gifts. Every dog lover understands that the loss of a dog is the loss of a family member and is an occasion to be marked with support and an acknowledgment of a life well lived.

However, I have observed that dogs that are lost due to behavior issues seem to be mourned less. Sometimes, this is because their families do not share the reason for their dog's death. Or they share the news with only a small group of close friends and family. Some families may feel embarrassment surrounding the issues they had with their dog. And almost all of them feel so much guilt at making the decision to euthanize their dog for behavioral illness that they can barely stand to talk about it. The opportunity to mourn for the dog is lost.

Even the dogs that are known, may not be known well. Especially those dogs that are not people friendly. The dogs who are "put away" when company comes. Those dogs that do not have a lot of friends. The dogs that do not get to be in the video with the mail carrier.

Sadly, those of us who live with these dogs know or suspect that there are people that simply did not like our dogs and are not sad they

## I Know Your Dog Is a Good Dog

are gone. It would be mighty difficult to share our loss and grief with those folks. And even those who liked our dog or at least understand that we loved our dog, may be relieved for us that the struggles are over

The missed chance to mourn our dog and to share our loss makes my heart hurt and is one of the driving reasons for writing this book. A dog with a behavior diagnosis is a dog with a mental illness. The dog that is euthanized for behavior has succumbed to a chronic, debilitating condition that impacted that dog's life as much as a dog that is diagnosed with a serious physical illness. For any serious illness, sometimes the treatment helps the dog get better and the dog will improve and survive. But sometimes the treatment does not help, and the dog cannot be saved.

And just like Beatrix Kiddo, the street cat, all animals have the right to be loved, grieved, and celebrated. I hope you can honor and memorialize your dog rather if it is in a small way or a big way.

My friend Susan lost her dog Kermit near the same time that my dog Thelma died. We were talking about what special dogs they both were, each in their own way. Thelma had been my first behaviorally challenged dog. She was fearful of strangers and her interaction with anyone outside of the family had to be well managed. Thelma had been my great teacher.

Susan's dog Kermit arrived to her already elderly. She met him at an animal sanctuary where she spent time volunteering. Kermit was a big black dog with a crooked face. He had suffered a stroke at some point in his life and that caused his muzzle to not quite line up with the rest of his head. A goofy dog, Kermit was built like he had been put together with spare parts. Susan

**Toys ready for the food pantry**

## 23. *Celebrate Your Dog*

fell in love with this guy and brought him home so that he could live out his senior years in comfort.

Susan and I wanted to do something special to commemorate our dogs' lives, so we formed the Toy Chest for Pets. Each holiday season we would sponsor a pet toy drive to collect toys for all kinds of pets. The toys were donated to our local pet food pantry.

We did this by setting up simple donation boxes at pet supply stores, dog day cares, veterinary offices, and any place we could think of. Thelma and Kermit's pictures were prominently displayed on the front of each box with a link to a Facebook page we had set up with details about the toy drive, the pet food pantry, and the stories of our wonderful dogs. We were surprised and pleased at how fast the boxes filled. We had great fun delivering the hundreds of toys to the pet food pantry. During the years we conducted the toy drive, each family that utilized the pet food pantry in December would receive toys for their cat or dog, along with food. It was a wonderful way to celebrate our best friends.

You do not have to do something so organized. You may want to make a donation to your favorite animal organization in your dog's

**Kermit, imperfect face, perfect heart**

memory. Perhaps, in your dog's honor, you would like to pay the adoption fee for a dog that has been at a shelter for too long. You may choose to place a rock with your dog's name at their favorite walking spot. Feel free to honor the dog that is with you now and to remember the dog that is gone. I know you love your dog. I know your dog was a good dog.

\* \* \*

Although I have reviewed the process for training a few techniques in this book, please remember that it is highly recommended, when working with a dog who has behavior concerns, that a professional trainer, behavior consultant or veterinarian be consulted, for the safety of all the people and dogs involved.

Some names have been changed to protect privacy.

**Thelma the First**

# Recommended Reading

American Veterinary Society of Behavior Position Statements found at https://avsab.org/.
*Animals in Translation: Using the Mysteries of Autism to Decode Animal Behavior* by Temple Grandin and Catherine Johnson.
*Behavior Adjustment Training 2.0: New Practical Techniques for Fear, Frustration, and Aggression in Dogs* by Grisha Stewart.
*Brain Games for Dogs: Fun Ways to Build a Strong Bond with Your Dog and Provide It with Vital Mental Stimulation* by Claire Arrowsmith.

The author with Thelma

# Recommended Reading

*Canine Body Language: A Photographic Guide Interpreting the Native Language of the Domestic Dog* by Brenda Aloff.
*Chill Out, Fido! How to Calm Your Dog* by Nan Kene Arthur.
*Click to Calm: Healing the Aggressive Dog* by Emma Parsons.
*Clicking with Your Dog: Step by Step in Pictures* by Peggy Tillman.
*Control Unleashed: Creating a Focused and Confident Dog* by Leslie McDevitt.
*Decoding Your Dog: Explaining Common Dog Behaviors and How to Prevent or Change Unwanted Ones* by American College of Veterinary Behaviorists.
*Don't Shoot the Dog: The Art of Teaching and Training* by Karen Pryor.
*Fired Up, Frantic and Freaked Out: Training the Crazy Dog from Over the Top to Under Control* by Laura VanArendonk Baugh.
*The Genius of Dogs: How Dogs Are Smarter Than You Think* by Brian Hare and Vanessa Woods.
*A Guide to Living with and Training a Fearful Dog* by Debbie Jacobs.
*How to Find Your Dream Dog* by Dixie Tenney.
*Inside of a Dog: What Dogs See, Smell, and Know* by Alexandra Horowitz.
*Love Has No Age Limit: Welcoming an Adopted Dog into Your Home* by Patricia McConnell and Karen London.
*Mine! A Practical Guide to Resource Guarding in Dogs* by Jean Donaldson.
*On Talking Terms with Dogs: Calming Signals* by Turid Rugaas.
*The Other End of the Leash: Why We Do What We Do Around Dogs* by Patricia McConnell.
*Pets on the Couch: Neurotic Dogs, Compulsive Cats, Anxious Birds, and the New Science of Animal Psychiatry* by Nicholas Dodman.
*Puppy Start Right, Foundation Training for the Companion Dog* by Kenneth Martin & Debbie Martin.
*Reaching the Animal Mind: Clicker Training and What It Teaches Us About Animals* by Karen Pryor.
*Separation Anxiety in Dogs: Next Generation in Treatment Protocols and Practices* by Malena DeMartini-Price.
The Whole Dog Journal online at https://www.whole-dog-journal.com/.

# Chapter Notes

## Introduction

1. Please see the list of recommended reading at the end of this book.
2. Nicholas Dodman, *Pets on the Couch: Neurotic Dogs, Compulsive Cats, Anxious Birds and the New Science of Animal Psychiatry* (New York: Atria, 2016), 158–162.
3. You can find the We Rate Dogs Twitter account at @dog_rates. The Instagram account is at https://www.instagram.com/weratedogs/?hl=en.

## Chapter 1

1. Malena DeMartini is one of the leading experts on separation anxiety in dogs. Her in-person, virtual, and printed resources can be found at https://malenademartini.com/.

## Chapter 2

1. Mariana Bentosela et al., "Sociability and Gazing Toward Humans in Dogs and Wolves: Simple Behaviors with Broad Implications," *Journal of Experimental Analysis of Behavior* 105, no. 1 (January 2016): 68–75, https://doi.org/10.1002/jeab.191.
2. "Pet Clothing Market Size, Share & Covid 19 Impact Analysis, By Product Type (Coats, & Jackets, Sweaters & Hoodies, Shirts & Tops, and Others), Pet Type (Dogs, Cats, and Others), and Regional Forecast, 2021–2028," Fortune Business Insights, accessed October 24, 2022, https://www.fortunebusiness insights.com/pet-clothing-market-104419.
3. Miho Nagasawa, Mofi Kazutaka, and Takefumi Kikusui, "Continued Distress Among Abandoned Dogs in Fukushima," *Scientific Reports* 2, no. 274 (October 11, 2012): https://doi.org/ 10.1038/srep00724.
4. Ibid.
5. Ibid.
6. Brian Hare, "Find the Genius in Your Dog," Dognition, accessed April 8, 2022, https://www.dognition.com/.
7. Brian Hare and Vanessa Woods, *The Genius of Dogs: How Dogs Are Smarter Than You Think* (New York: Penguin Group, 2013), xii.
8. Karen Overall, "Natural Animal Models of Human Psychiatric Conditions: Assessment of Mechanism and Validity," *Progress in Neuro-Psychopharmacology & Biological Psychiatry* 24, no. 5 (2000): 729, https://doi.org/ 10.1016/s0278-5846(00)00104-4.
9. Ibid.
10. James Dao, "After Duty, Dogs Suffer Like Soldiers," *New York Times*, December 1, 2011, https://www.nytimes.com/2011/12/02/us/more-military-dogs-show-signs-of-combat-stress.html.
11. Jaak Panskepp, "Consciousness and Cognition," *Neurobiology of Animal Consciousness* 14, no. 1 (2005): 30–80.
12. Gregory Berns, Andrew Brooks, and Mark Spivak, "Functional MRI in Awake Unrestrained Dogs," Plos *One* (May 11, 2012), https://doi.org/10.1371/journal.pone.0038027.
13. Dodman, *Pets on the Couch*, 51.

## Chapter 3

1. Greg Bouhl, "What Licenses Does a Dog Training Business Need?" Start

# Notes—Chapter 5

ingyourbusiness.com, last updated November 22, 2022, https://startingyourbusiness.com/what-licenses-does-a-dog-training-business-need/.

2. "Earning a Certification Can Help You Enter or Advance Many Careers," Career One Stop, accessed January 31, 2023, https://www.careeronestop.org/FindTraining/Types/certifications.aspx.

3. "Dog Trainer Certification," Certification Council for Professional Dog Trainers, accessed July 23, 2022, https://www.ccpdt.org/certification/dog-trainer-certification/.

4. Ibid.

5. The American Veterinary Society of Animal Behavior, "Position Statement on Humane Dog Training," 2021, https://avsab.org/resources/position-statements/.

6. "Ten Questions to Ask Your Dog Training Professional—Before You Hire Them!" Pet Professional Guild, last updated 2020, https://www.petprofessionalguild.com/Top-Ten-Questions-To-Ask-a-Potential-Dog-Trainer.

7. Susan Friedman, "Behavior+ Works," https://www.Welcome to BehaviorWorks.org.

8. "Application of the Humane Hierarchy Position Statement," Certification Council for Professional Dog Trainers, accessed June 13, 2022, https://www.ccpdt.org/wp-content/uploads/2015/01/Application-of-the-Humane-Hierarchy-Position-Statement.pdf.

9. Karen Overall, *Manual of Clinical Behavioral Medicine for Dogs and Cats* (St. Louis: Mosby, 20013), 184, 187, 491. Physical diagnoses that can impact or mimic behavior issues are numerous, and any medical diagnosis should be given by a veterinarian. Dr. Karen Overall lists pain, mobility issues, vision and hearing deficits due to aging as primary "rule outs" when assessing for a behavior concern. Neurological disease and thyroid issues should also be considered although these are less common.

10. The International Association of Animal Behavior Consultants is one of the primary professional organizations supporting LIMA, along with the Association of Professional Dog Trainers and the Certification Council of Professional Dog Trainers.

11. Pet Professional Guild, http://www.petprofessionalguild.com.

12. The International Association of Animal Behavior Consultants, http://www.iaabc.org.

13. The Certification Council for Professional Dog Trainers, http://www.ccpdt.org.

14. "CAABs Are Uniquely Qualified," Certified Applied Animal Behaviorists, accessed January 13, 2022, http://corecaab.org/qualifications/.

15. "What Is a Board Certified Veterinary Behaviorist?" Animal Health Begins with Behavior, accessed April 8, 2022, https://www.dacvb.org/page/AnimalOwners.

16. "Taking the 'Pet' Out of 'Petrified': Fear Free™ Veterinary Certification Programs," Fear Free, accessed July 29, 2022, https://fearfreepets.com/.

## *Chapter 5*

1. Overall, *Manual of Clinical Behavioral Medicine*, 53.

2. Ibid.

3. Ibid.

4. Ludovica Pierantoni, Mariangela Albertini, and Federica Pirrone, "Prevalence of Owner-Reported Behaviours in Dogs Separated From the Litter at Two Different Ages," abstract *Vet Rec* 169, no. 18 (October 29, 2011): 468, https://doi.org/10.1136/vr.d4967.

5. Joyce Yau et al., "Chronic Treatment with the Antidepressant Amitriptyline Prevents Impairments in Water Maze Learning in Aging Rats," *Journal of Neuroscience* 22 (February 15, 2002): 1436–1442, https://doi.org/10.1523/JNEUROSCI.22-04-01436.2002.

6. Overall, *Manual of Clinical Behavioral Medicine*, 53.

7. Temple Grandin and Catherine Johnson, *Animals in Translation: Using the Mysteries of Autism to Decode Animal Behavior* (Orlando: Harcourt Books, 2005), 95.

# Notes—Chapters 7, 8, 9 and 10

## Chapter 7

1. Brenda Aloff, *Canine Body Language: A Photographic Guide Interpreting the Native Language of the Domestic Dog* (Wenatchee, WA: Dogwise, 2005), 10.

2. Sarah Kalnajs, "The Language of Dogs: Understanding Canine Body Language and Other Communication Signals," DVD set, Blue Dog Training and Behavior, 2006.

3. Martina Scholz and Clarissa von Reinhardt, *Stress in Dogs: Learn How Dogs Show Stress and What You Can Do to Help* (Wenatchee, WA: Dogwise, 2007), 27.

4. The website for Family Dog Project can be found at https://familydogproject.elte.hu/. The website provides the history of this organization as being founded by Vilmos Csany, Adam Miklosi and Jozsef Topal in 1994 to study the behavioral and cognitive aspects of the dog-human relationship.

5. Mary Burch, "A Toast to Most: Konrad Most, a 1910 Pioneer in Animal Training," *Journal of Applied Behavior Analysis* 23, no. 2 (Summer 1990): 263–264, https://doi.org/ 10.1901/jaba.1990.23-263.

6. Blanche Saunders, *The Novice Obedience Training Course Textbook* (New York: Howell Book House, 1969).

7. John Paul Scott and John L. Fuller, *Genetics and the Social Behavior of the Dog* (Chicago: University of Chicago Press, 1965).

8. Karen Pryor, *Don't Shoot the Dog: The Art of Teaching and Training* (New York: Bantam, 1999), xii.

9. Ibid., xi.

10. Ibid., x.

11. Pat Miller, "Train Your Dog Using Imitation," *The Whole Dog Journal*, accessed May 9, 2022, https://www.whole-dog-journal.com/training/cognitive-skills/train-your-dog-using-imitation/.

12. Emma Parsons, *Click to Calm: Healing the Aggressive Dog* (Waltham: Sunshine, 2005), 6.

13. Ibid.

14. Ibid., 7.

15. The American Veterinary Society of Animal Behavior, *Position Statement on the Use of Dominance Theory in Behavior Modification of Animals* (2019), accessed on June 3, 2022, http://avsab.org/wp-content/uploads/2019/01/Dominance_Position_Statement-download.pdf.

16. Irwin Bernstein, "Dominance: The Baby and the Bathwater," *Journal of Behavioral Science* 4 (1981): 419–457, https://doi.org/10.1017/s0140525x00009614.

17. The American Veterinary Society of Animal Behavior, *Position Statement on Humane Dog Training*, https://avsab.org/resources/position-Statements/.

## Chapter 8

1. Overall, *Manual of Clinical Behavioral Medicine*, 261.

2. Dodman, *Pets on the Couch*, 31.

## Chapter 9

1. Overall, *Manual of Clinical Behavior*, 66.

2. Leslie McDevitt, *Control Unleashed: Creating a Focused and Confident Dog* (Hadley, MA: Clean Run Productions, 2007).

3. Grisha Stewart, *Behavior Adjustment Training: BAT for Fear, Frustration, and Aggression in Dogs* (Wenatchee, WA: Dogwise, 2012). Stewart has published several new editions since I added this book to my library. Stewart also provides multiple online videos and seminar information that can be found at her website, https://grishastewart.com/bat-overview/.

4. Nan Keene Arthur, *Chill Out, Fido! How to Calm Your Dog* (Wenatchee, WA: Dogwise, 2007).

5. Overall, *Manual of Clinical Behavioral Medicine*, 83.

## Chapter 10

1. Ibid., 708.

2. Christopher Wittich, Christopher Burkle, and William Lanier, "Ten

# Notes—Chapters 11, 12, 15, 19 and 20

Common Questions (and Their Answers) About Off-Label Drug Use," *Mayo Clinic Proceedings* 87, no. 10 (October 2012): 982–990, http://doi.org/10.1016/j.mayocp.2012.04.017.

3. Lauren Mehram and Peter Sculli, "The Benefits of Enrichment on an Animal's Physical and Mental Well-being," Potter Park Zoo (blog), January 23, 2022, https://potterparkzoo.org/benefits-of-enrichment/.

4. Nicole Wilde is one of the leading experts on canine play. Professionals and owners alike use her DVD set, *Dissecting the Dynamics of Dog-Dog Play* (Boise: Tawzer Dog, 2012).

5. "Adaptil," accessed January 11, 2022, https://www.adaptil.com/us.

6. Grandin, *Animals in Translation*, 117.

7. *Ibid.*

8. Alexandra Owens, "Tell Me All I Need to Know About Oxytocin," *Psycom*, September 23, 2021, https://www.psycom.net/oxytocin.

9. "Calming Care Can Help Performance Dogs Displaying Anxious Behaviors," Purina Pro Club, accessed July 7, 2022, https://www.purinaproclub.com/resources/dog-articles/todays-breeder/calming-care-helps-dog-anxiety#:~:text=The%20Calming%20Probiotic%20Effects%20of%20.

10. Nicole Kirchoff, Monique Udell, and Thomas Sharpton, "The Gut Microbiome Correlates with Conspecific Aggression in a Small Population of Rescued Dogs (Canis Familiaris)," PubMed.gov (January 9, 2019), https://doi.org/10.7717/peerj.6103.

11. Erica Mondo et al., "Gut Microbiome Structure and Adrencortical Activity in Dogs with Aggressive and Phobic Behavioral Disorders," *Heliyon* (January 29, 2020): https://doi.org/10.1016/j.heliyon.020.e03311.

12. Ragen McGowan et al., "Tapping into Those 'Gut Feelings': Impact of BL999 (Bifidobacterium Longum) on Anxiety in Dogs," Symposium, ACVB Veterinary Behavior, Denver, CO, January 6, 2020.

## Chapter 11

1. American College of Veterinary Behaviorists, *Decoding Your Dog: Explaining Common Dog Behaviors and How to Prevent or Change Unwanted Ones*, ed. Debra Horwitz and John Ciribassi with Steve Dale (Boston: Mariner, 2015).

## Chapter 12

1. "Learned Helplessness," *Psychology Today*, accessed November 16, 2021, https://www.psychologytoday.com/us/basics/learned-helplessness.

2. Chirag Patel, "The Bucket Game," https://www.The Bucket Game—Domesticated Manners.

3. "The Family Dog," https://www.The Family Dog.

4. Susan Friedman, quoted in Pat Miller, "Training a Dog to Make Choices," *Whole Dog Journal* (October 28, 2016).

## Chapter 15

1. Patricia McConnell, *The Other End of the Leash: Why We Do What We Do Around Dogs* (New York: Random House, 2002), 211.

2. James O'Heare, *Aggressive Behavior in Dogs: A Comprehensive Technical Manual for Professionals*, 2nd ed. (Ottawa: BehaveTech, 2014), 313.

3. Regulations concerning laws related to pet ownership can usually be found on city, county, or state government websites or by calling your local city hall.

## Chapter 19

1. Overall, *Manual of Clinical Behavioral Medicine*, 60.

## Chapter 20

1. To learn more about Champ's life read the book by his owner Beth Miller, *The Most Painful Choice: A Dog Owner's Story of Behavioral Euthanasia* (Jefferson, NC: McFarland, 2023).

## Chapter 21

1. Lily Velez, "Grieving the Loss of a Pet: Why It's So Hard and Tips for Coping," Veterinarians.org (blog), updated January 26, 2023, https://www.veterinarians.org/loss-of-a-pet/.

## Chapter 22

1. Dixie Tenney, *How to Find Your Dream Dog* (St. Louis: Authors Unite, 2016).

2. Kathleen Morril et al., "Ancestry-Inclusive Dog Genomics Challenges Popular Breed Stereotypes," *Science* 376, no. 6592 (April 29, 2022), https://doi.org/10.1126/science.abk0639.

3. Kenneth Martin and Debbie Martin, *Puppy Start Right: Foundation Training for the Companion Dog* (Waltham, MA: Sunshine Books, 2011).

4. Patricia McConnell and Karen London, *Love Has No Age Limit: Welcoming an Adopted Dog into Your Home* (Wenatchee, WA: McConnell Publishing, 2011).

# Bibliography

Aloff, Brenda. *Canine Body Language: A Photographic Guide Interpreting the Native Language of the Domestic Dog.* Wenatchee, WA: Dogwise, 2012.

American College of Veterinary Behaviorists. *Decoding Your Dog: Explaining Common Dog Behaviors and How to Prevent or Change Unwanted Ones.* Edited by Debra Horwitz and John Ciribassi with Steve Dale. Boston: Mariner, 2015.

The American Veterinary Society of Animal Behavior. Position Statement on Humane Dog Training. Retrieved on February 17, 2022, from AVSAB-Humane-Dog-Training-Position-Statement-2021.pdf.

The American Veterinary Society of Animal Behavior. Position Statement on the Use of Dominance Theory in Behavior Modification of Animals. Retrieved on February 21, 2022, from Dominance_Position_Statement-download.pdf. (avsab.org).

Arthur, Nan Kene. *Chill Out, Fido! How to Calm Your Dog.* Wenatchee, WA: Dogwise, 2009.

Bentosela, Mariana, et al. "Sociability and Gazing Toward Humans in Dogs and Wolves: Simple Behaviors with Broad Implications." *Journal of Experimental Analysis of Behavior* 105, no. 1 (January 2016): 68–75. https://doi.org/10.1002/jeab.191.

Berns, Gregory, Andrew Brooks, and Mark Spivak. "Functional MRI in Awake Unrestrained Dogs." *Plos One* (May 11, 2012). https://doi.org/10.1371/journal.pone.0038027.

Bernstein, Irwin. "Dominance: The Baby and the Bathwater." *Journal of Behavioral Science* 4 (1981): 419–457. https://doi.org/10.1017/s0140525x00009614.

Bouhl, Greg. "What Licenses Does a Dog Training Business Need?" Startingyourbusiness.com, last updated November 22, 2022. https://startingyourbusiness.com/what-licenses-does-a-dog-training-business-need/.

Burch, Mary. "A Toast to Most: Konrad Most, a 1910 Pioneer in Animal Training." *Journal of Applied Behavior Analysis* 23, no. 2 (Summer 1990): 263–264. https://doi.org/10.1901/jaba.1990.23-263.

"Calming Care Can Help Performance Dogs Displaying Anxious Behavior." Retrieved January 4, 2022, from https://www.purinaproclub.com/resources/dog-articles/todays-breeder/calming-care-helps-dog-anxiety.

Certification Council for Professional Dog Trainers. Application of the Humane Hierarchy Position Statement. Retrieved September 29, 2022, from https://www.ccpdt.org/wp-content/uploads/2015/01/Application-of-the-Humane-Hierarchy-Position-Statement.pdf.

Certified Applied Animal Behaviorists. "CAABs Are Uniquely Qualified." Retrieved January 13, 2022, from http://corecaab.org/qualifications/.

Dao, James. "After Duty, Dogs Suffer Like Soldiers." *New York Times*, December 1, 2011. https://www.nytimes.com/2011/12/02/us/more-military-dogs-show-signs-of-combat-stress.html.

Dodman, Nicholas. *Pets on the Couch.* New York: Atria, 2016.

# Bibliography

Fear Free Pets. https://fearfreepets.com/.

Grandin, Temple, and Catherine Johnson. *Animals in Translation: Using the Mysteries of Autism to Decode Animal Behavior.* Orlando: Harcourt Books, 2005.

Hare, Brian. Dognition. https://www.dognition.com.

Hare, Brian, and Vanessa Woods. *The Genius of Dogs: How Dogs Are Smarter Than You Think.* New York: Penguin Group, 2013.

Kalnajs, Sarah. "The Language of Dogs: Understanding Canine Body Language and Other Communication Signals." DVD set. Blue Dog Training and Behavior, 2006.

Kirchoff, Nicole, Monique Udell, and Thomas Sharpton. "The Gut Microbiome Correlates with Conspecific Aggression in a Small Population of Rescued Dogs (Canis Familiaris)." PubMed.gov (January 9, 2019). https://doi.org/10.7717/peerj.6103.

Martin, Kenneth, and Debbie Martin. *Puppy Start Right: Foundation Training for the Companion Dog.* Waltham, MA: Sunshine Books, 2009.

McConnell, Patricia. *The Other End of the Leash.* New York: Random House, 2002.

McConnell, Patricia, and Karen London. *Love Has No Age Limit: Welcoming an Adopted Dog into Your Home.* Wenatchee, WA: McConnell Publishing, 2011.

McDevitt, Leslie. *Control Unleashed: Creating a Focused and Confident Dog.* South Hadley, MA: Clean Run Productions, 2007.

McGowan, Ragen, Hallie Barnett, Gail Czarnecki-Maulden, Xuemei Si, Gerardo Perez-Camargo, and Francois Martin. "Tapping Into Those 'Gut Feelings': Impact of BL999 (Bifidobacterium Longum) on Anxiety in Dogs." Symposium, ACVB Veterinary Behavior, Denver, CO, January 6, 2020.

Mehram, Lauren, and Peter Scull, "The Benefits of Enrichment on an Animal's Physical and Mental Wellbeing." Potter Park Zoo (blog), January 23, 2022. https://potterparkzoo.org/benefits-of-enrichment/.

Miller, Pat. "Train Your Dog Using Imitation." *The Whole Dog Journal* (2018). https://www.whole-dog-journal.com/training/cognitive-skills/train-your-dog-using-imitation.

Miller, Pat. "Training a Dog to Make Choices." *The Whole Dog Journal* (2016). https://www..whole-dog-journal.com/training/cognitive-skills/training-a-dog-to-make-choices/.

Mondo, Erica, M. Barone, M. Soverini, F. D'Amico, M.Cocchi, C. Petrulli, M. Mattioli, G. Marliani, M. Candela, and P. Accorsi. "Gut Microbiome Structure and Adrencortical Activity in Dogs with Aggressive and Phobic Behavioral Disorders." *Heliyon* (January 29, 2020). https://doi.org/10.1016/j.heliyon.020.e03311.

Morril, Kathleen, Jessica Hekman, Xue Li, Jese McClure, Brittany Logan, Linda Goodman, Mingshi Gao, Yinan Dong, Marjie Alonso, Elena Carmichael, Noah Snyder-Mackler, Jacob Alonso, Hyun Ji Noh, Jeremy Johnson, Michelle Koltookian, Charlie Lieu, Kate Megquier, Ross Swofford, Jason Tuner-Maier. Michelle White, Zhiping Weng, Andres Colubri, Diane P. Genereux, Kathryn Lord, and Elinor Karlsson. "Ancestry-Inclusive Dog Genomics Challenges Popular Breed Stereotypes." *Science* 376, no. 6592 (April 29, 2022). https://doi.org/10.1126/science.abk0639.

Nagasawa, Miho, Mofi Kazutaka, and Takefumi Kikusui. "Continued Distress Among Abandoned Dogs in Fukushima." *Scientific Reports* 2, no. 274 (October 11, 2012). https://doi.org/10.1038/srep00724.

O'Heare, James. *Aggressive Behavior in Dogs: A Comprehensive Technical Manual for Professionals*, 2nd ed. Ottawa: BehaveTech, 2014.

Overall, Karen. "Natural Animal Models of Human Psychiatric Conditions: Assessment of Mechanism and Validity." *Progress in Neuro-Psychopharmacology & Biological Psychiatry* 24 (2000): 727–776. https://doi.org/10.1016/s0278-5846(00)00104-4.

Overall, Karen L. *Manual of Clinical*

# Bibliography

*Behavioral Medicine for Dogs and Cats*. St. Louis: Mosby, 2013.

Owens, Alexandra. "Tell Me All I Need to Know about Oxytocin." *Psycom*, September, 23, 2021. https://www.psycom.net/oxytocin.

Panskepp, Jaak. "Consciousness and Cognition," *Neurobiology of Animal Consciousness* 14, no. 1 (2005): 30–80.

Parsons, Emma. *Click to Calm*. Waltham, MA: Sunshine Books, 2005.

Pet Professional Guild. "Ten Questions to Ask Your Dog Training Professional— Before You Hire Them!" Retrieved on November 27, 2020, from https://www.petprofessionalguild.com/Top-Ten-Questions-To-Ask-a-Potential-Dog-Trainer.

Pierantoni, Ludovica, Mariangela Albertini, and Federica Pirrone. "Prevalence of Owner-Reported Behaviours in Dogs Separated From the Litter at Two Different Ages." Abstract *Vet Rec* 169, no. 18 (October 29, 2011): 468. https://doi.org/10.1136/vr.d4967.

Pryor, Karen. *Don't Shoot the Dog!* New York: Bantam Books, 1999.

Psychology Today. "*Learned Helplessness*." Retrieved on February 17, 2022, from https://www.psychologytoday.com/us/basics/learned-helplessness#.~.text=Learned%20 helplessness%20occurs%20when%20an, The%20ability%20to%20do%20so

Saunders, Blanche. *The Novice Obedience Training Course Textbook*. New York: Howell Book House, 1969.

Scholz, Martina, and Clarissa von Reinhardt. *Stress in Dogs*. Wenatchee, WA: Dogwise, 2007.

Scott, John Paul, and John J. Fuller. *Genetics and the Social Behavior of the Dog*. Chicago: University of Chicago Press, 1965.

Scroggins, Linda. *Mental Illness in Dogs: a Guide for Trainers*. Sarasota: First Edition, 2017.

Stewart, Grisha. *Behavior Adjustment Training: BAT for Fear, Frustration, and Aggression in Dogs*. Wenatchee, WA: Dogwise, 2012.

Tenney, Dixie. *How to Find Your Dream Dog*. St. Louis: Authors Unite, 2016.

Tillman, Peggy. *Clicking with Your Dog*. Waltham, MA: Sunshine Books, 2000.

Velez, Lily. Veterinarians.org. "Grieving the Loss of a Pet. Why It's So Hard and Tips for Coping." Retrieved on December 8, 2020, from http://www.veterinarians.org/loss-of-a-pet.

Wilde, Nicole. *Dissecting the Dynamics of Dog-Dog Play* DVD. Boise: Tawzer Dog, 2012.

Wittich, Christopher, Christopher Burkle, and William Lanier. "Ten Common Questions (and Their Answers) About Off-Label Drug Use." *Mayo Clinic Proceedings* 87, no. 10 (October 2012): 982–990. http://doi.org/10.1016/j.mayocp.2012.04.017

Yau, Joyce, June Noble, Carina Hibberd, Wayne B Rowe, Michael J. Meaney, Richard G.M. Morris, and Jonathan R. Seckl. "Chronic Treatment with the Antidepressant Amitriptyline Prevents Impairments in Water Maze Learning in Aging Rats." *Journal of Neuroscience* 22 (February, 15, 2002): 1436–1442. https://doi.org/10.1523/JNEUROSCI.22-04-01436.2002.

# Index

advice 36, 121, 140, 143, 163, 174
advocate 21, 123, 128, 130, 131, 142, 173
aggression 11, 20-22, 72, 74, 75, 114, 146
American Kennel Club 3, 186, 188
The American Veterinary Society of Animal Behavior 29, 32, 74, 75
The Animal Behavior Society 28, 29, 32
Arlo 115

Beatrix Kiddo 188
behavior consultant 9, 11, 26, 27, 31, 32, 39, 145, 180, 192
behavior modification 38, 39, 44, 45, 53, 56, 57, 59, 62, 63, 78, 86, 88, 90, 97, 99, 100, 102, 103, 106, 112, 126, 148, 156
behaviorist 27-29, 32
body language 4, 5, 27, 34, 40, 50, 59, 60, 62, 63, 109, 137

CAAB 28, 38, 147
Calming Care 114
Canine Cognition Center 21
Canine Good Citizen 3
CBCC-KA 11
Certification Council for Professional Dog Trainers 10, 23, 24, 27, 32
Certified Professional Dog Trainer 2, 10, 80
Champ 168
choice 36, 77, 78, 83, 119, 120, 126-129
consent 127, 128
cortisol 45
cost 144, 145
counter conditioning 86-89, 97, 104

Dao, James 20
DAP 112
day care 30, 40, 45, 109, 110
desensitization 86, 88, 97
displacement 4, 5
Dodman, Nicholas 21, 81
Dognition 20

environment 21, 25, 33, 35, 36, 43, 44, 49, 54, 61-63, 71, 86, 106, 107, 110, 111, 153, 170, 174, 184
euthanasia 156, 157, 166, 177, 178

The Family Dog 63, 128
Fear Free 31
Fishbein, Susan 45
Freckles 79
Friedman, Susan 25
Fukushima 19

genetics 43, 44, 64, 174, 184
glucocorticoids 19
goals 41
Grady 151
Grandin, Temple 46, 112, 113
growling 25, 63, 83

Hare, Brian 20
history 39
holistic 112
Humane Hierarchy 25, 26, 89

Jack 15

Keene Arthur, Nan 97

Lap of Love 177
learned helplessness 1266
LIMA 25, 26

Maizy 47
management 26, 39, 54-57, 63, 96, 100, 104, 139, 185
Martin, Debbie 185
Martin, Kenneth 185
Maya 33
McConnell, Patricia 144, 185
medication 29, 30, 102-105, 131, 145
mental enrichment 31, 105, 106, 111, 118, 145
muzzle 132-135

# Index

nutrition  25, 39, 105, 113, 114

observation  40
O'Heare, James  146
Overall, Karen  20, 80, 86, 97, 104
oxytocin  113

Panksepp, Jaak  20
Patel, Chirag  127
Pet Professional Guild  24, 25, 27, 32
Pink  1
pit bull  1, 2, 15, 105, 125, 183, 185
PTSD  19, 20, 80, 81, 178
punishment  24, 26, 57, 63, 65, 72, 74, 75, 77, 78, 89, 91, 92

reactive  11, 58, 92, 93, 96, 103
rehome  144, 146, 147, 150
reinforcement  25, 26, 45, 51, 54, 57, 63, 69, 72, 73, 77, 89, 90, 92, 94, 96, 100, 170
relax on mat  3, 96, 97, 99
rule of five  100

separation anxiety  17, 21, 30, 145
sniffing  4, 5, 46, 61, 95, 108, 111
social deprivation  44
Stewart, Grisha  32, 92
stress  11, 19, 31, 44, 45, 54, 57, 62, 75, 76, 107, 167, 171; signals 60, 61

Tenney, Dixie  182
Tex  158
Thundershirt  113
trainer  24, 28, 58, 89, 145, 185
trigger  11, 39, 40, 54, 60, 87, 90, 92, 103
trigger stacking  93

veterinary behavior specialist  26, 29, 38, 48, 58, 86, 97, 105, 117, 145, 147, 171, 173

Walt  136
We Rate Dogs  13
Woods, Vanessa  20
wraps  112, 113

www.ingramcontent.com/pod-product-compliance
Ingram Content Group UK Ltd.
Pitfield, Milton Keynes, MK11 3LW, UK
UKHW042004140426
5217IPUK00015B/970